Henry

ALSO BY DAVID STARKEY
FROM CLIPPER LARGE PRINT

Monarchy: From Middle Ages to Modernity

Henry

Virtuous Prince

David Starkey

W F HOWES LTD

This large print edition published in 2009 by
W F Howes Ltd
Unit 4, Rearsby Business Park, Gaddesby Lane,
Rearsby, Leicester LE7 4YH

1 3 5 7 9 10 8 6 4 2

First published in the United Kingdom in 2008
by Harper*Press* as *Henry: Virtuous Prince*

A CIP catalogue record for this book is available
from the British Library

ISBN 978 1 40744 232 7

Typeset by Palimpsest Book Production Limited,
Grangemouth, Stirlingshire
Printed and bound in Great Britain
by MPG Books Ltd, Bodmin, Cornwall

FSC
Mixed Sources
Product group from well-managed
forests, controlled sources and
recycled wood or fiber
SA-COC-1565
www.fsc.org
© 1996 Forest Stewardship Council

To Mark Pigott
a fellow Henrician

CONTENTS

INTRODUCTION

Henry and I go back a long way.

My first and second undergraduate essays at Cambridge, written in late 1964, were on his grandmother, Lady Margaret Beaufort, and his second wife, Anne Boleyn. My doctoral dissertation, begun in 1967 and finally completed in 1973, grew directly out of that second essay and was an in-depth study of his privy chamber and its staff. This was the department of the royal household that provided both the king's body service and his personal political aides. It was thus rather like the modern Downing Street or White House staff, and included individuals just as silky and shamelessly self-serving as their present-day equivalents.

One of them, William Compton, has a bit part in this book.

He was Henry's groom of the stool and I have only to write the words to be carried back almost four decades to the Cambridge University Library tea-room circa 1970. It is about 3.30 p.m. and I have met up with my fellow members of Geoffrey Elton's research seminar. We are a noisy, gregarious,

1

grub-loving group. I am eating home-made lemon-cake with a gooey icing and filling and bits of grated lemon rind that occasionally get stuck between the teeth. I am also drinking lemon tea. And I am talking. And talking. About Henry and his groom of the stool.

'Did you know the groom was *act*-ually' – I overemphasize the first syllable as though I were already on TV – 'in charge of Henry's close-stool? What? Oh that's the royal loo. Yes. And that he certainly attended the king when he used it? How do you know, you say? Well, the groom says so. He even describes the contents – solid as well as liquid. He may very well have wiped the royal bottom . . .'

No wonder my dissertation became known as doctoral faeces (say it fast!).

Happy days. And even they were not the beginning. Instead, another Cambridge scene, this time from my undergraduate days. I am sitting in one of Geoffrey Elton's lectures and nodding off. Suddenly, I jolt awake. 'Henry VIII', Elton announces, 'is the only king whose shape you remember.' Then he turns to the blackboard behind him and draws a quick sketch. First, a trapezium for the body. Then two splayed lines for the legs. A pair of triangles form the arms. The head and neck are a single oblong, surmounted by an angled line for the hat.

Pause for laughter. Then, playing to the audience,

Elton adds another, inverted triangle for the codpiece. More laughter and applause.

Elton was of course right. Holbein's portrait of Henry VIII. which he here reduced, brilliantly, to the bare essentials of its almost cubist geometry, *is* memorable. Almost too memorable indeed. For it not only eclipses other English monarchs, with the exception of Henry's daughter Elizabeth. It also obscures the other Henry.

The point is this: there are *two* Henrys, just as there are *two* Elizabeths, the one old, the other young. And they are very, very different. Especially in the case of Henry. Holbein's Henry is the king of his last dozen or so years, when he was – in Charles Dickens's glorious phrase – a spot of blood and grease on the history of England. This is the hulking tyrant, with a face like a Humpty Dumpty of nightmare, who broke with Rome and made himself supreme head of the church; who married six wives, of whom he divorced two and divorced *and* executed two others; who dissolved six hundred monasteries, demolished most of them and shattered the religious pieties and practices of a thousand years; who beheaded nobles and ministers, including those who had been his closest friends, castrated, disembowelled and quartered rebels and traitors, boiled poisoners and burned heretics.

This is also the king who reinvented England; presided over the remaking of English as a language and literature and began to turn the English Channel into the widest strip of water in the world. He carried the powers of the English monarchy to their peak. Yet he also left a *damnosa hereditas* to his successors which led, not very indirectly, to Charles I's execution one hundred and two years almost to the day after Henry's own death, and on a scaffold in front of the palace that Henry had made the supreme seat of royal government and where he himself had died.

But this is not the Henry of this book. This book is about the other Henry: the young, handsome prince, slim, athletic, musical and learned as no English ruler had been for centuries. This Henry loved his mother and – most unusually for a boy at the time – was brought up with his sisters, with all that implies about the civilizing and softening impact of female company. He was conventionally pious: he prostrated himself before images, went on pilgrimages and showed himself profoundly respectful of the pope as head of the church. He proclaimed that 'I loved true where I did marry', and meant it. He determined to knit up the wounds of the Wars of the Roses and restore the dispossessed. He abominated his father's meanness, secrecy and corrosive mistrust. Instead he modelled himself on Henry V, the greatest and noblest of his predecessors. Or he would be a new Arthur with a court that put Camelot in the shade. At the least, he determined that his reign, which began when he was only seventeen years and ten months old, should be a fresh start.

And it was. Or at least it was believed to be. Lord Mountjoy, his *socius studiorum* ('companion of studies'), hailed his accession as the beginning of a new golden age. Thomas More, who had known Henry since the future king was eight years old, went further. Henry, he proclaimed in the verses he wrote to celebrate the coronation, was a new messiah and his reign a second coming.

Mountjoy we can perhaps discount. But More was nobody's fool. If he saw these extraordinary qualities in Henry then they, or something like them, must have been there indeed.

But there is a double difficulty. The first is of image. For there is no decent representation of the young Henry. There are a few panel portraits, but they are journeymen's work and do not hold a candle to Holbein's blazing genius. And without an image it is difficult to turn the paeans of praise about the young Henry from a cold, idealized abstraction into a thing of warm flesh and blood.

Here I have tried to flesh out Henry through words – including as much as possible of Henry's own words and those of his contemporaries. Often these were in Latin. Once this presented no difficulty. Now it is an obstacle, not only to the reader but to many scholars as well. For my own part, I pretend to little Classical scholarship. Instead I have freely resorted to translations, where they exist, and to the help of translators where they do not. The result has been enlightening and some of the most original material in the book has come from newly translated Latin sources. I am particularly grateful to Justine Taylor for her help in this regard.

The other problem is one of explanation and is more fundamental. For to talk of two Henrys is only a figure of speech. They were in fact the same person. Or at least they were the same man when old and young. But how to explain the spectacular change from one to the other?

Was the young Henry a sort of aberration? Was he 'really' what he was to be in old age? Or was it all down to changing circumstances?

It can be put rather differently. Should we read him backwards, from what he became? Or forwards, from what he was?

Really there should be no question which. Modern scholarship is resolute that events must be read forward. It recognizes that the actors at the time were not gifted with foresight and it is clear that historians must not impose their own knowledge of what was to come on contemporaries who were necessarily ignorant of it. To do so is teleology. And to do so persistently is the ultimate sin of Whiggishness.

And yet. The truth is that the old Henry – with the horror, the soap opera and the drama – is immediately fascinating in a way that the young Henry is not. The young Henry is too conventional, too much a man of his own time. Or indeed of the age before his own. If he had been successful, he would have been a triumphant late-medieval king, a Henry V *redivivus*; as he failed, which he largely did, he merely represents a sort of fag-end.

So historians are constantly hunting for signs of what was to come. For heterodoxy. For scepticism about the externals of faith. For doubts about his first marriage. For high views of royal power and low ones of papal authority.

It is all, it seems to me, a wild-goose chase.

The Henry who swears unquestioningly the traditional coronation oath of an English king in 1509 is not the same as the man who revises it, line-by-line and word-by-word, twenty-odd years later. The man who went on pilgrimage – whether to Our Lady of Walsingham in Norfolk in 1511 to give thanks for the birth of his son or to Master John Shorne at North Marston in Buckingham in gratitude for his recovery from the sweating sickness in 1521 – is not the same as the king who demolishes Becket's shrine and every other place of pilgrimage in England in the 1530s. Nor is the man who would write the *Assertio Septem Sacramentorum* in 1521 – with its forceful argument that papal power was historically rooted, necessary for the unity of the church and the

7

ultimate guarantor of uniformity of faith – the same as the man who, less than a decade later, rejected each of those propositions in turn to substitute his own kingly authority over the church for that of the pope.

In short, Henry's reformation – the king's reformation as it has recently and rightly been called – begins in 1527, and not in 1509 or 1515. True, in the latter year Henry (who liked rolling phrases) delivers himself of a ringing declaration: 'By the ordinance and sufferance of God, we are king of England, and kings of England in time past have never had any superior but God only.'

Ringing indeed. But Henry is saying no more than the most pious of his medieval ancestors, though he may be saying it rather better. For in 1515 the 'imperial' authority of the English crown meant only that it had no temporal superior; it did *not* mean that it was superior to the spiritual power of the church. This of course is what Henry – the ageing Henry – made it mean in the 1530s. But the latter proposition is not 'implicit' in the former. Nor is it 'latent', 'prefigured' or whatever other Whiggish weasel-words historians choose to use to mask their teleology.

On the contrary, far from being 'implicit', it took a revolution – and one made in blood – to achieve it.

But things have an end as well as a beginning. And it is equally clear that the Wars of the Roses ended with Henry's accession in 1509. They had not ended with his father's victory at Bosworth in 1485. Or with his parents' marriage the following year. Or with Lincoln's defeat at Stoke in 1487. Or with the crushing of the Cornish rebels in 1497 and the subsequent capture of Perkin Warbeck. They had not even ended with the surrender of Suffolk, the last pretender, to Henry VII in 1506.

But they did end when Henry came to the throne. And that they did so was personally and directly due to him. His own conjoined descent from York as well Lancaster was important. But so too were his decisions – which had been conditioned by his repeated youthful experiences of pretenders and plots and destructive insecurities – to let bygones be bygones, to knit up old wounds and to restore the surviving members of the house of York (always excepting the inveterate traitor Suffolk and his siblings) to their wealth and dignities.

And, what has been insufficiently appreciated, it worked. The spectre of dynastic conflict, which had stalked England for the last fifty years, is suddenly laid. And it does not walk again. There are later dynastic problems of course. But they are not about York and Lancaster. They are about religion. Some of the Yorkists that the young Henry had restored *are* involved. But not as Yorkists. Instead, they rebel – or rather dream of rebelling – against him because they disagree with his religious policies.

Between these ends and beginnings, Henry's is a life which naturally falls in halves. Hence my decision to write it in two volumes. This first volume is intended to establish the authenticity and integrity of the young Henry; the second will be to show what he became and why.

Throughout the subject and focus is Henry – not his wives, his ministers, his courtiers or his children. All of course appear. And I have written at length about most of them elsewhere. Here, however, they only figure in so far as they help to explain Henry. And the same goes for everything else. I have drawn on an enormous variety of sources, from music and poetry to theology, architecture and marine engineering. But there are no separate studies of these subjects. They are there – as indeed are the politics, the diplomacy, the finance and the administration – only because they illuminate Henry.

This is, after all, a biography; it is not a life and times or, still less, a history of the reign.

I have incurred many debts in writing and researching this book: to my old friend Margaret Condon for allowing me to use her unpublished 'Itinerary' of Henry VII; to Sean Cunningham and Adrian Ailes of The National Archives for checking references and documents; to Adrian Ailes for his further help with heraldry; to Andrea Clarke of the British Library for checking documents and references there and for translating Spanish; to Steven Gunn of Merton College, Oxford for blazing a trail through the obscure last years of Henry VII which the rest of us gratefully

10

follow; to the staff of the London Library who have made it possible for me to write this book here in Kent; to my editor, Arabella Pike and my agent, Peter Robinson for their encouragement, criticism and support, and, above all, to my partner, James Brown, who as usual has read and commented on each chapter as it was written and – not least – put up with me while I was writing them.

The Red House
Barham, near Canterbury
August 2008

CHAPTER 1

ENTRY INTO THE WORLD

Henry, son of Henry VII and Elizabeth of York, was born on 28 June 1491 at Greenwich, the royal manor on the south bank of the Thames some five miles to the east of London. He was their third child and second son, and he was christened in the adjacent church of the Friars Observant by Richard Foxe, then bishop of Exeter, lord privy seal and one of his father's leading ministers.

These bare facts are all that has been known hitherto about Henry's birth. But somehow they have never seemed quite enough. Fortunately, another piece of evidence has turned up which makes clear that Henry was christened with all the pompous ritual laid down in the handbook of court protocol, known as *The Ryalle Book*.

How really could it have been otherwise?

The christening, like most of the ceremonies of the Tudor court, combined the sacred with the secular. And each reinforced the theatricality of the other. First a stage was built, consisting of a tall circular wooden platform with tiers of steps and a central iron post. The assisting clergy stood on the lower steps, leaving the upper step and the reinforced top, with the massive silver font in its centre, free for the stars of the show: Bishop Foxe and Henry.

And heaven help any officious priest or deacon who spoiled the view!

Next, the Tudors' love of rich, many-textured fabrics came into play. These were the principal source of decoration in a court that was always on the move: they could transform a bare and empty chamber in a long unlived-in palace in an hour or two; they could also turn, equally briskly, the plain box of the Friars' church into a setting worthy of the prince that Henry was to be. In charge of these fabrics were the specialist staffs of the royal wardrobes, who now took over.

Benjamin Digby, yeoman of the queen's wardrobe of the beds, and his men covered the wood and iron of the platform with gaily coloured cloth; hung a fringed and embroidered cloth-of-gold canopy over the font from 'line' or cords; lined and wrapped the font with fine linen or 'lawn' and trimmed its edge with a sheer, almost translucent stuff known as 'Cypress' from its original place of manufacture. Finally, other household officers clad the walls of the church with cloth-of-gold and tapestries and laid rich carpets on the floor.

The stagery complete, the performance could begin. Henry was undressed in the 'traverse' or tent-like green room, where more Cypress had been used to cover and draught-proof the adjacent windows. Then Foxe gave him his name and plunged him bodily three times into the waters of the font. Even this had been stage-managed, as the water had been gently warmed beforehand so as not to shock Henry and make him spoil the show by crying.

A new Christian had entered the world, and a new royal prince was ready to take his place in the firmament. Trumpets sounded, the attendants lit their torches, the heralds put on their gold-embroidered tabards and Henry, wrapped in a mantle of cloth-of-gold furred with ermine and clutching a decorated and lighted candle in his hands, was carried in triumph in a burst of light and sound.

Henry had come into the world on a stage; he would live on one and die on one.

Not, it must be admitted, that anybody at the time took much notice.

No chronicler, herald or contemporary historian gave the event more than a passing – and usually retrospective – mention. None of his father's poets laureate was inspired to commemorative verse. Even his grandmother, Lady Margaret Beaufort, only noted the bare details of his birth in the calendar of the book of hours which she used as a sort of family chronicle.

★   ★   ★

How did it come to pass that the Tudor who would make most noise in the world should enter it so quietly and almost unobserved? Partly it was a matter of accident: Henry happened to be born at the wrong time and in the wrong place. It was high summer, and most people who mattered were about to leave stinking, plague-ridden London for the country delights of the Long Vacation. Nor did Greenwich help. Still officially known as *Placentia* or 'Pleasure' in medieval Latin, it was a semi-private riverside retreat, more the queen's than the king's and emphatically off the beaten track.

Nevertheless, intention came into it as well. That Greenwich was used for Elizabeth of York's confinement in the first place suggests that a decision had already been taken to downplay the event. For Henry was the wrong baby to attract attention anyway. In the fullness of time he would be a royal star, effortlessly drawing all eyes and becoming the prime mover of the political cosmos and the axis round which English history turns. Then, he was only the spare and not the heir.

And the spare did not matter – or, at least, did not matter very much.

But there is a paradox, as there will be so often in Henry's story. What made Henry relatively unimportant to others, including his own parents, was supremely important to him. For his status as second son was to condition almost everything

15

about his first dozen years: his upbringing, his education, his relationship with his parents and his siblings, his attitude to women, even where he was brought up.

In short, in so far as the Henry we know was a product of nurture rather than nature, that nurture was determined by his also-ran place in the family pecking order.

On the other hand, of course, all this matters – to us and indeed to Henry – only because in circumstances unimaginable, or at least unimagined, at the time of his birth, Henry was to become the eldest surviving son.

And that changed everything – for England as well as for Henry.

CHAPTER 2

ANCESTORS

Among Henry's earliest memories were stories of his own turbulent family history. Some probably came from the horse's mouth of his parents and relations, and especially his mother; others formed a staple of the teaching of his first boyhood tutor, the poet John Skelton.

Henry, Skelton reminded him in the written materials he prepared for his pupil's instruction, was of 'noble' – that is, royal – blood on his mother's side as much as his father's. This was unusual. But then so was the whole of Henry's family story. For not only were his parents both royal; they both had a claim to the throne. Henry's mother, Elizabeth, eldest daughter of Edward IV, was heiress of the house of York; his father, Henry VII was, much more remotely, heir of the house of Lancaster. And the two claims, of course, were incompatible.

For the last few decades, their – and Henry's – ancestors had struggled for possession of the crown in a conflict known, after their respective emblems – the red rose of Lancaster and the white rose of York – as 'The Wars of the Roses'. Four kings, two princes and a dozen royal dukes had met violent deaths; others, of similar status, had been imprisoned, dispossessed or driven into exile. As well, there were the women who mourned their menfolk, or, at great risk to themselves, plotted and schemed on their behalf. All were Henry's relations: his father, mother, uncles, grandfather, grandmothers, great-grandfather and cousins innumerable.

And if present comfort and prosperity tempted him to forget, men like Skelton were on hand to remind him. 'Although you are of a famous family, nonetheless remember,' he admonished the boy, 'that ruin and exile are no more impossible for you than similar fates were for your fathers.' He then listed the perils of sovereignty in a series of crashing rhymes: *vulnera funerea miserabilia, suspecta tempora formidabilia, occulta odia instimabilia* . . . miserable deadly injury, formidable uncertain times, inestimable hidden hatreds'.

There must have been moments when Henry felt that his tutor had come near to rubbing his nose in it.

Now, of course, the victory of Henry's father at Bosworth and the subsequent marriage of his parents was supposed to put an end to all this. But passions were too entrenched for there to be any such swift and easy conclusion. Instead the aftershocks continued through Henry's childhood and youth, and provided the other great theme in his upbringing.

They determined the why and when of his entry into public life, of the offices he held and the titles he bore. They shaped his extended family and with it his own developing sense of identity and political affiliation. They even helped him choose between his parents: he would incline to his mother rather than to his father and, as a young man at least, preferred York to Lancaster.

It was a rebalancing which, more than anything else, would allow the union of York and Lancaster – sketched only imperfectly under his fiercely partisan father – finally to flourish and become a reality.

Henry's father and mother were a striking couple on their wedding day on 18 January 1486. Aged nineteen going on twenty, Elizabeth of York was one of the beauties of the age: tall, statuesque, with blonde hair, blue eyes, fair skin and pure, regular features. She was singularly attractive as a character too, and in a royal family of strident and assertive personalities, she was a healer and reconciler. King Henry VII, though nine years older, was in the prime of life. He too was well above average height, slim, even spare, but strong and with a full head of brown hair, worn rather long, a brilliant eye and a mobile, expressive face. He had also just shown many of the key qualities of kingship: bravery, decisiveness and the ability to master men and events.

Above all, he had had luck. And he had had it time and time again.

For really nothing was less likely than that this homeless, penniless, long-exiled adventurer, of dubious blood on both sides, more Welsh than English and more French than either, should become heir of Lancaster, king of England and marry the heiress of York.

Henry Tudor was lucky, in the first place, even to have survived the dire circumstances of his birth. This took place on 28 January 1457 at Pembroke Castle on the extreme south-west coast of Wales. His father, Edmund Tudor, earl of Richmond, had died of the plague three months earlier. His mother, Lady Margaret Beaufort, was only thirteen and had taken refuge with her brother-in-law, Jasper Tudor, earl of Pembroke. With her youth and diminutive stature, the birth was evidently a difficult one. At any rate, despite two further marriages, she would have no other children. And it was the depths of winter and the plague still raged.

But, out of these dreadful experiences, the closest bond was forged between Margaret and her only child. Even decades later, their correspondence reads more like the letters of two lovers than of mother and son.

Both of Henry Tudor's parents belonged to satellite families of the house of Lancaster. His father was the issue of a scandalous (and dangerous) liaison between the queen dowager, Catherine of France, mother of Henry VI and widow of Henry V, and a handsome young Welsh squire of her household, Owen Tudor. His mother, Lady Margaret Beaufort, descended from John of Gaunt, duke of Lancaster's equally scandalous relationship with his long-term mistress and eventual third wife, Catherine Swynford. Their many children were legitimated; given the surname Beaufort and promoted first to the earldom and later the dukedom of Somerset.

But they were deliberately excluded from the succession.

Fifty years later, however, their cousin, Henry VI, was having second thoughts. Henry VI was the third king of the house of Lancaster. In 1399, Henry 'of Bolingbroke', eldest son of Duke John of Gaunt by his first marriage to Blanche of Lancaster, had dethroned his childless cousin, Richard II and made himself king as Henry IV. Henry IV's reputation never recovered from the taint of the usurpation and subsequent murder of Richard II. But he did manage to hang on to the throne.

Any remaining doubts about Lancastrian legitimacy were swept aside under his son, Henry V. Henry V was the greatest general to have sat on the throne of England, and arguably her greatest king. He won a second kingdom by his victories in France, compelling the French king to give him his daughter, Catherine, in marriage and recognize him as heir to his kingdom.

Our Henry rejoiced to bear the name of his all-conquering predecessor. Almost a century later, tales of Henry V's exploits, passed on by his mother's aged lord chamberlain, filled his ears as a boy and gave him his ideal of kingship: he too, he resolved, would conquer France and make the name of the king of England the most feared in Europe.

France, alas, eluded him: feared, however, he became indeed – for reasons good and bad.

At his moment of triumph, Henry V died, leaving as heir to both his kingdoms a six-month-old son, Henry VI. Henry VI turned out to be utterly unworthy of his inheritance: he was peace-loving, morbidly religious, and inherited a streak of madness from his French grandfather, Charles VI. Despite eight years of marriage to Queen Margaret of Anjou, he had even failed to produce an heir.

This left the house of Lancaster dangerously exposed, since none of Henry VI's uncles had had legitimate children either. In these circum-stances, he had decided to bolster the dynasty by brokering the marriage between his cousin Margaret Beaufort and his half-brother, Edmund Tudor.

Was Henry VI really thinking of establishing a

strengthened junior branch of the royal line? It is possible. Of course Edmund – despite his close relationship to the king – had no English royal blood at all, and Margaret's was tainted. But – in the absence of anything better – their offspring might be half-plausible Lancastrian heirs in the event of the failure of the senior line.

The arrangements for the marriage were completed in March 1453. By then, it transpired, Margaret of Anjou was already pregnant with the longed-for prince of Wales, Edward, who was born on 13 October 1453. But that did not save his father. Henry VI had already lost most of France; now his incompetence and occasional madness were threatening to cost him England as well. Leader of his increasingly disloyal opposition was Richard, duke of York.

Richard descended twice over from Edward III. Edward III, as he rather smugly informed parliament in 1362, had been blessed 'in many ways and especially in the engendering of sons who are come to manhood'. There were five of them in all. Edward III endowed them with vast estates and borrowed the quasi-royal title of 'duke' from France to distinguish them from the rest of the nobility. Through his father, Duke Richard sprang from Edward III's *fourth* son, Edmund, duke of York. But through his mother he descended from his *second* son, Lionel, duke of Clarence. This, since the Lancastrian kings only descended from

Edward III's *third* son, John of Gaunt, arguably gave him a better title to the throne than Henry VI himself.

And argue it Duke Richard did. From about 1448 he adopted the royal surname 'Plantagenet', and in 1460 he claimed the throne itself. Six months later, however, he was dead and his severed head – derisively crowned with a paper crown – was displayed over the gates of York.

But Duke Richard's son, Edward, earl of March, succeeded where his father had failed. He dethroned and imprisoned Henry VI in 1461 and, reigning as Edward IV, made himself first king of the house of York.

Edward IV, who was only eighteen when he won the throne in battle, was a natural leader of men. He was six feet four inches tall and broad in proportion, with reddish-brown hair, a pink-and-white complexion and a broad, handsome, albeit flattish face. He was charming, too, especially to women, who found him irresistible. But the sunny mood could turn without warning to terrifying violence: he even, the all-too-plausible story goes, held a knife to the woman who would become his queen. He was a great builder, lived luxuriously and maintained a magnificent court as a matter of both policy and personal preference. This lover of life also loved his food, and he became grossly fat in his declining years.

No one, in short, since Edward III had looked

or behaved more like a king. And no one looked more like his future grandson, Henry VIII.

He even married for love.

His bride was a young widow, Elizabeth Woodville, whom he wed secretly in 1464, after a whirlwind courtship. She was bold, beautiful and came from famously fertile stock. Eighteen months later she presented Edward IV with a daughter, who was named Elizabeth after her mother and would become our Henry's mother in turn. Two more daughters followed.

But the marriage was controversial from the start, Elizabeth Woodville, as a subject and a widow, was wholly unsuitable as a royal bride. And she was personally contentious as well. Arrogant, low-born and grasping – with eleven brothers and sisters to provide for as well as the two sons of her first marriage – she went out of her way to alienate powerful Yorkist supporters, including the king's mother and brothers.

The result was that in 1470, affronted Yorkists joined with renegade Lancastrians to drive Edward IV into exile and restore Henry VI to the throne.

The 'readeption' of Henry VI, as it was known, turned the world upside down – not least for our Henry's future parents. For his father, Henry Tudor, then in his early teens, it meant a return to quasi-royal status. Back in 1461, with his powerful Lancastrian connexions, he had been part of the spoils of Yorkist victory, and had been made the ward of the Herbert family of Raglan Castle. They were the Tudors' Yorkist rivals in south Wales. But, paradoxically, his years at Raglan Castle were the most stable of Henry Tudor's youth: the Herberts looked after him well, brought him up carefully and intended him to become their son-in-law as husband of their eldest daughter.

But, as the Yorkist following started to splinter in the late 1460s, Henry Tudor's guardian was among the first to be killed in the struggle. The boy was rescued by his uncle, Jasper Tudor, earl of Pembroke, who escorted him to London to have an audience with his other uncle, the restored King Henry VI. The audience took place on 27 October 1470. And it was then, if later Tudor accounts are to be believed, that Henry VI prophesied that 'This . . . is he unto whom both we and our adversaries must yield and give over the dominion.'

For Henry's future mother, on the other hand, the 'readeption' spelt humiliation and disaster. Probably, as she was then aged four, it was among her earliest memories. She had been with her mother, Elizabeth Woodville, and two younger sisters in the Tower of London, where the queen was getting ready for the elaborate ceremonies of her fourth confinement. But on 1 October 1470

26

news came of her father's flight into exile. Immediately, vicious rioting broke out, and not even the Tower seemed safe. That night, the queen, with Elizabeth and her two sisters, 'secretly' took boat to Westminster 'and there registered her and such as her belonged as sanctuary folk'.

Elizabeth and her mother had begun the day as queen and princess of England; they ended it as refugees. But as York sank, Lancaster rose. On 3 October, Henry VI was released from his prison, where he had not been 'so cleanly kept as should seem such a prince', and was ceremoniously conducted to 'the king's lodgings where the queen before lay'.

No doubt he slept in her very bed.

Meanwhile, in the sanctuary, Elizabeth and her mother found themselves dependent on the charity of friends and foes alike. A London butcher, William Gould, gave them out of 'great kindness and true heart' the carcasses of half a cow and two sheep to feed their household each week; Thomas Millyng, the abbot of Westminster, went out of his way to befriend them; even Henry VI's government provided (and paid for) the services of Elizabeth, Lady Scrope of Bolton, as the queen's lady-in-waiting.

A month later, on 2 November, Elizabeth Woodville was safely delivered of a son. Her own doctor and midwife were in attendance. But, since she was a mere ex-queen, there was no ceremony. There was 'little pomp' either when the child was christened in the Abbey, with Millyng and the prior as godfathers and Lady Scrope as godmother.

Nevertheless, he was named 'Edward' after his father – and in the hope of better times.

And the good times soon returned. Only two years earlier, in July 1468, Edward IV's sister Margaret had married Charles the Bold, the most magnificent and ostentatious ruler of the day. As duke of Burgundy, Charles was a prince of the blood royal of France. But his real power came from his control of the Netherlands, a patchwork of cities and territories which included not only the modern Netherlands, but also present-day Belgium and much of north-eastern France. It was the richest area of Europe outside Italy, and was England's principal trading partner.

Here Edward IV found refuge in his exile. Nevertheless, despite their close relationship, Charles's initial welcome was cool. It became much warmer in December 1470 when Louis XI of France, the ally and patron of the new Lancastrian regime, declared war on Charles. Duke Charles riposted by agreeing to support Edward IV in a bid to recover England.

Things were going Edward IV's way in England as well. Henry VI 'readepted' was no more effectual than he had been the first time round. And the unholy alliance of Yorkists and Lancastrians that had restored him was coming apart. The result was that when Edward IV landed in Yorkshire in March 1471 his invasion soon turned into a promenade. As he marched south, troops flocked to join his little army of 1,500 men and he entered London unopposed.

Once again, it was all change, as Henry's grandfather confronted his great-uncle. Edward IV took the surrender of Henry VI, unkinged him for a second time and sent him back to his prison in the Tower. Then he went to Westminster to liberate his queen and children from the sanctuary. Elizabeth Woodville's first gesture was to present him with his first-born son Edward – the son he had never seen – 'to the king's greatest joy . . . [and] his heart's singular comfort and gladness'.

Elizabeth, for her part, probably never forgot that moment either.

It was the eve of Easter, and Edward IV's enemies expected him to pause for the court's customary elaborate devotions. Instead, he took them off-guard and defeated both groups in turn: the ex-Yorkists at Barnet and the Lancastrians at Tewkesbury.

This time, he decided, there would be no survivors. The Lancastrian prince of Wales and the last Beaufort duke of Somerset were killed in the battle, and Henry VI himself was done to death in the Tower with a heavy blow to the back of the head. No one, a Yorkist chronicler exulted, of 'the stock of Lancaster remained among the living' who could claim the throne.

No one, that is, apart from Henry's father, Henry Tudor.

He and his uncle Jasper, earl of Pembroke, were in south Wales at the time of Tewkesbury. In the wake of the disaster, they retreated first to Pembroke Castle and then, in late September 1471, took ship from Tenby. It would be fourteen years before Henry Tudor saw either England or his mother, Lady Margaret Beaufort, again.

Jasper and Henry Tudor had intended to seek refuge in France. Instead, autumn storms drove them ashore in Brittany. Brittany was the last of the great French duchies to retain its virtual independence from the kingdom of France. King Louis XI, 'the Spider', was determined to end its autonomy; Duke Francis II was equally resolved to keep it. To do so involved a careful balancing act between the three great powers bordering the Channel: England, France and Burgundy.

Henry Tudor was a useful counter in the game – too useful for the duke ever to give him up entirely.

There were narrow scrapes, however, as in 1476 when Duke Francis was bullied into agreeing to surrender him to Edward IV. But once again his luck held, and illness – real or feigned – provided sufficient breathing space for Henry Tudor to escape into sanctuary and Duke Francis to countermand his decision. The crisis over, Jasper and his nephew returned to live at the ducal court, as part-prisoners, part-honoured guests, and wholly dependent on the whim of their host and the shifting balance of power among his nobles and councillors.

Though it might not have seemed so at the time, this too was valuable training. Here Henry Tudor grew up, polished his French and, above all, learned the ways of courts and men. He became reserved, self-reliant, watchful, suspicious of the motives of others, and trusting – if he fully trusted anybody – only the handful of those who had shared the risks and sacrifices of exile with him.

These were admirable qualities for winning a throne. It was less clear how useful they would be in keeping one.

With the virtual destruction of the house of Lancaster, Edward IV's second reign was much smoother than his first. His family continued to grow, with the birth of a second son, Richard, duke of York, and three more daughters. He became steadily richer. And the execution in 1478 of his restless and insatiably ambitious brother, George, duke of Clarence, seemed to remove the last remaining threat to the dynasty.

But then disaster struck. At Easter 1483 Edward IV went on an angling trip on the Thames and caught a chill. Ten days later he was dead. He was succeeded by his son and heir, Edward V. Edward V was a bright and promising boy. But at thirteen he was at least three years short of his majority.

The impending royal minority tore apart the smooth façade of Yorkist England. For who should have the regency: the queen mother, Elizabeth Woodville? Or Edward IV's youngest and only surviving brother, Richard, duke of Gloucester? Both feared and mistrusted each other. Gloucester struck first. He intercepted the boy-king on his journey to London, arrested his Woodville guardians, who were despatched for eventual execution, and lodged Edward V in the Tower.

Possession of the king was nine-tenths of power in late medieval England, and on the back of it Richard had himself proclaimed lord protector or regent. But he could not go further without control as well of Edward V's younger brother and his own namesake, Richard, duke of York.

Once again, as in 1470, Elizabeth Woodville sought sanctuary at Westminster with her remaining children. Then Elizabeth of York had been a little girl of four; now she was a young woman of seventeen. Then, too, the rights of sanctuary had been respected even by Edward IV's worst enemies of the house of Lancaster. Not so in 1483 by his brother Richard, duke of Gloucester. Instead, Gloucester used moral blackmail and the threat of real force to compel the queen mother to surrender her second son. Prince Richard was immediately sent to join his elder brother, Edward V, in the Tower. With both boys in his clutches, Gloucester's way to the throne was clear.

He was crowned as Richard III on 6 July with the materials that had been prepared for his nephew, Edward V's coronation.

For Elizabeth of York, the handover of her little brother Richard was probably even more distressing than Gloucester's previous detention of Edward V. As the eldest son, Edward had been escorted by his parents at the age of only three to Ludlow Castle in the Marches of Wales, there to be put through a rigorous programme of literary, political and religious education to fit him for the throne. He was given his own household and council, and formal 'ordinances' or regulations were issued which spelled out the arrangements for his upbringing in minute detail.

Thereafter, brother and sister met only on the rare occasions that Edward came to court.

Richard, in contrast, had been part of Elizabeth of York's life from the moment of his birth in August 1473. As the second son, he had remained at home with his mother and his sisters. And he had been the liveliest and most attractive of brothers. Years later, a foreign visitor recalled seeing the family together, with Richard at its heart: 'He was, the visitor remembered, a very noble little boy and that he had seen him singing with his mother and one of his sisters and that he sang very well. He was also, the visitor added, very pretty and the most beautiful creature he had ever seen.'

Now he too was swallowed up in the Tower.

While Elizabeth as sister mourned, the queen mother as dynast plotted revenge. She found a willing fellow-plotter in Henry Tudor's mother, Lady Margaret Beaufort. Despite her Lancastrian blood, Lady Margaret had quickly accommodated herself to the realities of power in Yorkist England. Indeed, following her third marriage to Thomas, Lord Stanley, Edward IV's lord steward, she became a leading light in it.

But with Richard's usurpation and the disappearance of the princes in the Tower, it was clear that the tide had turned. Lady Margaret was not one to be left behind. Using the Welsh physician and necromancer Dr Lewis Caerleon as intermediary, agreement was quickly reached. Margaret Beaufort's son Henry Tudor would be betrothed to Elizabeth Woodville's eldest daughter Elizabeth of York; a joint rising would overthrow Richard III and Henry Tudor and Elizabeth of York, now king and queen, would inaugurate a new unified regime in which York and Lancaster would sink their ancient differences.

The marriage of Henry's parents now seemed a serious possibility.

★　★　★

It proved easier said than done. Richard was a competent and energetic general, and saw off with ease the series of badly coordinated regional revolts which was all the confederacy could throw against him. If Henry Tudor had joined them, as had been planned, he would most likely have been captured or killed. And even if he had escaped, his cause would have been damned by personal failure.

But, once again, his luck held. Or rather, a catalogue of mishaps turned out to be for the best. He did not set sail till things were almost over; when he arrived off England, he found the coast occupied by troops loyal to Richard III and decided not to land; finally, storms blew him back to the French coast and – as it turned out – to safety and the opportunity to fight again another day.

There was even a grain of comfort in the defeat of the English risings. Some four hundred of the participants escaped and fled abroad to join Henry Tudor back in Brittany. Almost all the leaders were men of substance: there were Woodville relations, veterans of Edward IV's household and important figures in the local government of the south-eastern shires. Augmented with recruits of this number and calibre, Henry Tudor's following started to look like a half-plausible government in exile.

Things were put on a formal footing during

Christmas 1483, when the exiles held a quasi-parliament at Rennes, the Breton capital, and exchanged oaths: Henry swore to marry Elizabeth of York; his followers, old and new, took an oath of allegiance to Henry Tudor as king of England.

But the strange course of Henry Tudor's fortunes had some way yet to run. Only three months after the meeting at Rennes, his cause suffered a heavy blow. Elizabeth Woodville – tired of the limbo of sanctuary and setting aside whatever moral scruples she felt (they were probably not many) – came to an agreement with Richard III. Still worse, at Christmas 1484 she introduced her daughter and Henry Tudor's proposed bride, Elizabeth of York, to Richard III's court, where both her beauty and the king's treatment of her made a sensation. There were even rumours, which Richard III had to deny publicly, that he intended to marry her after the divorce or death of his queen.

Was Henry's mother a pawn in the hands of others? Revolted at the thought of a marriage of convenience to her brothers' likely murderer? Or did she simply see a marriage – whether to Richard III or to Henry Tudor – that would make her queen consort as the only hope of rescuing the shipwreck of her family's fortunes? All are possibilities.

And where Elizabeth Woodville led, her son by her first marriage, Thomas, marquess of Dorset, tried to follow. After the failure of the revolts of 1483, he, like the other rebel leaders, had fled to join Henry Tudor in Brittany. Now he tried to slink across to England to reconcile himself with Richard III. But he was caught and hauled back to Henry Tudor in disgrace. After this double perfidy, Henry Tudor never fully trusted the Woodvilles again.

Meanwhile, Richard III was making serious attempts to extract Henry Tudor from Brittany. His chosen instrument was Duke Francis II's low-born minister, Pierre Landais, whom he won over by backing him against his aristocratic opponents. By autumn 1484 the minister was ready to deliver his side of the bargain by handing over Henry Tudor to a certain death. But Richard III's proved a Pyrrhic victory. Henry Tudor was warned of what was in store and fled across the border to France. Then, characteristically, Duke Francis changed tack and allowed the other English exiles to follow him.

The flight to France was the making of Henry Tudor. Brittany did not have the resources to back a serious invasion of England; France did. And, as Henry Tudor's luck would have it, circumstances there meant that he was received with open arms.

Louis XI had died in 1483, leaving as his successor his only son, Charles VIII, who was aged thirteen. This resulted in a minority, which as usual provoked a struggle over who should enjoy the regency. The losing side in the struggle then sought an alliance with Richard III. This, on the principle of tit-for-tat, was enough to turn the new French government into enthusiastic supporters of Henry Tudor.

The French court went to Normandy. There, with Henry Tudor present alongside the French king, the provincial estates voted taxation to finance his conquest of England. Men and ships followed. On 1 August 1485 the little armada set sail from Honfleur for Milford Haven.

England, Henry Tudor hoped, would be taken through Wales; it would also have to be conquered by French troops, since Englishmen made up less than a fifth of his army of two or three thousand. This too was lucky, for French infantry tactics were considerably ahead of English.

Henry Tudor came face to face with Richard III's army at Bosworth in Leicestershire. Richard's army was much bigger. But, inhibited by a justifiable fear of treachery, the king's leadership had been uncharacteristically confused and indecisive. The night before the battle he was also troubled by dreadful dreams, and slept badly. As 22 August dawned, however, Richard III recovered himself: it was, he realized, all or nothing.

Twice Richard III launched his forces against Henry Tudor's little army. In the first attack, the king's vanguard broke against Henry Tudor's front line which, stiffened by his seasoned French pikemen, had assumed a dense, wedge-shaped formation.

Richard III's army was now on the back foot. But the king thought he saw a way to retrieve the situation. He caught sight of Henry Tudor with only a small detachment of troops and at some distance from the rest of his army. The chance was too good to miss, and Richard III decided to try to end the battle at a single stroke by felling his opponent in combat, man-to-man.

There followed the second assault, led by Richard III himself.

For the last time in England, a king in full armour and wearing his battle crown and surcoat of the royal arms charged at the head of his heavily-armed and mounted household knights. The impact, psychological as well as physical, must have been terrifying. But, once again, Henry Tudor's pikemen assumed a defensive position – this time in squares – and protected him against the first shock. How long they could have continued to do so is an open question.

At this moment of utmost need, fortune once again smiled on Henry Tudor. Lord Stanley and his brother Sir William had brought a substantial army of their own followers to the battle. Hitherto – torn between their allegiance to York and Stanley's position as Lady Margaret Beaufort's husband – their forces had held aloof.

But now Sir William Stanley charged to rescue his nephew by marriage.

That carried the day. Richard III, despite overwhelming odds, fought on, cutting down Henry Tudor's standard-bearer and coming within reach of Henry himself. But finally numbers told. Richard III was unhorsed, run through and hacked to death. His naked, muddy and mutilated body was slung across a horse and put on public display before receiving a hasty burial. Meantime, his battle crown, which had fallen off in the struggle and become caught in a hawthorn bush, was retrieved and put on the victor's head by Lord Stanley.

Henry Tudor, the only surviving and improbably remote heir of Lancaster, was king.

Events now moved at breakneck speed. On 27 August 1485 Henry VII, as he now was, entered London and offered up his battle standards at St Paul's, on 30 October he was crowned, and a week later, on 7 November, he met parliament. Its first act was to confirm his title to the throne, though without going into awkward details about his exact hereditary claim, while its last, just before it was prorogued on 10 December, was to petition him to marry Elizabeth of York. 'Which marriage,' the speaker declared, 'they hoped God would bless with a progency of the race of kings, to the great satisfaction of the whole realm.'

Five weeks later, the deed was done.

*　　*　　*

The story of how Henry Tudor survived against the odds, and won his throne and his bride against even greater odds, is one of the world's great adventure stories. It made possible our Henry's very existence. But, in the fullness of time, it would also present him with a problem. For his relations with his father were to be complex at best. Yet he could not deny the greatness of his achievement. Indeed, even forty years later he would take him as the yardstick against which to measure his own record.

As well he might. His father had won his throne in battle, in man-to-man combat with his rival. And he would defend it in battle twice more. It was the ultimate test of kingship – and of manhood.

Would Henry be able to do more? Would he be able to do as much?

CHAPTER 3

THE HEIR

The wedding of Henry's parents was followed by scenes of popular rejoicing. 'The people,' Bernard André writes in his contemporary life of Henry VII, 'constructed bonfires far and wide to show their gladness and the City of London was filled with dancing, singing and entertainment.' At last, and after so long, it was possible to hope for peace.

But the marriage was only the first step to the union of the roses. To complete it, the royal couple needed children: the 'progeny of the race of kings' to which the speaker had looked forward in his petition of 10 December 1485.

And, bearing in mind the uncertainty of the times, they needed them quickly. Here again Henry VII's extraordinary luck held. Among his immediate predecessors, Henry VI had had to wait almost eight years for a son, and even the strapping Edward IV for six. Elizabeth of York, instead, gave Henry VII his son and heir within eight months.

He was named Arthur, and the king idolized him. Arthur was unique. Matchless. Perfect in body and mind. Nothing was too good for him, and no limit was placed on the hopes invested in him. He would be more honourably brought up than any king's son in England before. And, in time, he would outdo them all. Never, in short, have so many eggs been placed in one basket.

In time, his father's unapologetic favouritism towards his elder brother would be deeply invidious to Henry. But, in a backhanded way, it gave him space. He was never allowed to share Arthur's glory. But equally, Arthur was never on his back either. Nor was his father. It was a *quid pro quo* that was to have profound effects for both Henry's upbringing and his character.

All queens, of course, were expected to bear children: that – as many of Henry's wives would find to their cost – was their job. But in 1486 the pressures on Elizabeth of York had been particularly intense, as Andre makes clear in his account: 'Both men and women prayed to Almighty God that the king and queen would be favoured with offspring, and that eventually a child might be conceived and a new prince be born, so that they might heap up further joys upon their present delights.'

The prayers were answered. And sooner than anybody dared hope. For 'the fairest queen' became pregnant almost immediately: *non multis post diebus* ('after only a few days').

★　★　★

The celebrations for Elizabeth of York's pregnancy were. Andre claims, almost greater than those for the wedding itself. Everyone, high and low, in court and country and church and state joined in:

> Then a new happiness took over the happiest kingdom, great enjoyment filled the queen, the church experienced perfect joy, while huge excitement gripped the court and an incredible pleasure arose over the whole country.

For the queen, no doubt, the joy was mingled with relief. But Henry VII knew nothing of such modest emotions. Instead, his forthcoming fatherhood only opened up new prospects: greater, grander even than anything yet.

The birth of his first child, the king decided, would be no ordinary affair. It would take place at Winchester. And it would invoke the atmosphere of history and romance that hung around the place. For Winchester was believed to be the site of King Arthur's castle and capital of Camelot. After all, as Caxton had just pointed out in his new edition of Sir Thomas Malory's *Morte d' Arthur, published only the month before Bosworth, the Round Table itself was still there to prove it.*

Then, having been born in Arthur's capital, the child would be christened Arthur too, and Britain's golden age would be renewed.

It was a giddy prospect indeed. But it depended on one enormous assumption: that the child the queen was carrying was a son. Presumably the royal doctors and astrologers had declared this to be the case. And the king must have believed them. For if he were not confident that the child could be christened Arthur, what was the point of dragging the court, the heavily pregnant queen, and the whole bulky apparatus of royal ceremonial some sixty-odd miles to Winchester, over roads that had turned into muddy quagmires in the torrential autumn rains?

It was a tremendous gamble (imagine the shame and confusion if the child had turned out to be a girl!). Yet the gamble paid off, as Henry VII's gambles always seemed to.

But only just. The court arrived at Winchester at the beginning of September. Less than three weeks later, Elizabeth of York went into labour and the child was born in the early hours of 20 September 1486, 'afore one o'clock after midnight', as Lady Margaret Beaufort noted in her book of hours.

The birth was at least a month premature.

Perhaps the queen had been shaken by the journey, in her gaily decorated but springless carriage or, when the going got really rough, in her litter slung between two horses. Or perhaps it was merely the difficulties of a first pregnancy.

★   ★   ★

But at least the child was healthy, and – above all – it was the promised boy. The *Te Deum* was sung in the cathedral, bonfires lit in the streets and messengers sent off with the good news to the four corners of the kingdom.

It remained only to get the ceremonies of his baptism – dislocated by his premature birth – back on track. The main problem was the whereabouts of the intended godfather, the earl of Oxford. He was still at Lavenham, the immensely rich cloth-making town that was the jewel in the crown of the de Vere family's principal estates in Suffolk. Lavenham was over a hundred miles from Winchester, and the roads were getting slower by the hour as the rains continued. To give Oxford time to make the journey, the christening was put back to Sunday, 24 September.

On the day appointed, the other actors assembled: the prince's procession formed in his mother's apartments; while the clergy and his godmother, the queen dowager Elizabeth Woodville, who had been restored to the title and lands which had been forfeit under Richard III, prepared to receive the baby in the cathedral. The earl, they were then informed, was 'within a mile'. It was decided to wait for him.

They kept on waiting. And waiting.

Finally, after 'three hours largely and more', and with still no sight of Oxford, Henry VII intervened. As protocol dictated, the king was out of sight. But he was never out of touch, and, losing

46

patience at last, he ordered the ceremonies to begin. The prince was named and baptised with a substitute godparent, Thomas Stanley, the king's stepfather, who had been made earl of Derby as a reward for his family's behaviour at Bosworth, as his sponsor.

At this moment, Oxford entered. John de Vere, 13th earl of Oxford, was probably the most powerful man in England after the king; he was certainly the noblest, with an earldom going back to 1142. He had been a Lancastrian loyalist even in the dark days after the destruction of the house of Lancaster at Tewkesbury in 1471, and had been imprisoned by Edward IV. In 1484 he escaped and joined Henry Tudor in France. Almost all of his other supporters were tarnished with accommodation at the least with Edward IV; Oxford was unblemished and Henry, who trusted so few, felt he could trust him implicitly, as one 'in whom he might repose his hope, and settle himself more safely than in any other'. It was a relationship that endured, and Oxford became both Henry VII's most important military commander and – by virtue of his hereditary office of lord great chamberlain, to which he was restored – his leading courtier as well.

Oxford now assumed his intended role in the ceremonies. He 'took the prince in his right arm' – the arm that had fought so often for

Lancaster – and presented him for his Confirmation. That done, another procession formed and the child was carried to the shrine of St Swithun, the patron saint of the cathedral, in whose honour more anthems were sung.

The adults then took refreshments – 'spices and hypocras, with other sweet wines [in] great plenty' – while the prince was handed back to the Lady Cecily, the queen's eldest sister, who carried him home in triumph with 'all the torches burning'. The procession passed through the nursery, 'the king's trumpets and minstrels playing on their instruments', and brought him at last to his father and mother, who gave him their blessing.

Arthur's christening was the first of the many spectacular ceremonies that Henry VII used to mark each stage of the advance and consolidation of the Tudor dynasty. Like its successors, it was carefully planned, staged and recorded. It also showed Henry VII's bold eye for theatre – and his willingness to take the risks that all great theatre involves.

Finally, and above all, its scale and ambition make clear why Henry's own christening cere-monies at Greenwich, which were almost domestic in comparison, were so comprehensively ignored by contemporaries.

The court remained at Winchester for the next five or six weeks. Partly this was out of necessity. The queen was ill with an 'ague', which was almost certainly a *post-partum* fever following a difficult birth, and was taking time to recover. Indeed, she seems to have attributed her recovery and her child's survival only to the attentions of Alice Massy, her *obstetrix* or midwife, whom she insisted on using for all her future births. There were also the formalities of her 'churching', or ceremonial purification from the pollution of childbirth, to go through. For most women, the church would only perform the ceremony after sixty days had elapsed from the time of delivery. For the queen this was normally abbreviated to about forty, as indeed seems to have been the case on this occasion.

The time appears to have been put to good use as well to finalize the details of Arthur's upbringing during his infancy – and perhaps beyond.

The basic arrangements for the upbringing of the little prince were already in place. One of the ladies who had attended the christening was 'my lady Darcy, lady mistress'. This was Elizabeth, Lady Darcy, the widow of Sir Robert Darcy. She was the best-qualified person possible for the job, since she had fulfilled the same function, which carried overall charge of the royal nursery, for Edward IV's eldest son, Edward. The substantial fee, of 40 marks, or £26. 13*s*. *4d* a year, was commensurate with the responsibilities of the post.

Almost as well paid, with £20 per annum, was Arthur's wet-nurse, Catherine Gibbs, who as was then customary suckled the boy on his mother's behalf. This was double the amount that would be paid to the nurses of subsequent royal children, including Henry himself, and it was a sum which the cash-strapped exchequer of these years frequently had difficulty in raising. But Catherine became expert at extorting it. On one occasion she resorted to a sob-story. The treasurer was instructed to pay the £10 outstanding on the nail as Catherine 'is now in Our Lady's bonds nigh the time of her deliverance' – in other words, she too was pregnant and near term. Assisting Catherine were Arthur's two 'rockers', Agnes Butler and Evelyn Hobbes, whose job was to rock the prince in his cradle.

No doubt Lady Darcy was *the* practical expert on the Yorkist nursery. But many others in Winchester for Arthur's christening were well informed as well. Elizabeth Woodville, the queen dowager, had been instrumental in setting it up. Elizabeth of York had been on the receiving end as a conscientious eldest daughter. But most interesting is the role of John Alcock, bishop of Worcester, who had just christened Arthur 'in pontificals' or full priestly vestments.

Alcock belonged to the other elite of late medieval England. Aristocrats and gentlemen, like Oxford, supplied the brawn and (occasionally) the beauty and style in public life; the brains and organization came from university-educated clergymen like Alcock.

Their origins were from almost the opposite end of the social spectrum to Oxford: they owed their position to talent and education, not pedigree and breeding, and they wielded their authority by the pen, not the sword. But, despite its very different sources, their power was commensurate with that of the titled aristocracy. They had a virtual monopoly on the two greatest offices in the council, the positions of lord chancellor and lord privy seal; they even had comparable incomes, since the richest bishoprics, like Canterbury and Winchester, which enjoyed princely revenues, were generally reserved for them.

The greatest, the richest, the most splendid of such clerical ministers was to be Henry's own cardinal-chancellor, Thomas Wolsey, who did more, built more and impressed himself more vividly on his contemporaries than any of his predecessors.

But he was also the last – and in part for reasons that were already present in the kind of sophisticated, Latinate education which was even now being planned for Henry's elder brother, and was in time to be enjoyed by Henry himself.

Alcock was thus part of an Indian summer. Born in about 1430, he was the son of a burgess of Hull. He received his early education at the grammar school attached to Beverley Minster, and then continued to Cambridge, where he stuck through the whole programme of degrees, from bachelor to doctor. By then he was about twenty-nine.

The result, however, was anything but otherworldly. Hardly any of Alcock's contemporaries opted for theology; instead, like him, they chose law.

The result was honed, organized, hungry minds.

But Alcock had to wait over ten years for the first crumbs of patronage. Then it fell like manna from heaven. The turning point was the crucial year 1470-71, when Alcock, then an up-and-coming lawyer, seems to have been one of the select group who showed kindness to Elizabeth Woodville and her children when they took refuge in the Westminster sanctuary. Neither Edward IV nor Elizabeth Woodville ever forgot it. In quick succession Alcock became dean of St Stephen's, Westminster, master of the rolls or deputy chancellor, and bishop of Rochester.

This was the prelude to the decision in 1473 to give Alcock joint custody of Edward, prince of Wales and the presidency of his council at Ludlow. His co-adjutor was Elizabeth Woodville's brother, Anthony, Earl Rivers. Rivers had 'the guiding of our son's person', Alcock the responsibility for managing his household as well as presiding over his council. He had also probably had a major hand in drafting the 'ordinances' which laid out their joint roles.

Understandably, in view of his closeness to the Woodvilles and Edward V, Alcock was marginalized by Richard III. But Henry VII restored him to full favour. He was acting lord chancellor at the beginning of the reign and, as a notable preacher (one sermon to the University of Cambridge lasted more than two hours), he became the principal propagandist for the new regime in the pulpit.

Now he, the former guardian of the Yorkist prince of Wales, had been chosen to name and baptize the new Tudor prince. Probably he still had records of the upbringing of Prince Edward; if not, as a seasoned administrator, he knew where to find them.

Alcock's knowledge clearly informed Henry VII's decisions about the rearing of his own son. But Alcock's episcopal colleague, Peter Courtenay, bishop of Exeter, who had just confirmed Arthur in the second half of the ceremonies in the cathedral, also had an important part to play in how the new prince would be brought up.

Courtenay's career was a bolder, bigger version of Alcock's. He was a cut above socially, as a member of the cadet line of the earls of Devon. He had also studied abroad, at Cologne and Padua, the latter then the most famous law school in Europe. There he became rector, and put the finances of the faculty on a sound footing. In the 1460s he had been Edward IV's proctor or legal agent at the papal court; in the 1470s he acted as Edward's own secretary.

Then, in 1483 he took the most important decision of his career. He joined in the risings against

Richard III, and after their failure fled to join Henry Tudor in Brittany. With his position, talents and combination of top-level administrative and political experience, he immediately became one of Henry Tudor's most influential advisers. He was with him at Bosworth, when he was described (rather strangely for a bishop) as 'the flower of knighthood of his country'. A fortnight later he was made lord privy seal, alongside Alcock as chancellor. And he supported the new king's right hand throughout the coronation service.

Now, in Winchester, he was about to get his reward.

Or rather, he was about to get Winchester. William Waynflete, the scholar-bishop who had held the see for almost forty years, had died at his palace at Bishop's Waltham, five miles to the south-east of Winchester, on 11 August, only three weeks before the arrival of the court in the city. Winchester was the plum of the English church, with an income of £4,000 a year – almost three times that of the Earl of Oxford, who for all the antiquity of his title had only £1,400 a year. And it had buildings to match. There was a splendid town palace, Winchester House, in Southwark on the south bank of the Thames opposite St Paul's, and three grand country residences, apart from Bishop's Waltham, at Farnham, Wolvesey and Esher.

The formalities of Courtenay's 'translation' to

Winchester, as it was known, were not completed till April 1487. But the king had probably taken the decision to appoint him on the spot. Part of the deal seems to have been that Courtenay should make Farnham Castle available as a nursery residence for Arthur.

It was ideally suited to the purpose. It was on the way back to London; it was near, but not too near, the city; it had extensive parkland; and it had recently been extended and beautified by Waynflete, who was a great builder.

The king and queen left Winchester in the third week of October, and arrived at Farnham on the twenty-sixth. Arthur, with his nurse Catherine Gibbs and his little household headed by his lady mistress, Lady Darcy, was settled into his new home, and the court continued to Greenwich to celebrate the great feasts of All Saints and Christmas. His mother visited him in January 1487 to make sure that all was well. And in February the townsmen of Farnham successfully petitioned for permission to set up a chantry or endowed chapel with a priest to pray for the king and queen and Arthur himself, who was 'now being nursed' in the town. The same month the king assigned 1,000 marks ($£666.13s.4d$) for the expenses of the household of his 'most dear son the prince'. It was the kind of solitary upbringing that befitted the heir. And it was one that Henry would never experience.

★   ★   ★

But even before the final details of Arthur's household were in place, the political settlement which had been dramatized by his christening had crumbled. One of his godparents had been the great Lancastrian stalwart, the earl of Oxford; the other was the principal survivor of the Yorkist political establishment, the queen dowager Elizabeth Woodville. This was the union of the red rose with the white as it was intended to be.

It lasted for less than six months.

On 2 February 1487, Henry celebrated the feast of the purification of the Blessed Virgin Mary, colloquially known as Candlemas because of the lavish deployment of candles in the ritual, at his favourite palace of Sheen. Candlemas was one of the 'days of estate' or unusual ceremony at court. Large numbers of nobles were in attendance on such occasions, and now Henry took advantage of the fact to call a 'great council'. A 'great council' was, in effect, a parliament without the commons, and this one had more impact, both on the country and on Henry's family, than most parliaments.

The background was a sudden escalation of Yorkist opposition. This had never entirely died away, but now it took on disturbing echoes of Henry Tudor's own successful campaign for the throne. An impostor appeared in Ireland, and was successfully passed off as a Yorkist prince. Survivors of Richard III's regime offered support in England, and the Duchess Margaret in the

Netherlands gave refuge and help to Yorkist exiles, just as Brittany had done to Lancastrian émigrés a few years earlier.

The great council agreed a series of counter measures. Most dramatic was the decision to strip Elizabeth Woodville of her recently regranted dower lands. These were given instead to her daughter the queen, while Elizabeth Woodville herself withdrew from court to live in retirement at St Saviour's Abbey, Bermondsey, on a comfortable pension.

Did Henry VII really fear that Elizabeth Woodville might join in the developing Yorkist conspiracy? That she was on the point of turning against her own daughter and grandson, to whom she had just stood as sponsor at his christening? It seems hard to believe. On the other hand, he may have simply decided it was better to be safe than sorry.

Whatever the case, the effect was the same. With Elizabeth Woodville's retirement, followed by her death in 1492, Lady Margaret Beaufort emerged as the unchallenged matriarch of her son's court. Henry would have only one grandmother. Bearing in mind Lady Margaret's imperious character, he was probably grateful.

The great council had another important result: it flushed out John de la Pole, earl of Lincoln. Lincoln was the son and heir of the duke of Suffolk; he was also, through his mother Elizabeth

Plantagenet, the nephew of both Edward IV and Richard III. He was especially close to the latter, who may have nominated him as his heir. Despite this, Lincoln had accommodated himself to the new Tudor world. He presented his aunt, Queen Elizabeth Woodville, with the towel after her ceremonial washing at Arthur's christening, and a few months later he was one of the ornaments of the court at the celebration of All Saints' Day at Greenwich.

He had attended the great council too. But the Yorkist revival had tested his allegiance too far. Immediately after the council, he absconded from court and fled to join the other Yorkist émigrés in the Netherlands.

It was the beginning of a deadly feud between the Tudors and the de la Poles that only ended thirty years later. Part of the trouble was that the de la Poles proved only too adept at copying Henry Tudor's tactics in exile. Lincoln raised a force of professional German troops in the Netherlands, sailed with it to Ireland, crowned the impostor as Edward VI and then invaded England at the head of an army swollen with Irish soldiers.

For the second time in two years, Henry VII had to prepare to fight for his crown in battle.

He took as his base the mighty fortress of Kenilworth in Warwickshire. Thence, in May 1486 he wrote to the earl of Ormond, the queen's lord chamberlain, to order him to escort Elizabeth of

York and Lady Margaret Beaufort, who were staying at Chertsey Abbey in Surrey, to join him. A month later, the king and queen separated once more. Henry VII moved east to Coventry as he prepared to close in on the rebels. But the queen, accompanied by Peter Courtenay, bishop of Winchester, hastened back to be with her son Arthur at Farnham, where she arrived on 11 June. It also looks as though a detachment of the household was sent ahead to Romsey Abbey, eight miles north of the Solent, to prepare an escape route abroad for the queen and prince if things went badly.

It proved an unnecessary precaution. Henry met the rebels at Stoke, near Newark in Nottinghamshire, on 16 June. The royal army was much larger and the Yorkists were crushed. Lincoln was killed in the battle, while the pretender was captured, uncrowned and, in an act of ironical mercy, sent to spend the rest of his life in the royal kitchens.

Stoke had confirmed the result of Bosworth, and Henry's crown sat that much more firmly on his brow. To celebrate he had a new one made – a 'rich crown of gold set with full many rich precious stones' – which he wore for the first time on 6 January 1488, the feast of the Epiphany and the most important of the four 'crown-wearing' days at court.

This, almost certainly, was the diadem later known as the Imperial Crown. In the fullness of time, the Imperial Crown would become the supreme symbol of Henry VIII's own monarchy and of his revolutionary claims to authority over church as well as state. For his father, on the other hand, it was much more straightforward: a second victory in battle had made his claim to the throne more solid, and he would wear a crown of unusual size, weight and richness to prove it.

Another royal visit to Arthur's nursery at Farnham followed in March 1489. By this time Elizabeth of York was pregnant again. Once more the birth and baptism would be made to symbolize Tudor power, this time in a setting that was even more magnificent than that chosen for Arthur: Westminster.

Since the thirteenth century the palace of Westminster had been the principal seat of the English monarchy – being, at one and the same time, the king's main residence and the head-quarters of royal government, where parliament, the law courts and the exchequer all sat.

The royal birth was to be only one element in an autumn of ceremony. On 14 October, parliament, which had been prorogued on 23 February, reassembled. A meeting of parliament brought together everybody who mattered in Tudor England: nobles and knights, clergy and layfolk. The opportunity was too good to miss. Not only would the lords and commons provide a ready-made audience for the birth of the second royal child, they would also, the king decided, dignify the creation of his first-born as prince of Wales.

The decision to invest the three-year-old Arthur was taken soon after the assembly of parliament; the date was set for St Andrew's Eve (29 November), and summonses were sent out. It is clear that this date was expected to coincide quite closely with the birth of the king and queen's second child. But was it assumed that the birth and baptism would take place before the creation? Or afterwards?

No one, however, would have been bold enough to predict what actually happened – unless, perhaps, one of Henry VII's astrologers had worked his apparent magic again.

On Halloween, 31 October, the queen commenced her confinement with the ceremony known as 'taking to her chamber'. 'The greater part of the nobles of the realm present at this parliament' were in attendance. A month later, on 29 November, the rituals of Arthur's creation began. First he was to be made a knight of the Bath. The ceremonies started 'when it was night' and lasted to the following morning.

But, just as the ceremonies got under way, the queen went into labour. As the king was giving his son 'the advertisement [or solemn admonition] of the order of knighthood', the chapel royal were reading psalms for Elizabeth of York's safe delivery. At a quarter past nine that night a healthy daughter was born.

The following morning, Arthur was created prince of Wales in the parliament chamber, and immediately afterwards his sister was baptised in the adjacent church of St Margaret's Westminster. She was named Margaret after Lady Margaret Beaufort, who stood as her godmother.

After the christening, the infant Margaret was carried back in triumph to the palace, 'with noise of trumpets . . . [and] with Christ's blessing'. And indeed God (or the stars) seemed to be on the side of the Tudors: the double family event was a powerful signal of their strengthening grip on the throne; it also meant that the first two pieces on the dynastic chessboard were in place.

It remained to be seen how much room there would be for the third child, Henry, whose entry into the world – so understated in comparison with the ceremonies for Arthur and Margaret – followed eighteen months later in June 1491.

CHAPTER 4

INFANCY

Immediately after his birth and christening, Henry, like his elder siblings and indeed almost all elite children from the dawn of time to the beginning of the twentieth century, was handed over to be suckled by his wet-nurse. Her name was Anne Uxbridge, and for the first two years or so of his life she was the person closest to Henry. She would have acted as his surrogate mother emotionally as well as physically, and his very survival depended on her good health and assiduity.

Unfortunately, despite her importance to Henry, almost nothing is known about her. We are even ignorant of her maiden name. She had married into a family of minor Sussex gentry, and within a few years would be widowed and remarried to Walter Luke. Assisting Anne were Henry's two 'rockers', Margaret Draughton and Frideswide Puttenham. Theirs was a merely menial duty, and they were paid only a third as much as Anne Uxbridge: £3.6s.8d a year as against £10 for Henry's nurse.

But, menial or not, at least one of them was to

remain around long enough to become a fixture in Henry's boyhood and youth.

These staffing arrangements were more or less identical to those for Henry's elder siblings, Arthur and Margaret. And much the same physical provisions would have been made for Henry as well. These are described in great detail in *The Ryalle Book*. The royal child was to have a nursery apartment consisting of two main interconnecting rooms – an inner or sleeping chamber and an outer or receiving chamber – and smaller service rooms. Dominating both principal chambers were Henry's cradles, known respectively as the 'great' and 'little' cradles.

The 'little cradle' stood in the inner or sleeping chamber of Henry's two-room apartment. It was made of painted and gilded wood, and was just under four feet long. There were four silver-gilt pommels, one at each corner, and two similar pommels on top of the U-shaped frame in which the body of the cradle swung. The bedding consisted of a mattress, sheets, pillows and a rich counterpane of cloth-of-gold furred with ermine. Sensibly, two sets of each were provided. There were also five 'swathing' bands, each with its silver buckle, to hold the child in place and, it was thought, encourage him to grow straight and strong. Over the cradle hung a 'sparver' or canopy, while a traverse, or curtain, could be drawn round it.

And that was the little cradle! The 'great cradle

of estate', which stood in the outer or receiving chamber, more than lived up to its name. It was a third larger than the other, and covered in cloth-of-gold: the royal arms were placed at its head, rich carpets surrounded it on the floor and its cloth-of-gold canopy was fringed in silk and suspended from a silver-gilt boss.

These features – the cloth-of-gold, canopy and carpets – were the essential elements of the chair of estate, or throne, which stood in the Presence Chamber of Henry's father and mother. Even when empty, etiquette dictated that the chair be treated with the same respect as though the sovereign or consort sat in it. The same went for Henry's cradle of estate: gentlemen doffed their hats and bowed; ladies curtsied. And when Henry lay there the bows and curtsies would have been extra deep. Henry might not have been born to a throne. But he was swaddled in the infant equivalent of one.

The equipment of the smaller service rooms of the nursery apartment was more practical, and took account of the fact that the occupant of the nursery was a baby as well as a prince, with the mundane need of all babies for washing, bathing and feeding. There were 'two great basins of pewter for the laundry in the nursery', a 'chafer' (to heat water) and a brass basin in which to wash the child, and a liquid- and stain-proof 'cushion of leather, made like a carving cushion, for the nurse', on which Anne Uxbridge sat while breast-feeding Henry.

Such an infancy – with its wet-nurse and rockers, its cloth-of-gold and ermine, its rituals and deference – seems almost impossibly strange. But then it was par for the royal course: it was neither peculiar to Henry, nor can it have contributed much to what would make him distinctive.

For that we need to look elsewhere, to aspects of Henry's upbringing that were less bound by rules and conventions. Should he, for instance, be brought up with his elder brother? Or his sister? The choice was a real one, since separate establishments already existed for the two older children.

Arthur, as we have seen, had had his own independent princely household from the earliest days of his infancy. For the first two years or more of his life, it had been based at the bishop of Winchester's castle-palace at Farnham, Surrey. A year or two later, by the time of Arthur's creation as prince of Wales, it seems to have moved a score or two miles east and to have been situated in or near Ashford in Kent.

Even less is known about the location of Margaret's much smaller nursery establishment. But it seems a safe bet that it moved from palace to palace with her mother, Elizabeth of York, who normally followed a much less hectic itinerary than her husband, the king. This meant that Margaret was living at Greenwich at the time of her little brother Henry's birth elsewhere in the palace. As she was only eighteen months old herself, she still had her wet-nurse, Alice Davy, as well as her rockers, Ann Mayland, Margery Gower and Alice Bywymble.

At some point in the latter half of 1491, Margaret was weaned and her nurse, Alice Davy, paid off. This still left her with her three rockers, who were duly paid their half-year wages of £1.13s.4d on 31 December. But the 'warrant', or instruction to pay their wages, also lists Henry's own nursery establishment, headed by Nurse Uxbridge. A similar joint warrant for both Henry and Margaret's servants was issued a half-year later, in July 1492.

What was going on? Henry, it seems clear, had been moved in at birth with his sister Margaret. They always kept their separate rooms and, to begin with, their staffs also retained their distinct identities. But the move towards a collective nursery had begun.

It accelerated in the course of the year. By early July 1492 Henry had a younger sister as well. His mother began her fourth confinement at Sheen (which Henry's father was later to rename Richmond) in early June. Shortly after, Henry's maternal grand-mother, Queen Elizabeth Woodville, who had been forced into a discontented retirement at

Bermondsey Abbey in 1487, died on 8 June. Because of her condition, Elizabeth of York was unable to attend the funeral. Her new daughter, born on 2 July, was christened Elizabeth, after both her mother and her grandmother. She also seems to have inherited the Woodville good looks.

Elizabeth joined Henry and Margaret in the new collective nursery, and a warrant was issued to pay the salaries of all three groups of attendants. First to be named was Cecily Burbage, 'nurse to our right dearly beloved daughter the Lady Elizabeth', who enjoyed the accustomed £10 per annum; then came the remaining 'servants attending upon our right dearly well-beloved children, the Lord Henry and the Ladies Margaret and Elizabeth'.

Henry, as the male, came first. But he was outnumbered, as he was to remain for all his boyhood, by his sisters.

The name of one royal child is, of course, conspicuous by its absence from these warrants: Henry's elder brother, Arthur, prince of Wales. He, it seems clear, was still being brought up elsewhere and alone. Quite where at this point we have no idea. But the uncertainty vanishes with the other great event of 1492: Henry VII's campaign against France.

To go to war with France was the natural destiny for a late medieval English king. When it came

68

Henry's own turn, he would embrace it with enthusiasm. His father, however, did so hesitantly and reluctantly. He knew the reality of war in a way his son never would – and, as a usurper who had won his crown on the field, he was all too aware of the risks of battle as well. Go, however, Henry VII finally did, though he put off embarking till October, when the campaigning season had at most only a few more weeks to run.

Henry, who was barely eighteen months old, was of course far too young to understand anything of this. But he could not escape its consequences. Indeed, the war and its aftermath turned out to be the dominant event of his childhood, creating a poisonous web of intrigue and danger of which he found himself the unwitting centre.

The more immediate effect of the campaign, however, fell on the already overburdened shoulders of Henry's elder brother, Arthur. When, seventeen years earlier, Henry's grandfather Edward IV had invaded France in a similarly brief and inglorious campaign, he had made his eldest son Edward, prince of Wales, lieutenant and governor of the realm (that is, regent) during his absence. Predictably, Henry VII did the same, and Regent Arthur, aged six, found himself holding the same resounding powers as Regent Edward, aged five, had done. He was sent to Westminster, perhaps to preside over meetings of the council and certainly to 'attest' or give formal sanction to certain of its acts.

Arthur's regency lasted only a few weeks, until his father's return to England on 17 December automatically brought it to an end. But it had evidently been deemed a success, and it emboldened Henry VII to take the next and crucial step in his son and heir's career. Edward, prince of Wales had been only three when he was sent to receive his academic and political education as head of a devolved administration in the Welsh Marches. Now, in the course of 1493, Arthur, aged six, followed in his wake and, wherever possible, in his footsteps. He too took up residence at Ludlow, the great castle which Edward IV had rebuilt for his eldest son; the powers of Arthur's council were closely modelled on those of Edward's, and some of the personnel were the same. The boys even shared the same physician, Dr Argentine, who was the last person known to have seen the dethroned Edward V, as he then was, alive in the Tower.

Arthur's departure for the Welsh Marches was also the turning point in his relations (or rather lack of them) with his younger brother. Henry was now developing fast. In the summer of 1493 he was weaned, and bade farewell to his wet-nurse Anne Uxbridge, who was described as 'late' nurse to Henry early the following year. In 1494 he learned to ride and (less confidently) to walk.

But Arthur was not there to see it. Instead, he became the brother that Henry scarcely knew.

They met only on high days and holidays at their parents' court. There is no evidence that they ever exchanged letters or even tokens.

Did they, I wonder, spend more than a few weeks in each other's company?

Instead, Henry's world was shaped by his sisters, his mother and her women. And it was as feminine as Arthur's was male: cloth and bedding was brought for Henry and his sisters; linen was purchased to make shirts for him and smocks for them.

Once again, the war of 1492 was pivotal in defining this separation between the experiences of the two boys, Just before his departure for France on 2 October, the king, Bernard André reports, spoke feelingly about his family to the lords of the council, and 'carefully provided for his most noble queen and most illustrious children'. Arthur, we know, he had made regent. But he entrusted Henry and his sisters to their mother, who remained with them at Eltham, near Greenwich, for the duration of the war. Thence she bombarded her husband with letters, and, André claims, her 'tender, frequent and loving lines' played a part in his decision to return home speedily.

Elizabeth of York's feelings we should take at face value; her husband's reaction to them with a grain of salt. But, more importantly, how are we to take André's statement about Henry VII's provision for his family? My guess is that it represented a fairly formal settlement. And at all events, it became so over the next year or two.

Hitherto contemporaries had applied the name 'nursery' only to Arthur's youthful establishment, which, as we have seen, had followed Yorkist precedent and was run by ex-Yorkist personnel, like the 'lady mistress' or head officer of the nursery, Dame Elizabeth Darcy. Arthur's departure for the Welsh Marches and the public stage left this royal nursery empty. It was soon taken over by Henry and his sisters. Their little establishment was first called 'our nursery' in 1494, and within a couple of years the term became common form. At about the same time, a head officer, the 'lady mistress of our nursery', was appointed. But it was not Dame Elizabeth Darcy. Instead, one of the queen's ladies, Elizabeth Denton, got the job. Moreover, Mrs Denton continued to serve and be paid as one of Elizabeth of York's attendants even after her appointment as lady mistress.

This would point to the closest possible connexions between Henry's nursery and his mother's household; it also suggests that the two were usually physically close as well. Which is perhaps why Eltham, where Elizabeth had stayed with her younger children during her husband's absence in France, seems to have been the principal site of Henry's upbringing. It was next door to his birthplace and Elizabeth's favourite residence of Greenwich, and conveniently close to London. The short journey was safe for the youngest royal infant, and ladies of the queen's household could come and go at will. As could the queen herself.

Elizabeth of York, in short, may not have been a hands-on mother, but she was close at hand. And at moments of crisis she could – and did – take charge of Henry herself.

But the choice of Eltham was probably impelled by sentiment as much as convenience. It had been a favourite residence of Elizabeth of York's father and Henry's grandfather, Edward IV, who had carried out extensive building works there including the great hall, with its magnificent hammerbeam roof, and the stone bridge. Nowadays most of Eltham is ruinous, though Edward IV's hall and bridge survive. In Henry's day, when Edward IV had been dead for only a decade, his grandfather must have been a vivid memory. Men who had been his servants probably still worked at Eltham; items of his household stuff were perhaps still in use.

By the choice of Eltham, Elizabeth had made sure that her second son would be brought up in the shadow of the grandfather he so much resembled.

In this little world of the nursery at Eltham, Henry was undoubtedly king of the castle. He was the real king's second son; he was also, for almost all of the time, the only boy in a household of women, and as such was probably spoiled outrageously.

But, despite his primacy, he was always aware of his siblings. His elder sister Margaret was a given in his life. Though slight in stature, like her godmother and namesake Lady Margaret Beaufort, she was (also like Lady Margaret) a formidable character and well able to secure her share of attention.

Then there was the excitement, which Henry experienced at least three times, of the arrival of a new baby, with its nurse and rockers. Room had to be made for a fresh face in the circle and a new name had to be learned. Or, equally mysteriously, it must have seemed to Henry, a playmate would disappear. A temporary hush would descend on the noise of the nursery, and perhaps he would glimpse a blackrobed procession bearing a tiny coffin.

This first happened in autumn 1495, when Elizabeth, the then youngest child, suddenly sickened and died. Infant mortality was heavy under the Tudors, and the death of children was all too common an affliction. But this was the first time that Henry's parents had had to bear it. They were deeply affected. The enormous sum of £318 was spent on the funeral of 'our daughter Elizabeth, late passed out of this transitory life'. A monument was erected to her in the chapter house at Westminster Abbey. The epitaph spoke wistfully of her childish beauty.

Henry was then four years old. Old enough for the death of a pretty young sister to have made an impression, but too young for it to have been a serious blow.

And in any case, a replacement soon arrived, as his mother was already pregnant with another child. She was delivered on 18 March 1496 of a daughter who was christened Mary – presumably in honour of the Virgin, to whom her father bore a special devotion. In the course of the next year, the wording of the warrants for wages for the staff of the nursery was adjusted to reflect the new arrival, and the name of 'Mary' replaced 'Elizabeth' as one of Henry's two 'sisters'.

Finally, on 21 February 1499, Henry at last acquired a baby brother, named Edmund, after his grandfather Edmund Tudor, earl of Richmond. Edmund's wet-nurse was Alice Skern, who had previously suckled Mary, the next youngest child. In 1499–1500 Alice, together with Edmund's two rockers, duly figured in the list of wage-payments for the nursery, alongside the attendants on Henry, Margaret and Mary. A younger brother would have had a much greater impact on Henry's life than the arrival of another sister. He would have been a rival for attention in the nursery; he might have been a political rival when they grew up. But (as we shall see) it was not to be.

Also important in defining Henry's social world were the servants of the nursery, led by his wet-nurse and lady mistress. Nurse Uxbridge's parting from Henry some time in the first half of 1493

75

was probably tearful. But it was sweet sorrow, as the success of Anne's nursing led to a life-time of royal patronage that was the making of her and her second husband. The patronage was started by Henry's father, and was continued on an even more generous scale by Henry himself. Clearly he felt affection, even love, towards her. And while there is no record of reunions between Anne and her former charge during Henry's boyhood, she was to have an honourable place at his coronation.

But his feelings for Anne seem to have been eclipsed by his regard for his lady mistress, Elizabeth Denton. Anne, after all, had left him while he was still only an infant and well below the age of memory. Elizabeth Denton, on the other hand, was the dominant figure of Henry's early boyhood and beyond. This would not necessarily have been to her advantage. Henry, I would guess, was not always an easy child to handle: he was royal and knew it, yet Elizabeth was required to keep him in bounds. In the event, she seems to have got the balance right and Henry was to cherish an abiding affection for her, which he would show by rewarding her lavishly when he became king.

But is there a darker side to the story? Was the scale of these rewards a sign that Henry, neglected by his parents, turned to the women of his nursery for the love that should have come from his own father and mother? Hardly. It was entirely conventional for a king to reward his former wet-nurse and the others who had looked after him in infancy: even Henry's own son, Edward VI, who was the coldest of young fish, did so. Moreover, as so much depended on the royal offspring, their parents would have been mad to neglect them.

Henry VII and Elizabeth of York were not mad. Instead, according to their own lights, they were conscientious and loving parents. If a criticism can be made, it is that they tried too hard, especially with Arthur. They were also bound by the conventions of their times. But these were less harsh than the more schematic historians of the family have assumed. For writers like Lawrence Stone, parental love was an invention of the eighteenth-century bourgeoisie: in earlier centuries and higher social classes it scarcely existed. Henry's parents would have been astonished to hear this: the king's feelings about his family entered into his calculations about the French war in 1492, and the royal couple's grief for the death of their daughter Elizabeth in 1495 is palpable. And when their eldest son also died seven years later, they were nearly broken by the event.

What really shaped their parents' attitudes to the upbringing of Henry and his elder brother was not indifference or neglect, but precedent. As a usurper, Henry's father was more than usually anxious to do the right thing. And the right thing was generally defined as what Edward IV, Henry VII's most recent predecessor to be recognized as legitimate, had done. This is why, as has often been pointed out, the upbringing of Henry VII's eldest son, Arthur, was so closely modelled on that of Edward IV's first son, Edward, prince of Wales.

Much less remarked on, however, is the fact that Henry in turn as second son was being groomed to follow the path blazed by Edward IV's younger son, Richard, duke of York. It was almost, Henry must have felt as soon as he was old enough to understand such things, as though he had a ghostly mentor in whose steps he was fated to tread.

But was Richard, duke of York, so young and handsome, and of whom memories were still so green, a ghost at all? Was he *really* dead? Or was Henry, and still more his father, stepping into shoes that rightfully belonged to another? Were they a king and a prince? Or a usurper and his whelp?

These questions – and others just as inconvenient and seditious – were raised by the campaign of 1492. Henry VII had sent an army into France; the French would riposte by launching a pretender into England.

CHAPTER 5

DUKE OF YORK

In November 1491 a young, French-speaking Fleming called Perkin Warbeck had an awkward confrontation with a group of townsmen in Cork, the major port on the south coast of Ireland. Not surprisingly, for he cut an exotic figure. Most people then, men and women alike, wore thick, drab, serviceable woollens. But Warbeck was clad from head to foot in shimmering silk. The clothes were not his own, but belonged to his master, a Breton merchant called Pregent Meno. Warbeck had just landed in Ireland with Meno, and was modelling the fine stuffs Meno had imported to sell to the Irish elite.

Such details did not concern the crowd, who had eyes only for Warbeck's impressive appearance. Wasn't he the earl of Warwick, son of the executed George Plantagenet, duke of Clarence? they cried. They were so persistent that Warbeck could only shake them off by swearing on the gospels and a crucifix before the mayor that he was no such person. Next two men, one English, the other Irish, appeared. Surely he was the bastard son of Richard III, they said, 'swearing great oaths that they knew well I was [he]'. Once again Warbeck answered, also 'with high oaths', that he was not.

At this point the pair revealed their hands. They were Yorkist conspirators against Henry VII. If Warbeck would act as their figurehead, they would offer him powerful support. Reluctantly, he claimed, he acquiesced. Then his grooming began. He was taught English and 'what I should do and say'. Finally, his assumed identity was changed: from Richard III's bastard to Richard, duke of York, the younger of the two princes in the Tower.

Meanwhile, almost six hundred miles away at Eltham, at the other extremity of his father's dominions, the six-month-old Henry lay in one of his grand cradles. His status too was denoted by magnificent fabrics and furs. And he also was destined by his parents to follow in the wake of his murdered uncle, Richard, duke of York. But Richard's name, title and inheritance were now in contention. Who would gain them? Henry? Or Warbeck?

The scenes in Cork were not spontaneous. In mid-November, Charles VIII of France had financed and equipped a Yorkist expedition to Ireland. This had landed at Cork just before Warbeck, setting the town on edge and creating the explosive atmosphere to which Warbeck's dazzling appearance was the spark.

But equally, Warbeck's epiphany was the fulfilment of the wildest dreams of the expedition's leaders, for in him they had found the most promising Yorkist impersonator yet. Others had tried before, but Warbeck was in a different league. Despite his relatively modest birth as son of a bourgeois of Tournai, he was handsome, literate and affable. He also had the right experience, being widely travelled, multilingual and familiar with the ways of courts from his time in service to the royal house of Portugal.

The conspirators wrote to Charles VIII with news of their good luck. Charles responded by sending an embassy to 'Richard, duke of York'. It bore a courteous invitation to him to take up residence in France, and was accompanied by a fleet to carry him there. Warbeck accepted, and landed in France in March 1492. Charles VIII 'received [him] honourably, as a kinsman and friend'.

Perkin Warbeck *alias* 'Richard, duke of York' had made his entry on to the European stage. And the stage would prove a broad and resonant one. As Warbeck put it himself, 'thence [from Ireland] I went into France, and from thence into Flanders, and from Flanders into Ireland, and from Ireland into Scotland, and so into England'. It was also a saga that would twice seem to threaten Henry's life and lead his mother to seek safety for her son, first in the Tower and then in the remote extremities of Norfolk.

★   ★   ★

Warbeck is – and was – an enigma. Prince? Pretender? Puppet? Pawn? He meant different things to different people; there may have been times when he himself was unsure who and what he really was.

Above all, he assumed a very different importance on either side of the Channel. For Henry VII, Warbeck was a dagger thrust at his very heart. For Charles VIII, he was a mere counter in Anglo-French relations. The result was that each monarch misjudged, almost comically, the reactions of the other. Charles's initial support for Warbeck had been intended to deter Henry from interfering with his takeover of Brittany by marrying its young duchess, Anne. Instead, it drove the English king to his full-scale invasion of France in 1492. Henry's peace terms of course required Charles to renounce all aid to Warbeck. But this too backfired. Fearing that they might be handed over to the English, in early December Warbeck together with his handlers and followers managed to escape across the French border to Malines (Mechelen in Flemish) in the Netherlands. There they found, to their delight and Henry VII's chagrin, a very different patroness to the fickle and calculating Charles VIII.

For Malines was the principal residence of Duchess Margaret of York. Her husband Charles the Bold, duke of Burgundy, had died in 1477, leaving her childless, rich and unfulfilled. But her life found new meaning with the fall of the house of York in 1483–85. Thereafter, the grand passion of her life, which she pursued recklessly and with unrestrained partisanship, became the restoration of her family to the English throne. To achieve this, she would do anything and use anybody.

Now providence, it seemed, had placed the ideal weapon in her hands, and she greeted Warbeck's arrival like manna from heaven: '[I] embraced him,' she wrote, 'as an only grandson or an only son' – the son, of course, that she had never had. She gave him a bodyguard, clad in the Yorkist livery of murrey and blue, an official residence and a high-ranking official to manage his affairs.

Relations between England and the Netherlands were close, and news of Warbeck's reception as duke of York spread like wildfire in England. If Margaret believed him to be her nephew Richard, it seems to have been reasoned, his claims must be true. And if Warbeck's claims were true, then he, and not Henry VII, was rightful king of England.

Even the leading officers of Henry VII's own household were persuaded, and by early 1493 were giving their support to Warbeck's cause. John Ratcliffe, Lord Fitzwalter, the lord steward, committed himself in January. Then, in March, Sir William Stanley, the lord chamberlain and Henry's saviour at the battle of Bosworth, threw his massive weight behind the conspiracy.

★   ★   ★

Henry VII, who had at least an inkling of these machinations, now faced a pincer movement as domestic treason threatened to combine with foreign invasion. One of his first responses, strikingly, involved Henry.

On 5 April 1493, Henry, as the king's *secundogenitus* ('second-born') son, was made lord warden of the Cinque Ports and constable of Dover Castle. The joint position, which was responsible for England's first line of defence against cross-Channel invasion, had been left vacant since the death of the previous holder, the earl of Arundel in 1487. It is easy to see why it needed filling as a matter of urgency to deal with Warbeck. But why the not-yet-two-year-old Henry? Was he simply a suitable dignified front for his deputy, Sir Edward Poynings, who was one of the strongmen of the regime and would do the real work?

Or had it already been decided that the Tudors would deploy second son against pseudo-second son: Henry against Warbeck?

In fact the feared invasion did not happen, since Margaret alone did not have the resources to support one. She was rich and influential, but she was not the acting ruler of the Netherlands. That was Maximilian von Habsburg, archduke of Austria and, as king of the Romans, quasi-elective ruler of the confederation of German states known as the Holy Roman Empire. As if all that were not enough, Maximilian had married Charles the Bold's only child by his first marriage, Mary. Mary had died in 1482 at the age of only twenty-five, leaving two children of the union: Philip the Fair, for whom Maximilian was acting as regent of the Netherlands, and Margaret.

Maximilian was Henry VII's intended ally in the war against France. Indeed, it was Maximilian, rather than Henry, who had been personally injured by Charles VIII's coup in seizing Brittany. The Duchess Anne, whom Charles had married, had already been betrothed to Maximilian; similarly, Maximilian's daughter Margaret was herself betrothed to Charles, and on the strength of that had already been sent to live at the French court as the prospective queen of France. But, despite the double insult of losing a wife and having his daughter repudiated and returned home like unwanted goods, Maximilian came to terms with Charles. Instead, his venom over the affair was redirected against his erstwhile ally, Henry VII.

This meant that when Warbeck was sent to meet Maximilian in Germany, he got almost as warm a welcome from him as he had from Margaret herself, and was received with royal honours. These were redoubled the following year when Maximilian returned to the Netherlands to present his son Philip, who at sixteen had attained his majority, to his subjects as their duke. Ceremony after ceremony unrolled, each grander than the last: at Malines in August, at Louvain in

September and finally at Antwerp on 24 October 1494. Throughout, Warbeck was treated as king-to-be of England. It was at Antwerp that the display reached its peak: his bodyguard of twenty archers wore the badge of the white rose, while the facade of his lodgings was hung with the royal arms of England, with an explanatory Latin inscription underneath: 'The arms of Richard, prince of Wales and duke of York, son and heir of Edward IV, sometime by the grace of God, king of England, France and lord of Ireland.'

This insolent display was too much for a couple of Englishmen loyal to Henry VII. They armed themselves with a pot filled with night-soil and flung the stinking contents at Warbeck's lodgings, before making good their escape. This small, if highly effective, piece of private initiative set Malines in uproar, and an innocent English bystander was stabbed to death for no other reason than his nationality. Across the Channel, however, Henry VII was preparing a much weightier official response.

'Oyez, oyez, oyez!' cried the heralds in early October 1494 as they issued the challenge to two days of martial sport: the first day to be a joust, in which the opposing knights charged at each other with wooden lances; the second a tournament, in which they fought, also on horseback, with heavy swords. A third day's sport was soon added, making the tournament the most ambitious to be held in England since the palmy days of Edward IV's reign. The heralds' cry went up in three several places: in the king's great chamber at the ancient royal palace of Woodstock, to the north of Oxford, where the court was then staying; at the fair in the town; and again in the city of London.

But the cry was also intended to echo round Europe, and 'all comers of what nation so ever they be, as well [Henry VII's] subjects as other' were challenged to respond. For the joust was to celebrate the forthcoming creation of the *real* duke of York, as opposed to the mere pretender of Malines.

Henry, the second son had acquired a dynastic purpose at last.

The background was the disputed inheritance of Richard of Shrewsbury, second son of Edward IV. Before Richard, the usual title of the king's second son was not York but Clarence. The title of duke of Clarence had first been given by Edward III to his second son Lionel in 1362. It had been revived for Henry IV's second son Thomas in 1411, and again for Edward IV's next brother, George, in 1461.

But with the birth of Richard of Shrewsbury the tradition was broken. George, duke of Clarence was still alive and had a son, the earl of Warwick, who could be expected to inherit the dukedom. Edward IV, who was the son, great-nephew and great-grandson of successive dukes of York, and had briefly borne the title himself before his accession, was also anxious to preserve the family 'name'. The result was the decision to create Richard of Shrewsbury duke of York at the age of only eight months.

The ceremony took place on 28 May 1474, the day after parliament had been prorogued for Whitsuntide, and was followed by a splendid joust. A year later, the boy was made, in quick succession, knight of the Bath and knight of the Garter. In 1478, following his child-marriage to the heiress of the Mowbrays, he was given the great and ancient office of earl marshal, which his wife's family had held in hereditary succession. Finally, in 1479, he followed in the footsteps of his namesake and grandfather Richard, duke of York, and was made lord lieutenant of Ireland.

The reasons for following the single precedent of 1474 and creating Henry duke of York, rather than the many and making him duke of Clarence, can be summed up in one word: Warbeck. But perhaps there were more positive motives at work as well. For, as the success of Warbeck's impersonation showed, loyalties to the house of York were still alive and well. Why not make a fresh attempt to incorporate them within the house of Tudor? And who better to do it than Henry? He was close to his mother, Elizabeth of York; he took after his Yorkist grandfather, Edward IV; even his principal residence, Eltham, was one of Edward IV's favourite palaces. At least it was worth a try – after all, in the face of the threat posed by Warbeck, almost anything was.

Warbeck is also why Henry VII decided to do more than simply slip Henry into Richard of Shrewsbury's shoes. Richard of Shrewsbury's accumulation of titles, offices and honours was impressive. But it had also been random and piecemeal. Henry VII would go one better: *his* second son would be inducted into his inheritance in a single, coherent programme of ceremony. There is evidence as well of unusually thorough preparation. Who was responsible for the detail we do not know. But there is no doubt that the inspiration came directly from the king. He kept a watchful eye throughout, and when anything threatened to go wrong, intervened swiftly and decisively himself.

He had to. For he was not only seeking to outdo the Yorkist court, he was also competing directly with the Burgundian. In the last half-century or so, the Burgundian court had reinvented court ceremony and chivalric display as political weapons. Now, with the Burgundian support for Warbeck, these weapons had been turned against Henry VII. Time after time in the summer of 1494, as Maximilian had given Warbeck an honoured place at an *entrée* or an oath-taking ceremony, he had increased Warbeck's standing in the eyes of Europe and diminished Henry Tudor's.

It was now time to strike back, and Henry's creation as duke of York provided the means.

The decision had been taken in the late summer. At that point the royal household split into two: part remained with the king at Woodstock; part joined Henry at Eltham. This sort of division frequently happened under Henry VII. The king could not, of course, be in more than one place at a time. But his household could be. And that was the next best thing. For the household did more than look after the king's domestic arrangements and royal ceremony. It was also a sort of ministry of all the talents, and the department of everything else. This meant that it was fast, responsive and able to tackle the king's principal concern of the moment – whatever and wherever it might be.

And in the autumn of 1494, that meant Henry's creation as duke of York.

The household with the king at Woodstock was in overall charge. It was there, for instance, that 'letters missives' and 'writs' were directed to those who had been chosen 'to give their attendance upon our dearest second son the Lord Henry for to take with and under him the noble order of knight of the Bath'. On 2 October the writs were forwarded in a batch to Robert Lytton, the under-treasurer of the exchequer and himself one of those nominated, together with a covering letter under the 'signet', the smallest and most personal of the royal seals. This instructed Lytton to 'send [the writs] forth in the haste ye goodly may' to the addressees. But first he was to keep a formal record of the writs 'for our interest in case any of them do default in that behalf'.

The king's 'interest' lay in the fines that would be due from any of those nominated who refused to take up the order of knighthood at the king's command. At first, this sounds like a typical piece of money-grubbing by the notoriously tight-fisted Henry VII. But, most likely, his intention was to secure not the largest amount in fines, but the best possible turnout for his son. And he succeeded: twenty-two of those chosen answered the summons; the remainder 'were pardoned or at their fines'. The number and quality of the knights attracted attention, as was also intended, and Sir John Paston's London agent sent him a full list, headed by 'My Lord Harry, duke of York'.

There is no such documentation for the activities of the household at Eltham. But it seems clear that it had two principal tasks. The first was to turn Eltham from a staging-post for the royal nursery into the seat of a new royal dukedom. The second was to prepare Henry himself for his forthcoming creation. And there was plenty to do. After all, it was little more than a year since he had been weaned. Now he had to ride, to walk, to bow, and to stand still; to memorize and repeat a strange oath; to wear robes, coronet and sword; and, most difficult of all perhaps, to remain awake through days of interminable ceremony.

And he had to be confident enough to do all this in public, under the relentless scrutiny of thousands of pairs of eyes. Henry's every move would be watched by the city chroniclers, the recording heralds, the man in the street and – no one quite knew where or who or how many – Warbeck's adherents.

The ceremonies had been timed to coincide with the great feast of All Saints on 1 November. This was one of the four crown-wearing days at court, when royal ceremony was at its most splendid and the court at its fullest. It would be all the fuller for Henry.

On 10 October, Henry's father, mother and grand-mother left Woodstock and began a slow and stately return to the capital. They took a week, with halts of a day or two at Notley Abbey near Thame, High Wycombe and Windsor. On the seventeenth, they reached Henry VII's favourite residence at Sheen. Here they stayed for another ten days before leaving by boat early in the morning of the twenty-seventh, arriving at Westminster in time for dinner.

Forty-eight hours later, on the twenty-ninth, the king sent formally to summons his second son from Eltham. Henry's initiation into public life had begun.

★　　★　　★

He began by making his formal *entrée* into London. The day for this had also been chosen to coincide with an occasion of major pageantry in the civic calendar, since on 29 October each year the newly elected lord mayor of London went in state to Westminster to be sworn in before the barons of the exchequer. The swearing-in took place in the morning. This left the 'mayor, the aldermen and all the crafts in their liveries' plenty of time to return to the City and get themselves in place to welcome Henry.

He arrived at 3 o'clock. He was accompanied by many 'great estates' or high-ranking noblemen, while the city in turn received him 'with great honour [and] triumph'.

One would expect no less, since the City then, like the City now, knew how to put on a show. But, case-hardened to spectacle though he was, the author of the *Great Chronicle of London* was impressed. It was not the pageantry that caught his eye, however, despite the many attendant 'lords and gentlemen'. It was Henry.

As the chronicler noted with surprise. Henry rode through the City 'sitting alone upon a courser'. Henry was always to be an excellent horseman, and his royal studs played an important part in improving the quality of English horseflesh. But in this first public display he excelled himself. For the boy riding by himself on the great warhorse, through narrow, potholed streets and between cheering crowds was not 'four years or thereabouts', as the chronicler thought. He was scarcely three years and four months old.

Henry continued his solo display by riding along Fleet Street, through Temple Bar, the gateway which marked the limit of the City boundaries, into The Strand and King Street before crossing the large open space of New Palace Yard to reach Westminster. It was here, in this supreme theatre of royal ceremony, that his brother Arthur had been created prince of Wales and his sister Margaret christened. Now it was Henry's turn.

First came his introduction to the ceremonies of the court. At dinner on 30 October Henry, together with the most important of those who were to be knighted with him, performed the honorific services for the king at table. One 'took the assay' or tasted the king's food; a second carried his soup; then, when the meal was done and the king was ready to wash his hands, a third bore the water and a fourth the basin. Finally, Henry gave his father the towel on which to dry himself.

By a happy coincidence, this was both the most honourable and the lightest task. Even so, he must have practised hard during the preceding weeks at Eltham: to hold the elaborately folded linen on his arm, to bow, to proffer it, to receive it again, to back away from the royal presence – and to do it all in the right order and with due decorum.

This moment in the king's chamber at Westminster

was, of course, only the start of Henry's training in protocol. But he was a fast learner, and soon knew the rules as well as any gentleman usher. On the other hand – unlike many princes – he never became their victim.

Etiquette, he thought, existed for him; not he for etiquette.

As the short, early-winter day drew to an end and night fell, it was time for the rituals proper of Henry's knighthood to begin. First came the eponymous ceremony of the bath. Twenty-three baths, one for each postulant knight, together with their adjacent beds, had been set up in and around the Parliament Chamber. Henry was undressed and placed in his bath, which consisted of a barrel-like wooden tub, lined and draped with fine linen. Then the earl of Oxford as lord great chamberlain 'read the advertisement' or formal admonition of knighthood to him: be strong in the faith of Holy Church: protect all widows and oppressed maidens: and, above all earthly things love the king thy sovereign lord and his right defend unto thy power'.

When Oxford had finished reading the solemn text, Henry's father dipped his hand in the water, made a sign of the cross on his son's shoulder and kissed it. It was a second, and perhaps higher baptism.

The same ritual was repeated with the other postulant knights, Meanwhile, Henry had been lifted from his bath into his bed and there dried. Then he was dressed in a rough hermit's gown, and accompanied by his twenty-two companions in similar attire, led in procession to St Stephen's Chapel on the east or river side of the palace. There, amidst its marble columns, gilded carving and superbly painted walls, Henry and the rest kept vigil till the small hours, before confessing, receiving absolution and hearing mass. They then returned to their beds and slept till daybreak.

When Henry was roused, he found Oxford, two earls and the lord treasurer by his bed. They proffered him his clothes and helped him dress, as they did with his companions. The knights-to-be then made their way through the private passages on the east side of the palace to New Palace Yard. There the postulants, headed as always by Henry, took horse and rode across the yard into Westminster Hall. The hall still stands much as Henry saw it. Its vast interior is like the apotheosis of the railway station. Compared to it, the hall at Eltham must have seemed as small as his own chamber. At the foot of the dais, he dismounted. Clearly he found riding easier than walking, especially when encumbered with elaborate robes, for, with the lesser or White Hall still to traverse, he was carried by Sir William Sandys into the king's presence. At Henry VII's command, the duke of Buckingham put on his son's right spur and the marquess of Dorset his left. The king himself girded him with the sword and dubbed him knight 'in manner accustomed'.

Then he picked him up 'and set him upon the table'. Was it fatherly pride? Or only a determination that everybody could see?

What, if anything, did the three-and-a-half-year-old Henry understand of all this, let alone remember? The higher symbolism – of physical cleansing, spiritual purification, sleep and awakening as a (re)new(ed) man – would have been beyond him, as indeed it was probably beyond most of his adult fellow-postulants as well. Perhaps instead the event lingered in his memory as a series of intense sensory experiences: cold and heat; wetting and being towelled dry; the scratchy fabric of his hermit's gown; the mysterious gloom of the chapel in the small hours and the weariness of staying up later than he'd ever done before; and, in the morning, the exhilaration of showing, once more, that he could ride all by himself.

Or maybe there *was* more. Maybe he even understood, more or less, what was going on. For in fact he had heard it all before, so many times, in the tales told by his nurse, his lady mistress and his women: of knights, of oaths, of maidens in distress, of vigils, watches, disguises and transformations; of hermits, monsters and kings. It was the world of romance and chivalry that he had inhabited already in his imagination and dreams. Now he was part of it indeed.

He was a knight! He had sworn the oath. Kept vigil in the church. Ridden the horse. Been touched by the sword. He was a knight! He would be athlete, hero, icon.

He was a knight!

The next day was 1 November, All Hallows' Day, and the day of high festival which had been chosen for Henry's creation as duke of York. After hearing matins, the king came robed and crowned into the Parliament Chamber and took up his position on the dais under the cloth of estate. He was surrounded by the lords spiritual, headed by John Morton, the cardinal-archbishop of Canterbury, and the lords temporal, including two dukes, four earls, and 'the substance of all the barons of this realm'. The assembled dignitaries also included the judges, the master of the rolls, the lord mayor and aldermen of London and a 'great press' of knights and esquires.

The place and the personnel (apart from the representatives of the City) were the same as for a parliament; the author of the 'Black Book of the Garter', a near contemporary, even mistook it for one, which was exactly what was intended. Richard of Shrewsbury had been created duke of York during a parliamentary session; Henry must at least appear to have been.

For the first of so many times, Henry was to meet the political elite of England. His procession formed in St Stephen's Cloister, marched through the gallery and entered at the lower end of the Parliament Chamber. First came the heralds, with Garter king of arms carrying the letters patent of creation. Then followed three earls in their crimson parliament robes: the earl of Suffolk, bearing a rich sword pommel upwards, the earl of Northumberland a rod of gold, and the earl of Derby a cap of estate and a coronet. Behind them walked the earl of Shrewsbury, again robed, carrying Henry. When Henry came into the Parliament Chamber he was conducted to the king by the marquess of Dorset and the earl of Arundel, who were also robed. After they had all bowed to the king, Oliver King, the royal secretary, read the patent which created Henry duke of York, 'with the gift of a thousand pound by year'. The king then invested his son with the sword, the rod, the cap and the coronet, and the whole company adjourned to St Stephen's for a solemn mass celebrated by the cardinal-archbishop in cope and mitre, assisted by eight bishops and yet more abbots, also in pontificals.

The service ended and a grand procession was formed. This was joined by the ladies of the court, headed by the queen, also crowned, and Lady Margaret Beaufort, in her coronet, both of whom had heard the service in the queen's closet or private pew.

At this climax of the ceremonies, Henry VII took direct charge. Standing in the dean's stall of

St Stephen's Chapel, he settled two disputed cases of precedence on the spot and 'ordered' the procession himself. We can judge the result thanks to the reports of two very different observers. The first was that of Sir John Paston's London agent, the priest Thomas Lyng, who must have joined the gaping throng in Westminster Hall. 'The king and queen went crowned on Hallowmas Day last,' he wrote, 'and my lord of Shrewsbury bare My Lord Harry, duke of York, in his arms; and ten bishops, with mitres on their heads, going before the king that day round about Westminster Hall, with many other great estates.'

Lyng's may be the voice of everyman. But the picture he conjures up, of the red-robed figures in their crowns, mitres and coronets, processing round the half-lit spaces of Westminster Hall, is an unforgettable one. The professional's judgment was more discriminating. The procession, in the view of the herald who drew up the account of the ceremonies, was 'the best ordered and most praised of all the processions that I have ever heard of in England'.

After the procession, the king changed out of his robes and dined. At the end of the second course, the heralds cried 'largesse' for the king and then for Henry in his new style. 'Largesse,' the cry went up in old French, 'largesse of the most high, mighty and excellent prince, second son of the king our sovereign lord, duke of York, lieutenant-general of Ireland, earl marshal, marshal of England, lord warden of the Cinque Ports, largesse.'

The careful preparations, the king's own intervention and his son's precocious ease and confidence in public had all had their effect. The result was that there was no doubt who had won the battle of ceremony: Henry, duke of York in London had faced down with ease the cardboard pretender in Malines.

But was ceremony enough? Henry's father was far too wise to rely on it alone. Instead, on 7 November and again on the eleventh, the king took advantage of the presence of so many dignitaries for his son's creation to hold two unusually large meetings of the council. The king himself presided and one of those present was Sir William Stanley, the lord chamberlain and Warbeck's latest and most important recruit. Each, king and councillor, was acting a charade. But, being public men, they probably played it well.

The minutes (which rarely tell the whole story) note the setting up of a sub-committee to prepare draft legislation for the next parliament; while suitors complained that, because 'there hath been so great council for the king's matters', Cardinal Morton, who was also the lord chancellor, had only sat in Star Chamber for one day out of seven.

Was the consideration of future legislation really so pressing? Or, whatever the formal record may say, were Warbeck and his English adherents on the agenda as well?

Despite these backstage machinations – or perhaps indeed as a deliberate screen for them – the round of celebrations continued regardless, though a little later than planned. The joust had originally been announced as taking place on 4, 9 and 12 November. But the fourth turned out to be the 'obit' or anniversary of the death of 'the full noble memor the king's father', Edmund Tudor, earl of Richmond, out of respect for whom the whole series was put back five days, to the ninth, eleventh and thirteenth.

There is no reason to suppose that the oversight was other than genuine. But it did leave useful time to prepare for the extraordinary meetings of the council.

Henry, no doubt, was frustrated at the delay. But on the ninth he took his place in the royal box alongside his parents as the first of the 'great estates of the realm'. It was his first joust, and he was not to be disappointed. The second day, on the eleventh, was especially exciting. The challengers pranced on to the field under new-fangled pavilions made of sumptuous fabrics and embroidered with different mottoes: 'For to accomplish' or 'Our promise made'. And they accomplished their promises indeed in the exuberant violence of the sport. Best was the tourney or mounted sword-fight between Sir Robert Curzon and Thomas Brandon. First their swords became locked together in Curzon's gauntlet, and Curzon nearly dragged Brandon out of the saddle in his struggle to extricate it. Brandon saved the day by pulling off Curzon's gauntlet, sword and all. Re-armed at the king's command, they then both broke their swords on each other's armour, before finishing the bout with new weapons.

And all this was done in *his* honour. The challengers wore *his* new 'colours of the duke of York, that is to say, blue and tawney'. And, when the prizes were awarded after supper, special thanks were given to the contestants in *his* name: 'the noble and mighty prince the second son of the king our sovereign lord, the duke of York, in the honour of whose creation this noble joust and tourney hath been holden'.

Henry could hardly wait to take part as a combatant himself.

Only one other member of the royal family was permitted to share in his glory: his sister Margaret, with whom he had been brought up since birth. She presented the prizes to the contestants at the end of the first two days of the joust. And on the final day of the tournament she herself was the focus of attention. The tournament was a kind of ladies' day: held, as the challenge stated, to give pleasure to the ladies of the court and in particular to 'their redoubted lady and fairest young princess, the eldest daughter to our sovereign lord the King'. The day began with a pageant of four ladies leading four knights, and it ended with proclamation of the prizes. Garter, the other kings of arms, heralds and pursuivants, 'standing on high on a form', offered thanks in the name of 'the right high and excellent princess the Lady Margaret', who again presented the winners with their prizes of a diamond and a ruby ring.

She was taking her place as the first lady of the court, just as her younger brother was to be its first gentleman.

The Christmas celebrations that year took place at Greenwich. Henry, rejoicing in his new dignity, may have made the short journey from Eltham to join his parents for the festivities. But he would not have stayed long, as the celebrations were kept to the bare minimum of twelve days, for the king had work to do.

Over the course of the holidays, Henry VII had received news that Sir Robert Clifford, one of Warbeck's principal adherents in Malines, had been turned and was being escorted back to England with proof positive of the treasonable communications between the pretender and his adherents in England. On 7 January 1495, the day after Twelfth Day, the king returned to London and took up residence in the Tower, 'in order', Polydore Vergil claims plausibly, 'that he might at once imprison in that safe place any members of the plot whom [Clifford] might name'. Clifford was brought to the king on 9 January and interrogated. Immediately afterwards, Sir William Stanley, who was discharging his duties as chamberlain at court, 'suddenly was arrested and put under sure keeping'.

The trap had snapped shut smoothly. Stanley, who had a powerful armed following and was well able to resist arrest, had entered the Tower voluntarily, in all his glory as lord chamberlain. He would leave it only as a condemned man. His trial took place on 6-7 February and he was executed nine days later. Lord Steward Fitzwalter's trial followed at the end of the month. His sentence was commuted to life imprisonment, but within two years he too was executed, on pretext of having tried to escape.

What, the London chronicler wondered, had Stanley, with his wealth, his property and his power, been thinking of when he threw it all away 'for a knave [Warbeck] that after was hanged'.

CHAPTER 6

RIVAL DUKES

The bloodlettings in England in early 1495 did nothing to dampen the ardour of Warbeck's support in the Netherlands. The result was that for the next few years there were two rival dukes of York: Henry at Eltham, and Warbeck almost anywhere as his quest for his kingdom began in earnest. One thing the two had in common was their need for money: Henry to maintain his state, Warbeck to recover it.

At Henry's creation as duke of York, his father had announced his intention to endow his second son 'with the gift of a thousand pound by year'. He did so, however, at no direct cost to himself. The king's uncle, Jasper Tudor, had received substantial land grants, both from his half-brother Henry VI, when he created him earl of Pembroke, and from Henry VII himself, when he promoted him to the duchy of Bedford. But Jasper was childless, while his wife was well provided for in her own right as dowager duchess of Buckingham.

This left the way clear for an act of parliament

of 1495 which, in effect, made Henry his great-uncle Bedford's heir: providing that, after his death, Bedford's lands were to pass to Henry, duke of York 'for the maintenance, supportation. relief and sustaining' of his honours and offices. Despite his nonage, the act gave Henry power to grant leases and offices. But the grants required the agreement and signature of the king, the duke's chancellor and three of his other councillors. In practice, the king seems to have kept the management of the duke's estates very much in his own hands. Henry VII also protected the longer-term interests of the crown by stipulating that, if Henry became heir apparent by the death of his brother Arthur, 'which God forbid', Bedford's lands were to revert directly to the crown.

As Bedford died on 21 December 1495, the day that parliament was dissolved, the act took immediate effect. In addition, Henry VII intended to add to his second son's lands by purchase. Henry, Lord Grey of Codnor, who died in 1496. had no children. Even before his death it looks as though the king was angling to obtain his lands. Five years later, in 1501, Henry VII agreed to pay Lord Grey's executors £1,000 for the castle of Codnor and other lands for the use of his second son, Henry. Codnor, in Derbyshire, is remote, and forty years later the castle was described as 'all ruinous'. But at the time it looks as though it was intended to become an outpost of Henry's dukedom.

★　★　★

Estates on this scale were sufficient to maintain a substantial establishment. The figures in Kate Mertz's *The English Noble Household, 1250–1600* suggest that a lord with an income of about £1,000 a year would spend about £600 on his house-hold. This tallies well with the fact that Henry VII assigned 1,000 marks (£666.13s4d) 'for the expenses of the household of our right dear and right well beloved son the duke of York'. The sum actually spent was usually a few pounds higher, and the difference was made up in arrears by annual payments from the exchequer and chamber. Expenditure at this level would support, again according to Mertz, a household of about fifty.

We know the names of only a few. As usual, the financial staff are best documented. The receiver of Henry's lands was John Heron, who was also treasurer of the chamber. In his capacity as Henry's receiver, he was paid a fee of £10 from about 1497, though he did not obtain a patent formally granting him the office and fee until 1503. William Fisher was treasurer of Henry's household in 1496, but he had been replaced by John Reading within a year. Reading received a commission to purvey, that is, obtain at preferential prices, victuals for the duke's household in 1498. Other casual references give the names of one of Henry's chaplains and of a couple of servants without specified duties. Finally there is mention of 'the duke of York's schoolmaster', to whom the king gave a reward of £2 in 1502.

How much difference in practice all this made

to Henry's position is unclear. The guess must be that it altered rather little. Henry continued to live with his sisters at Eltham, to share his upbringing with them and to be attended by their joint staff. What changed instead were words. The joint staff became the 'attendant[s] in our nursery upon our right dear and right entirely well-beloved son the duke of York and the lady Margaret and Mary his sisters'. And Henry's own title and mode of address changed too, of course.

But equally, words and titles matter – especially if you are royal.

Finally, there is something more indefinable. Henry's creation and endowment as duke of York marked his entry into his inheritance as a prince of the blood. It also made the rivalry with Warbeck evident and inescapable. The 'dukedom [of York],' one of Henry's future servants, Sir William Thomas, asserted flatly, 'belongs to the king of England's second son.' Only force could determine which of the rival dukes would possess it.

Warbeck and his handlers understood this too. But how to raise the funds necessary to mount a serious invasion of England? Warbeck had no resources, and the goodwill of Margaret of York and Maximilian would only stretch so far. Instead, at the turn of the year 1494–95, it was decided, in effect, to mortgage England to pay for its future conquest.

Two sets of deeds were executed. In the first, between the pretender and his 'aunt' Margaret of York, Warbeck pledged himself not only to compensate her for her outlay on the expeditions against Henry VII in 1486 and '87, but also to settle all her claims on England going back to the third of her dowry which was still unpaid at the time of Charles the Bold's death in 1477. The second agreement, between Warbeck and Maximilian, was even more extravagant. In this the pretender promised, in return for Burgundian hospitality and assistance, to nominate Maximilian and his son Philip as his heirs to the dominions of the English crown should he die before he had issue of his own.

With England as security, fundraising now proceeded apace. Maximilian made over, covertly as well as openly, some of his Netherlandish revenues. Commercial moneylenders were also encouraged to take a punt on Warbeck's success. The result was that by June 1495 a substantial amphibious force had been raised, consisting of fifteen ships and a mixed force made up of English exiles, mercenaries and international soldiers of fortune. Not, in short, very different from the expedition which Henry, earl of Richmond, had captained in 1485 when he set out to recover his right in England.

Back in England, however, early 1495 was not all trials and executions. By late January, Henry VII had discovered all he needed to know about

Warbeck's English adherents, and the court moved from the Tower to Henry's birthplace of Greenwich.

There, on 4 February 1495, the wedding of the year took place in the presence of the king and queen. The bride was the queen's sister, Anne Plantagenet, and the groom Lord Thomas Howard, son and heir of the earl of Surrey. Elizabeth of York had brokered the marriage, with the 'assent' of the king, while its financial terms were ratified by an act and an amending act of parliament, which were passed 'at the special desire' of the queen, in view of her 'very will and mind' that the money be paid in full.

Perhaps, bearing in mind his mother's enthusiasm, Henry, nearby at Eltham, was brought over to join in the family celebration. The marriage is forgotten now. But at the time it seemed the most significant in England since the wedding of Henry's own parents nine years earlier. For, like that wedding, it involved a union of political opposites.

The groom's father, Thomas Howard, earl of Surrey, was the most important survivor of Richard III's regime. He had fought at Bosworth alongside his father, John Howard, duke of Norfolk. Norfolk had been killed by Henry Tudor's forces and Thomas captured. Subsequently, both were attainted, that is, declared legally dead, by Henry VII, and their estates and titles confiscated. But Thomas was not executed; instead, he was given the opportunity to redeem himself. And he took it. It was a carefully calculated policy of *quid pro quo*: Thomas showed loyalty and usefulness, Henry VII gave him honour and favour. Step by step his estates were regranted and in 1489 his earldom itself was restored.

The year 1495 marked another major stage in Thomas's rehabilitation: he recovered a further large tranche of his lands, while his reconciliation with the king was confirmed by his son's marriage to the king's sister-in-law.

Thomas Howard, unlike Sir William Stanley, who went on trial for his life two days after the wedding, had decided that Henry Tudor was a better bet than Perkin Warbeck.

But the marriage was, still more, a reconciliation with the queen. For the inheritance of the Mowbrays, dukes of Norfolk and earls of Surrey, had been disputed between the Howards and the Plantagenets. And, once again, the brief life of Richard of Shrewsbury, Elizabeth of York's younger brother and our Henry's *alter ego*, was at the heart of the story.

Richard of Shrewsbury had been married to Anne Mowbray, daughter of the last Mowbray duke of Norfolk, in 1478, and given the dukedom of Norfolk (alongside his own duchy of York) in right of his wife. Anne died three years later, aged only eight and of course childless. But Richard of Shrewsbury kept the dukedom of Norfolk and the lands.

This was to challenge head-on the claims of John Howard. He descended in the female line from the Mowbrays; he had also been an ardent Yorkist. But Edward IV was more interested in protecting the rights of his son, Richard of Shrewsbury, than in recognizing faithful service. Howard's opportunity came with Richard III's usurpation. Howard supported him at every step, and was rewarded with the dukedom of Norfolk and its vast estates. This meant that the princes in the Tower posed as much a threat to the Howards as to Richard III. Some even suspect that Norfolk was their murderer. This seems unlikely. But certainly there was bad blood between the two families.

The marriage of Anne Plantagenet (Richard of Shrewsbury's sister) to Lord Thomas Howard (John Howard's grandson) was a vital step towards neutralizing this poisonous legacy. Even more important, however, had been his parents' decision about Henry himself. The previous autumn he had been given all of Richard of Shrewsbury's titles and offices – with one exception: the dukedom of Norfolk. That was left unfilled, as a final carrot to be dangled in front of the Howards.

And, as it happened, it was Henry himself who would restore it to them, along with the ancient office of earl marshal, which the Mowbray dukes had held in hereditary succession, and which Henry *had* been granted in 1494.

★　　★　　★

Henry, whether or not he was present at the wedding, was deeply interested in its outcome. Anne Plantagenet was his aunt and one of his mother's leading attendants; Lord Thomas was now his uncle; while their children would be his cousins and, apart from his own siblings, his closest relations near to his own age. Four were born, three of whom died at birth. The fourth lived and was baptized Thomas after his father. But this baby too died on 3 August 1508, and was buried at Lambeth with the monumental inscription 'Lord Howard, son of Thomas Lord Howard, and of his wife the daughter of Edward IV'.

One wonders what his pride would have been had he lived – or what kind of problems he would have presented to his cousin Henry.

Anne herself died in 1511, and her husband promptly set himself to find another wife who would keep him within the charmed – and dangerous – circle of royalty.

Henry may have had a second family wedding to attend in 1495 as Catherine Plantagenet, aged only sixteen and next to the youngest of the queen's sisters, followed Anne to the altar. Her husband was Lord William Courtenay, son and heir of the earl of Devon. Their marriage settlement was also ratified in the same parliament as the more complex one between Anne and Lord Thomas Howard. By the act, the earl transferred his principal estates to a group of trustees to the ultimate benefit of his son and daughter-in-law.

First of a distinguished list of names was Henry himself as duke of York.

On the other hand, the queen's involvement does not appear so explicitly as in the arrangement of the Howard marriage. But her role must have been similar, since she financed this marriage as well by supporting the whole young family: she paid for clothes for Lord William, gave Lady Catherine an annuity of £50 as one of her principal ladies and defrayed the entire cost of bringing up their children.

Once again, it was politics that spoke. The sixth and seventh Courtenay earls of Devon had been committed Lancastrians, and had paid the price: the former was beheaded after the battle of Towton in 1461; the latter was killed at Tewkesbury, that graveyard of Lancastrian hopes, ten years later. With the death of the seventh earl the direct line of the house was extinguished. The *male* heir was Edward Courtenay of Bocconock in Cornwall, who descended from a collateral branch. In 1483, like his kinsman Peter Courtenay, bishop of Exeter, Edward threw his lot in with the Tudor cause: he joined in Buckingham's revolt, escaped its failure by fleeing to join Henry Tudor in Brittany, returned with him in August 1485, fought at Bosworth and was restored to the earldom the following October.

Here then was a record of Lancastrian loyalism – both personal and familial – that was second only to the earl of Oxford's. The marriage between Earl Edward's son and Edward IV's daughter was thus both a reward, and a renewal of the union of the Roses in the face of Warbeck's rival appeal to Yorkist sentiment.

Unlike many political unions, the marriage seems to have been happy; certainly it was fruitful. There were three children: Henry, Edward and Margaret. They were brought up in the country near Havering-atte-Bower in Essex. The old royal residence had long been part of the queen's dower, and under Elizabeth horses were bred on the estate. This may be why Dame Margaret, the wife of Sir Roger Cotton, the queen's master of the horse, headed the little nursery that was a miniature version of the establishment for Henry and his sisters across the river at Eltham.

Plenty of clothes were bought for the children, and soap to wash them with. But, despite hygiene and healthy country air, Lord Edward died in infancy in July 1502. News of his death was brought to the queen, who paid for his funeral. In December 1502 the two surviving children were brought up from Havering to the court in London and settled in their own chamber, which was furnished with additional necessaries like candlesticks and cupboard cloths. Lord Henry promptly fell sick. With the life of the queen's only surviving nephew at risk, a surgeon was summoned and paid the substantial sum of 10 shillings 'for medicines by him ministered upon the Lord Henry Courtenay'.

Usually, sixteenth-century cures were worse than the disease. Nevertheless, the boy survived to play a momentous part in the reign of his cousin and namesake, Henry VIII, as his closest male relation.

Henry had been at most an onlooker at his aunts' weddings. But a few months later, in May 1495, he was once again the centre of attention at his installation as knight of the Garter. The Garter ceremonies were fixed for Sunday, 17 May. On 4 May the exchequer was instructed to pay 100 marks (£66. 13s.4d) for the feast. But payment was delayed, as was usual at this period. On the twelfth Henry VII sent an urgent reminder. 'The day of the said feast is at hand', he pointed out to under-treasurer Lytton, when 'we have appointed our dearest second son the Duke of York to be installed Knight of the Garter'. Further delay in payment was unacceptable, as 'this matter toucheth so near our honour'.

Once again, as when he had personally marshalled the procession for Henry's creation as duke, Henry VII was intervening to make sure that his second son entered public life in proper style. The records of the Garter, as the great register of the order known as the 'Black Book' notes, are 'a perfect silence' for this period. But Henry would have been

117

vested with the robes of the Garter: the kirtle or gown, the mantle and the hood, all of blue velvet lined with white damask; sworn his oath; had the Garter itself buckled round his left leg, and been conducted to his stall in the chapel by the two most senior knights present.

Whether his father the king was there in person or entrusted the installation of his son to deputies is unclear. But the payment on 18 May, the day after the feast, of £13.6s.8d to Sir Charles Somerset, the vice-chamberlain and captain of the guard, 'for offerings and expenses of my Lord Henry, duke of York, at his installation', probably argues against the king's own involvement. Two years later white damask was ordered for lining or relining a 'gown of garter' for Henry.

Could he have been boy enough to have spilt something on his new robes?

Less than a month after Henry's installation, the time for feasting was over as news arrived that Warbeck's invasion fleet was ready to set sail. Henry VII moved to Woodstock before beginning a progress through the Welsh Marches to Sir William Stanley's former stronghold of Holt Castle in Denbighshire. There he inspected its treasures, which had been carefully inventoried after Stanley's fall, and showed himself ready to face down any residual Yorkist sentiment.

None manifested itself. Warbeck's original aim seems to have been to try to land in East Anglia, in Richard of York's former duchy of Norfolk, to try to benefit from memories of the young prince. But adverse winds kept him south, and he put troops ashore instead at Deal in Kent. This formed part of Henry's jurisdiction as lord warden of the Cinque Ports. And it was perhaps their familiarity with Henry that led the men of Kent to take a robustly sceptical attitude to 'Duke Richard'. First they tricked Warbeck's landing party into thinking that they supported his cause. Then, having lulled the invaders into dropping their guard, they rained arrows on them, killing many and capturing more.

Warbeck watched from his ships, powerless to help and not – it seemed – very eager to try. He sailed off to the west, eventually landing near Waterford in Ireland.

Here too Henry was nominally in command. The lord lieutenancy, or viceroyalty, of Ireland had formed part of Richard of Shrewsbury's galaxy of offices and titles. Henry had duly followed in Richard's footsteps and been appointed lord lieutenant in September 1494, with, once again, Sir Edward Poynings as his deputy. Poynings had left for Ireland immediately, with a mission to bring it under direct English rule. The cowed Irish parliament passed the necessary legislation, known as 'Poynings' Laws', readily enough. Enforcing them was another matter, and the deputy soon faced a major revolt.

Warbeck, naturally, was trying to fish in these

troubled waters. But even here he failed. After his repulse from Waterford he vanishes from view for two months, lurking we know not where. Then, in November 1495, he reappeared at the court of James IV of Scotland.

There a new phase of the pretender's career began. James IV wanted to recover Berwick from England. He wanted to make a noise in Europe and be recognized as a major power.

Warbeck, he decided, offered the means.

'Richard IV' was received at Stirling Castle on 20 November with royal honours. He was married to Lady Catherine Gordon, the king's remote cousin by marriage. And he was given Falkland Palace as his residence and base for his following of 1,400 armed retainers.

In September 1496 the king and would-be king launched a joint invasion of England. But the north, where the earl of Surrey commanded the border, held firm, and first Warbeck then James IV withdrew to Scotland.

Meanwhile, Henry VII was trying to win James IV from his attachment by fair means and foul. First he offered him the hand of Henry's elder sister, Margaret. But the incursion into England by Warbeck and James was a provocation too far, and in 1497 Henry VII decided to launch a counter-invasion. Taxation was voted, preparations got under way and a massive army was assembled to crush the Scots.

But at this moment events suddenly turned in Warbeck's favour. The Cornish saw no reason why they should pay taxation to fight distant Scotland, and rose in revolt. They were joined by the men of Somerset and beyond. Still worse, with the king's army mustering in the midlands to fight the Scots, there was nothing to stop the Cornish rebels when they decided to march on London.

In the face of the sudden crisis. Henry's father and mother went in opposite directions. On 5 June the king left Sheen and rode to Aylesbury and beyond to shadow the advance of the rebels on London from the west. On the sixth the queen entered London with 'my lord duke of York her second son' and stayed at The Coldharbour, Lady Margaret Beaufort's town-house in Thames Street. She remained there almost a week, till Monday the twelfth, when news came that the rebels had entered Arthur's former nursery-town of Farnham.

Henry and his mother promptly decamped to the Tower, where they remained as the rebels and the royal troops, never more than a few miles apart, advanced round the south of the City.

For five days Henry's dukedom and his father's crown hung in the balance. He probably enjoyed his short stay in the Tower: there were battlements to explore and big guns to touch gingerly. It was a paradise for a small boy, and the experience may have laid the foundations for his lifelong interest in fortifications and ordnance. But for his mother these were uneasy days in a place of uneasy memories. Perhaps she told her son about them. If so, he would have found them more fascinating than the Tower and its armaments – and much more frightening.

This was the third time that Elizabeth of York, still only thirty-one years old, had taken refuge in London as the battle for the crown raged round about. The first occasion was in 1470, when her father, Edward IV, had been temporarily driven from his kingdom and Elizabeth, aged four, and her mother, Queen Elizabeth Woodville, had first sought the protection of the Tower, and then, as Edward IV's situation became hopeless, the spiritual safety of the sanctuary at Westminster. Then, after Edward's premature death in 1483, mother and daughter fled first to the Tower and then to the sanctuary once more as Richard of Gloucester cut a dreadful swathe through their family.

Now she was a refugee in the Tower again. Would it be the sanctuary next? Or worse? And what of Henry? Was he to follow in the footsteps of Richard of Shrewsbury for one last, terrible time?

At times, indeed, it was a close-run thing. The Cornish rebels swept across southern England, and not until they had reached Blackheath, within a mile or two of the royal nursery at Eltham, was Henry VII ready to give them battle. But the waiting game had paid off. Splits appeared among

122

the Cornish, and the rebels were crushed on 17 June.

Henry VII entered the Tower in triumph, not chains, later that day and was reunited with his wife and second son.

A month later, Henry VII, together with the whole royal family, including Arthur, moved to Woodstock – partly for recreation in the magnificent park, and partly to hold a watching brief on Warbeck and his reaction to the Cornish revolt.

While they were there they were visited by the Venetian ambassador, Andrea Trevisan. First he had audience with the king, who received him 'leaning against a tall gilt chair, covered with cloth-of-gold' and with 'the prince, his eldest son, by name Arthur' at his side. Then Trevisan paid a courtesy visit on Elizabeth of York. She was standing 'at the end of a hall, dressed in cloth-of-gold; on one side of her was the king's mother, on the other her son the prince'.

And 'her son the prince', the Italian original makes clear, was Henry, duke of York.

In other words, even when they were under the same roof, Arthur and Henry preserved their distinctive upbringings: Arthur was identified with his father, whom he would succeed; Henry, as always, with his mother, whose family 'name' he bore as duke of York.

★　★　★

Meanwhile, James IV of Scotland, who was tiring of 'Richard', Henry's rival duke of York, encouraged Warbeck to take advantage of the confusion in England by mounting another invasion. Warbeck sailed with his wife in July, gathered reinforcements from Ireland and landed in Cornwall. About 3,000 followers joined him, and he besieged Exeter.

As in the summer, the king and queen separated. The king marched west to relieve Exeter, which was ably defended by the earl of Devon. Meanwhile, Elizabeth of York, once again accompanied by Henry, found safety under guise of going on pilgrimage to Walsingham in the far north of Norfolk.

The precaution proved unnecessary. On hearing of the king's approach, Warbeck abandoned his followers and fled into sanctuary. He was promised his life, and he surrendered. 'This day came Perkin Warbeck,' the king's account book noted triumphantly on 5 October. The Tudors' throne was secure, and young Henry's dukedom safe.

One of the king's first acts was to send a messenger posthaste to his second son to tell him the tidings and bring him £66.13s.4d 'for certain considerations'.

CHAPTER 7

EDUCATION

Henry's education started early. On 2 November 1495, when the boy was not yet four and half, his father paid £1 'for a book bought for my lord of York'. Perhaps this was the book from which Henry first learned to read. Perhaps he had just acquired the skill. But who had taught him? Not a tutor, as there is no trace of a formally appointed teacher for some time. Instead, I would guess that Henry learned from his mother. There is also the strong possibility that she taught him to write as well.

Henry's own handwriting has always been a bit of a mystery. Its bold, square, rather laboured forms are quite unlike the hands of his known teachers, like John Skelton, and intellectual compeers like Thomas More. On the other hand, it is very like his sisters' writing. His is more 'masculine' and better-formed. It is also the hand of someone who wrote regularly, if (as we know) rather painfully and reluctantly. His sisters', in contrast, are typical women's hands: loose and unpractised, if only because they wrote little. But the resemblance is still striking. It is weaker in the case of Margaret, Henry's elder sister. But it is much closer in the case of the younger sister, Mary. Indeed, her hand at first sight would pass for Henry's own – especially when he was scribbling rough notes or making corrections. The size, rhythm and letter forms are identical; only the pressure is different. Henry's massive fist leans heavily on the page; Mary's little hand flutters.

The reason for the resemblance is obviously a common teacher. Henry and Mary did, as we shall see, share a tutor, William Hone. But he joined their service long after they were literate and had formed their hands.

The common teacher, instead, I would suggest, was someone who really had been with them from the beginning: their mother.

Elizabeth of York had been unusually well educated for a fifteenth-century woman – that is, if we believe the account given in the ballad of Elizabeth's life known as 'The Song of the Lady Bessy'. This claims that her father, Edward IV, had appointed a scrivener, 'the very best in the City', as tutor to Elizabeth and her sister Cecily, the next eldest. He had taught them 'both to write and read full soon . . . /Both English and also French,/And also Spanish, if you had need'.

Only a few fragments of her handwriting seem to survive. The most substantial is her inscription of ownership in a book of devotion: 'Thys boke ys myn Elysabeth the kyngys dawghtyr.' It consists of only eight words and thirty-nine letters. But it is characteristic enough – in weight, in letter forms and in rhythm – to point to her role in inducting her second son and his sisters into literacy.

Henry's encounter with formal education came a year or two later, with the appointment of his first tutor, the poet John Skelton.

Skelton's poetry is extraordinary: helter-skelter rhymes, rhythms and alliterations tumble down the page; brisk and brutal English alternates with polysyllabic Latin and sententious French. One of his principal subjects was himself, and he felt it a worthy one: he must be the only poet to have written, in *The Garlande or Chapelet of Laurell,* sixteen hundred lines of verse in praise of himself and his own works.

The title of Skelton's autobiographical poem comes from the practice in the ancient world of crowning poets with a 'garland' or wreath of laurel. The custom was revived in the renaissance, and Skelton himself received the honour on several occasions: from the universities of Oxford in 1488, Louvain in 1492 and Cambridge, where he had studied, in 1493. In 1488 Henry VII also bestowed the title of poet laureate on Skelton and gave him a gown of green and white (the Tudor livery colours) inscribed in gold with the name 'Calliope', the muse of epic verse.

But among the proudest achievements to be

listed in *The Garland* was the fact that Skelton had been 'creancer' or tutor to 'The Duke of York . . . Now Henry the viij, Kyng of Englonde'.

The date of Skelton's appointment as tutor is unknown. But it was certainly early – say in 1496 or '97. Years later, in a poem commissioned by Henry VIII himself, Skelton boasts that 'The honor of England I learnyd to spell', and that Henry had called him 'master . . . In hys lernyng primordiall'. Equally, it is important to note the rather precise limitations of this: Skelton claims to have taught Henry to spell; he does not claim to have taught him to read or write. That distinction instead, as we have seen, almost certainly belongs to Henry's mother.

Skelton's principal job as Henry's tutor was different. It was to consolidate Henry's skills in English and to use them as a foundation for a second, then much more highly regarded, literacy in Latin. Fluency in Latin was an end in itself; it was also the key to most other knowledge, since Latin was the universal language of intellectual expression.

But why appoint a poet, of all people, to do this? Here it is important to understand the real meaning of Skelton's repeated laureations. Skelton himself – understandably preoccupied with his identity and reputation as a poet – writes as though they were a seamless tribute to his poetic genius.

In fact, his laureations at Oxford, Louvain and Cambridge were primarily university degrees, conferred for his conspicuous achievement in the field of Latin and rhetoric. Facility in the composition of Latin verse was the summit of such distinction. But it was only a part of it.

Skelton himself gives only the briefest account of how he tried to share something of this knowledge with Henry.

> I yave hym drynke of the sugryd welle
> Of Eliconys waters crystallyne,
> Aqueintyng hym with the Musys nyne.

The phrases are, of course, commonplaces. This makes it difficult to be sure what is meant. Probably Skelton would have given Henry a good grounding in the basics of Latin grammar and vocabulary, and introduced him to examples of the principal literary forms of the ancient world.

This, certainly, was the approach adopted by Skelton's fellow laureate and tutor, the blind French poet Bernard André, whom we have earlier encountered as Henry VII's official biographer. André had been appointed royal laureate in 1485, three years earlier than Skelton, and was manifestly senior to him. He was also given the senior royal teaching post as well, with his appointment in 1496 as tutor to Henry's elder brother Arthur. By this time Arthur, who was in his tenth year, had already completed his 'secondary' instruction at the hands of a professional schoolmaster, John Rede; now it was André's job to give the prince's education a final, 'tertiary' polish.

He joined the prince's household in the Welsh Marches, and both teacher and pupil went to it with a will. 'Before he reached his sixteenth year,' André writes, '[Arthur] had either committed to memory or read with his own eyes and leafed with his own fingers, in grammar: Guarinus, Perottus, Pomponius, Sulpitius, Aulus Gellius and Valla; in poetry: Homer, Vergil, Lucan, Ovid, Silius, Plautus and Terence; in oratory: the *Offices, Letters* and *Paradoxes* of Cicero, and Quintilian; in history: Thucidides, Livy, the *Commentaries* of Caesar, Suetonius, Cornelius Tacitus, Pliny, Valerius Maximus, Sullust and Eusebius.'

As Skelton was responsible for Henry until the age of eleven or twelve at the most, the boy cannot have got nearly so far under his tuition. But his reading would have been a scaled-down version of his elder brother's curriculum.

All this, of course, was in Latin. But Skelton had a magpie mind, stuffed with curious learning of all sorts. It may be that he kept it to himself. But, given the irrepressible zest of his poetry, it does not seem very likely. Instead, he seems to have communicated many of his enthusiasms to Henry: his love of obscure astronomical and mathematical lore; his fierce patriotism and fiercer xenophobia; and, above all, something of his own sense of language and skill in English verse composition.

This last would have been regarded as a leisure activity. But as the adult Henry wrote verse and enjoyed Skelton's poetry, it is fairly safe to imagine the boy and his tutor whiling away the odd hour in writing doggerel. Something of Skelton is also present in Henry's prose: in its pungency at best and its prolixity at worst. Even his vocabulary sometimes has a Skeltonic ring, and when, in his great speech to parliament in 1545, the king enjoined the clergy to follow his own middle way in religion, inclining neither to the 'old Mumpsimus', on the one extreme, nor the 'new Sumpsimus' on the other, we seem to hear the old macaronic rhymester himself.

Skelton, like André and other fashionable teachers of the day, also wrote didactic works and aids to study of various sorts. One that André composed specially for Arthur survives. It is an index to André's own commentary on St Augustine's *City of God*, which is dated 17 June 1500 'in bello loco' – this latter phrase being a latinization of the name of Bewdley near Kidderminster, which was Arthur's usual residence at this time. *The Garlande or Chapelet of Laurell* lists several of Skelton's own contributions to the genre:

'Item New gramer in Englysshe compylyd.'
'Of Tullys Familiars the translacyoun.'
'Item the Boke to Speke Well or be Styll.'
'*In primis* the Boke of Horiorous Astate.'
'Item Royall Demenaunce Worshyp to Wynne.'

The first was a Latin grammar, though written in English; the second, a translation of one of the standard rhetorical works, Cicero's *Letters*; the third was probably an English version of the *Tractatus de doctrina dociendi et tacendi*, a popular rhetorical treatise written by Albertano of Brescia; while the fourth and fifth sound like variations on the ever popular themes of courtesy books or mirrors for princes, which dealt with the principles of proper etiquette and good conduct.

None has survived; nor is it possible to say which, if any, were written specifically for Henry. But these questions can be answered for another work, of which Skelton was very proud. This was his *Speculum Principis. The Garlande or Chapelet of Laurell* describes the circumstances of its composition:

The Duke of Yorkis creancer whan Skelton was,
Now Henry the viij, Kyng of Englonde,
A tratyse he devysid and browght it to pas
Callid *Speculum Principis*, to bere in his honde,
Therin to rede, and to understande
All the demenour of princely astate.
To be our kyng, of God preordinate.

132

The treatise was originally dated 'at Eltham, 28 August, in the year of Grace, 1501'; what survives is a later copy, made by Skelton for presentation to Henry when the little duke of York had become King of England.

Posterity has not shared Skelton's own regard for the work: even its first modern editor dismisses it as a flimsy piece 'whose composition . . . occupied probably not more than a day'. Actually, like its author (and like, too, the boy to whom it was addressed), the treatise is the strangest mixture of commonplace leavened with originality and insight.

The beginning is lost; the surviving text plunges straight into the assertion that virtue is more important to a ruler than wealth or nobility. The assertion is supported by a variety of examples drawn from approved authorities. Therefore, 'if you wish to excel the rest in majesty and are eager for glory', Skelton tells his little prince, 'you must exceed everybody in virtue and learning'. So far, so commonplace. The next step in the well-worn argument would have been to explain that the prince must choose similarly virtuous and learned councillors to help him in his task. But here Skelton breaks sharply with convention. For he has a low opinion of councillors. 'You will have councillors: either learned or ignorant, the ones irresolute, the others weak' – and all useless. Instead you must trust to yourself alone: you must be as firm as a rock, as solid as a stone. The lessons are driven home with a set of counter-examples of wicked rulers. There follows another sharp touch of reality, in which, as we have seen, Skelton warns Henry (after a perfunctory apology for his bluntness) that the greatness of his family will not protect him against the miserable fates suffered by his ancestors.

Skelton then summarizes his advice in a series of pithy maxims which were intended to be memorable and which Henry probably had to memorize. 'Above all, loathe gluttony,' the litany begins. 'Hear the other side.' 'Do not be mean.' 'Love poets: athletes are two a penny but patrons of the arts are rare.' Finally, turn to books and the past for wisdom: 'Peruse the chronicles; direct yourself to histories; commit them to memory.'

It is easy to smile at all this, particularly when one of the moral precepts enjoined Henry to 'choose a wife for yourself, and prize her always and uniquely'. Or when the ten-year-old boy was solemnly warned not to 'deflower virgins' or 'violate widows'.

But the knowingness may be misplaced. Actually, Henry valued marriage, which is why he married so often. Similarly, the injunctions about virgins and widows were not absurd. Instead, they would have lent authority to the rest, since Henry – as Skelton no doubt reminded him – had already sworn to protect them both in the solemn vows he had taken at his creation as a knight of the Bath.

Indeed, in general. Henry would appear to have taken Skelton's list seriously rather than otherwise. He longed 'to excel the rest in majesty and [was] eager for glory'. He loathed meanness – at least to begin with. And he found the idea crucial in defining himself against his father: he would pursue (in Skelton's words) the 'glory of virtue' as against his father's 'vain pride in riches'. He was aware of the turbulent history of his family, and did his best to knit up old wounds. He reverenced scholars, and when he was confronted with the most momentous problem of his reign, the dissolution of his first marriage, he turned to books for guidance and refashioned the royal library as a result. And for him, as for Skelton, history was the final court of appeal, and his revolutionary new title of Supreme Head on earth of the church of England was based on 'sundry old authentic histories and chronicles'.

In other areas, the record is more mixed: Henry's attitude to counsel, for example, swung between the conventional respect for advice and Skelton's heretical contempt for it. Finally, Skelton notched up one total failure. 'Above all, loathe gluttony,' the boy was told. Skelton probably put the injunction at the head of his list because it was already clear that Henry was that way inclined. If so, he wasted his breath. Even when Henry was young he was well-fleshed, and when he was old he was gross.

Still, if most teachers achieved Skelton's overall

success rate, they would be happy. On the other hand, we must not exaggerate his influence. Skelton's teachings may have stuck, but – as we shall see – there is little evidence that Henry had much regard for his teacher or looked back on him with much gratitude.

Skelton's appointment should have been a climactic moment for Henry – and not only because of the extraordinary personality of his teacher. Both contemporary theory and normal practice divided the upbringing and education of a Tudor boy of the upper classes into two: babyhood and infancy were in the hands of women; boyhood and youth were the responsibility of men.

Skelton's appointment should have signalled the moment that Henry crossed this threshold.

Those of a psychological bent have had a field day on this subject. They have blamed Henry's early sequestration from female company for the adult Henry VIII's fractured and abusive relation-ships with women, for his combination of prurience and sexual inhibition, even for the pathological fear of incest which some have attributed to him.

The only problem is that Henry was *not* sequestered from the company of women at the age of six or seven any more than he had been at birth. Instead, by the standards of the day he continued both to have his cake and eat it: his male teacher, Skelton, was appointed; at the same time he continued to be brought up with his sisters in the nursery at Eltham.

The resulting ménage was seen and described by no less an observer than Desiderius Erasmus, the great Dutch humanist, on his first visit to England in the autumn of 1499. Erasmus was staying at Sayes Court near Greenwich, the country house of his host and former pupil Lord Mountjoy, who was then acting as Henry's mentor or *socius studiorum* ('companion of studies'). Thomas More, Erasmus's new friend, came to see him, and the two walked or rode over to nearby Eltham. 'For there,' Erasmus continues his account,

> all the royal children were being educated, Arthur alone excepted, the eldest son. When we came to the hall, all the retinue was assembled; not only that of the palace but Mountjoy's as well. In the midst stood Henry, aged nine, already with a certain royal demeanour; I mean a dignity of mind combined with a remarkable courtesy. On his right was Margaret, about eleven years old, who afterwards married James, King of Scots. On the left Mary was playing, a child of four. Edmund was an infant in arms.

There the royal children stand, frozen by the magic of Erasmus's pen in a timeless *tableau vivant*, with

Henry at its centre. But then the group moves. Once more Henry is the focus. Thomas More stepped forward and presented him with a piece of writing he had brought. Erasmus, who had arrived empty-handed, was covered in embarrassment. And the embarrassment was deepened when, during dinner, to which the visitors were invited to stay, Henry took the initiative again and sent Erasmus a note 'to challenge something from my pen'.

This was a request which could not be refused. But it took Erasmus three days – fighting against both time and a total lack of inspiration – to knock together something suitable. What is probably the actual presentation copy survives. It is a little manuscript of ten leaves: illuminated, to make it a fitting gift for Henry; rather hastily and carelessly written because of the pressure of time, and (for the same reason) made up largely of reused materials, which Erasmus made a habit of carrying with him on his travels for just such an eventuality as this.

To the eleven already written poems, Erasmus added a new one, in praise of Henry's tutor John Skelton, and a prose letter of dedication to Henry himself. He also produced, separately, a more substantial ode, entitled *Prosopopoeia Britanniae maioris*, in which Britain sings her own praises and those of Henry VII and his children.

In the collection, Skelton, who had taken Erasmus by surprise by lauding him to the skies as a poet (which happened to be one of the few literary genre of which Erasmus was *not* a master), figures almost as much as Henry. Thanks to his patroness, the muse Calliope, he is the glory of English letters:

> The debt that ancient Greece
> To Homer owed, to Vergil Mantua,
> That debt to Skelton owes Britannia,
> For he from Latium all the muses led
> And taught them to speak English words
>   instead
> Of Latin; and with Skelton England tries
> With Roman poets to contend the prize.

Erasmus must have been well briefed, as he read no English.

Erasmus may have been an indifferent poet, but he was a master letter-writer. And it is the letter of dedication which speaks most directly to Henry (and to us). Erasmus turns the slightness of his gift to advantage. Why give gold?, he asks. All princes are rich, but few are famous. And it is the work of poets and scholars – not wealth or statues or paintings or genealogies – which confers immortality. Henry, Erasmus continues, adopting a tone that must have seemed deliciously confiding to the boy, can understand this, because he, unlike most modern princes, is appreciative of literature and is determined to pattern his life on ancient rather than modern models.

That was indeed one reading of Henry's behaviour. And, making the necessary allowances for Erasmus's flattery, it was true enough. Henry's book-learning *was* precocious, and he was to remain unusually bookish as a king. And – whatever else he might fail to absorb from the renaissance – fame and an appetite for greatness were and always remained his goal and spur.

But it was probably the other observer who got the full measure of the scene. Thomas More's favourite image of politics was as a play. And here we see Henry, barely in his ninth year, able to take an encounter and transmute it into a theatrical performance. He turned the dais of his grandfather, Edward IV's hall (on which he was surely standing) into a stage, the throng of attendants into the extras and his sisters and younger brother into the supporting cast. His visitors were at once fellow-actors in the rituals of gift-exchange and an appreciative audience for the display of both his charm and his talents. The resulting applause Henry knew was his by right; he also knew that his rightful place in the world (second son though he might be) was first. He was a star.

Erasmus's letter is a portrait of Henry in words, and a remarkably shrewd and vivid one at that. But there is also a real portrait, thought to be of Henry as a boy, which belongs to more or less the same date.

It is a painted and gilded terracotta bust in the royal collection, which shows a child of eight or nine. This would date it to 1499 or 1500, and make it exactly contemporary with Erasmus's visit. It is also when Guido Mazzoni, to whom the work is attributed, is known to have been in northern Europe at the court of France. The boy is finely dressed. His doublet is represented by a layer of gilding over-painted with green. This probably means that the original was of green cloth-of-gold. It was edged and trimmed with gold braid and lined with a red silk fabric. The lining shows on the revers at the high-collared neck and in the slashings at the shoulders. Here the lining is further decorated with gold. The doublet can be fastened at the left shoulder with a lace. But the lace hangs untied (was Mrs Denton off-duty that morning?). Underneath, a fine shirt is visible, gathered at the neck and trimmed with a neck-band, also of gold. For some reason the child has had his head shaved (had Henry caught lice from one of the stable lads?), and his scalp is protected by a skullcap of gold lace. The complexion is fair, the cheeks bulge with rude health, the lips are finely formed and the eyes blue-grey. They are also rather wide apart, as Henry's were.

And he is laughing. But it is not a simple childish laugh. The eyes are turned away, and despite the dimpled cheeks there is something knowing, adult, even a little disturbing, about his humour. It is, we can guess, how Henry looked when he pressed the reluctant Erasmus for his tribute of laboriously written verse.

A laughing child is not the first image that leaps to mind of the boyhood of Henry VIII. But then, the whole story of his early years turns out to be rather unexpected. The fact that he was brought up away from Arthur means that he was never overshadowed by his elder brother. And the presence of his sisters and their women helped to civilize him and give him poise and confidence.

It was in part a case of nurture working with nature – as a glance at the portrait bust shows. It also presents a sharp contrast to Arthur himself. As Arthur's one realistic portrait suggests, he took after the opposite side of the family to the 'Yorkist' Henry, and closely resembled his paternal grandmother, Lady Margaret Beaufort. He had the same hooked nose and deep-sunk, hooded eyes, with, even as a youth, heavy bags under them. He also inherited her slim build, though like his father he was rather tall for the times. And, above all, he had the cold Beaufort temperament as well.

So heredity alone would have made the brothers very different. The difference was intensified by Arthur's driven, solitary childhood. The result produced a model prince. But, like many models, one somewhat lacking in life. Instead, Arthur displayed the exaggerated sense of responsibility of the eldest child. His public manner was stiff, though formally gracious. He was intellectually precocious. But women, as we shall see, were a bit of a closed book. King Arthur would have been respected, perhaps feared, but not, one suspects, loved.

Henry, on the other hand, always aroused strong feelings: first of love and adulation; then, subsequently, of hate and terror. It was a matter of character. But it was also a question of upbringing. The years of childhood idyll at Eltham suggest that being a second son had its advantages – at least when you were young.

CHAPTER 8

WEDDINGS

'Choose a wife for yourself, and prize her always and uniquely,' Skelton had solemnly enjoined the little Henry. Actually, royal children rarely had much choice in the matter. Serious marriage negotiations for Henry's elder brother Arthur had begun when the lad was aged three; his sister Margaret had been offered to James IV of Scotland at the age of seven; now, it seemed, it was the turn of Henry and his little sister Mary.

The occasion was a one-day summit conference held at St Peter's church outside the walls of Calais on 9 June 1500. Henry's parents had first travelled to Calais a month earlier on 8 May, in a simple attempt to avoid an outbreak of epidemic disease which was playing havoc in London and the vicinity. Contemporaries called the disease the 'sweating sickness', after its principal symptom. It seems to have been a virulent form of influenza, with a mortality rate that matched that of the plague itself. Despite its inauspicious beginnings, the royal visit to Calais soon blossomed into a considerable diplomatic

144

event, which culminated in the summit conference between Henry and the Archduke Philip, ruler of the adjacent Netherlands and son of Maximilian.

For the meeting, which lasted only a few hours, the king transformed the interior of St Peter's church into a palace from the Arabian Nights. Chambers were formed out of richly figured tapestry, and the floor was strewn with roses and lavender. The banquet included seven horseloads of cherries and a holocaust of kids (young goats).

The aim was to repair the damage done to Anglo–Burgundian relations by Habsburg support for the Yorkist cause. All seemed to go well. Philip, who had always been less infatuated with Warbeck than his father Maximilian or his aunt, the Dowager Duchess Margaret of York, acknowledged Henry VII as his 'patron, father and protector'. And, to cement their good relationship, the two rulers discussed a double marriage alliance: between Henry, duke of York and Philip's daughter Eleanor, and between Henry's four-year-old sister Mary and Philip's infant son Charles.

It might even be that his father let Henry know something of these plans. In late July, six weeks after Henry's parents had returned from Calais, the king despatched Richard Weston, one of his most intimate body servants, to ride to 'my lord of York'. Was the king, following the death of Henry's short-lived brother Edmund, who had died during his parents' absence in Calais, anxious about the well-being of his second son? Or was he informing him of the wealthy bride that awaited him in the Netherlands?

At any rate, a month later the king sent the young duke a gift of £2, again by Weston's hands. And it was Weston too who gave a reward of 10 shillings to the servant Henry sent to court to thank his father for his present.

But the marriages of Henry and Mary were far from the mind of the special Spanish envoy, Gutierre Gomez de Fuensalida, as he spurred his horse from Paris to the Channel. Word of the Anglo–Burgundian summit had quickly spread on the diplomatic grapevine, and Fuensalida was desperate to reach Calais to find out what was afoot.

Fuensalida, like his masters Ferdinand and Isabella, had heard worrying rumours. The real purpose of the Calais meeting, everybody in France told him, was to arrange *another* Tudor–Habsburg marriage: between Henry's elder brother Arthur, prince of Wales, and Philip's sister, the Archduchess Margaret. And that, of course, would have meant breaking off the marriage which had already been contracted between Arthur and Catherine of Aragon, Ferdinand and Isabella's youngest daughter.

In fact, Fuensalida's worries were unnecessary. Henry VII, who was well aware of Spanish anxieties, might tease Spain's resident ambassador in London, De Puebla, with a deliberatively vague

146

account of the Calais meeting with Philip. 'It had,' he claimed airily, 'no other object than to show to the world their paternal and filial love, and to give something to guess at to their evil-wishers.'

But (as De Puebla well knew) Henry VII's commitment to the Spanish match for his eldest son and heir was absolute.

Ferdinand, king of Aragon, and Isabella, queen regnant of Castile, had unified Spain by their marriage and carried it to the front rank of European powers by their prowess in diplomacy and war. Henry VII, who had achieved something similar in England – though on a much smaller scale – with his victory over Richard III and marriage to Elizabeth of York, had first put out feelers to the pair in 1487, only two years after Bosworth. The proposal took the usual form for the day, of an alliance to be cemented by a marriage – between his one-year-old son Arthur and Ferdinand and Isabella's two-year-old daughter Catherine. Ferdinand and Isabella, still in the throes of the reconquest of the Islamic south of Spain and eager for allies against France, had responded favourably, and Henry VII sent an experienced embassy to Spain to conclude matters.

De Puebla was involved from the very beginning. He had been sent as ambassador to England in response to Henry VII's original overtures, and had helped negotiate the treaty of Medina del Campo in 1489, which first committed the parties to the marriage. Six years later he returned to

England as resident ambassador and brought England and Spain, who had drifted apart in the interim, together once more to renew the treaty.

Thereafter, De Puebla had been indefatigable in bringing it to fruition. He sweated blood in line-by-line negotiations about the terms – especially the financial terms – sometimes with Henry VII's councillors, often with the king himself. He performed with a rather ridiculous enthusiasm in the proxy weddings by which he sought to make the marriage contract unbreakable by even the most ingenious canon lawyer. And he spilled real blood too, when under his steady pressure Henry VII decided to smooth the way to Catherine's arrival in England by executing the two most obvious threats to the Tudor throne: the pretender, Perkin Warbeck, who had been gaoled in the Tower since his surrender in October 1497, and the earl of Warwick, son of the duke of Clarence, who for the last sixteen years had been imprisoned by both Richard III and Henry VII.

The two birds were killed with one stone. Warbeck and Warwick were accused of plotting a joint escape from the Tower, and were tried and condemned in November 1499. Warbeck was hanged on 23 November and Warwick beheaded on the twenty-eighth.

In January 1500, De Puebla wrote exultantly home: following the executions, he crowed, 'there does not remain a drop of doubtful Royal blood; the only Royal blood being the true blood of the king, the queen, and, above all, of the prince of Wales'. Henry does not even get a look-in.

But still there were delays – this time on De Puebla's own side. Ferdinand and Isabella were distracted by a major Islamic uprising, which took several months to put down. Still worse, there was a rebellion in Isabella's own heart: having seen so many of her children and grandchildren die, sacrificed in similar dynastic marriages, she was understandably reluctant to let go of her last unmarried daughter.

But by the late spring of 1501 the excuses had run out. On 21 May Catherine made her final farewells to her parents in Granada and began her journey to her new kingdom. First she had to cross the torrid plains and mountains of Spain, then to brave the storms and treacherous currents of the Bay of Biscay and the Channel. It was August before she arrived at the coast. There was another delay while she went on pilgrimage to the shrine of Santiago de Compostella, and it was not till the seventeenth that she set sail. Three weeks later she was back in Spain, driven ashore by terrifying storms. In desperation, Henry VII sent one of his best captains to escort her to England. This time it was the Channel which nearly shipwrecked the fleet. It was supposed to land at Southampton; instead, battered and storm-tossed, it put in at Plymouth, the first available major harbour, 150 miles to the west.

'This day [2 October]', Lady Margaret Beaufort noted in the calendar of her book of hours, 'my lady princess landed.'

It took Catherine another month, travelling at most ten or twelve miles a day and with frequent halts, to reach the environs of London. Everything about the journey – what route she should take, where she should stay, what she should travel in and who should meet and accompany her – had been worked out in advance in the minutest detail. But by the time she reached Dogmersfield near Fleet in Hampshire, Henry VII could contain his impatience no longer. Who was the woman to whom he had pledged the hope of his dynasty? What did she look like? He would interrupt Catherine's carefully prepared itinerary and find out with his son-Arthur.

Catherine sent word that the meeting was impossible, since Spanish custom and her father's commands meant that she must not show herself to Arthur or his family till her wedding morn. Henry VII, invoking his authority as king and pater-familias, overruled her, and threaten to confront her in bed if necessary.

Catherine yielded with good grace. First she met the king alone, and then together with the prince. As usual, a recording herald was present. But he says nothing about what either party thought of the other.

★　★　★

A week later, on Friday, 12 November, Catherine met Henry, who escorted her throughout her grand *entrée* into the city of London. It was the first encounter of two people who between them would change history.

Once again, a herald was present; once again he was silent about their thoughts.

But another observer used the decent obscurity of Latin to express himself very freely. This was Thomas More, whose genius for friendship was already ripening his acquaintance with Henry into something deeper. 'Catherine,' he wrote to another friend, the schoolmaster John Holt, 'lately made her *entrée* into London amid a tremendous ovation; never, to my knowledge, has there been such a reception.' 'But,' More exclaims, 'the Spanish escort – good heavens! – what a sight! If you had seen it, I am afraid you would have burst with laughter; they were so ludicrous. Except for three, or at the most four, of them, they were just too much to look at: hunchback, undersized, barefoot Pygmies from Ethiopia. If you had been there, you would have thought they were refugees from hell.'

Then, suddenly, More's mood changes as he contemplates Catherine herself: 'Ah, but the lady!' he sighs, 'take my word for it, she thrilled the hearts of everyone: she possesses all those qualities that make for beauty in a very charming young girl. Everywhere she receives the highest of praises; but even that is inadequate.'

More's judgment of Catherine, at least, never wavered.

The wedding was held two days later, on Sunday, 14 November in old St Paul's Cathedral. Isabella had already remonstrated with Henry VII about the excessive scale of the celebrations. In vain. For the king was determined to extract the maximum advantage from the marriage alliance between the Tudors and the most powerful dynasty in Europe.

And that required, in the first place, that as many people as possible should be able to see the ceremony. Hence the choice of St Paul's, which was the largest building in what was by far England's biggest and most populous city. And hence too the decision to take a leaf out of *The Ryalle Book* and copy the arrangements for the christenings of Henry and his siblings. As for these, a tall, many-tiered circular platform was built in the centre of the nave, on which the marriage itself would take place. But how to get the couple there, through the crowded church? The solution was to build a walkway at head-height the entire 450-foot length of the nave: from the west doors to the marriage platform, and again from the marriage platform to the steps of the choir screen.

This idea was inspired: the ceremony now became a series of sweeping processional movements, each accompanied by carefully cued musicians placed high up in the vaults to exploit the vast reverberations of the building.

The star of the processions was of course the bride, Catherine of Aragon. But accompanying her every move was Henry. He escorted her on her entry into the church: from the bishop's palace, where she had been staying, across St Paul's churchyard, through the west doors and along the elevated walkway to the wedding platform. Then, after the wedding, he led the other dignitaries to hear mass with the bridal couple in the choir. Finally, after the mass, as Arthur went privately to the bishop's palace to greet Catherine at the threshold of the bridal chamber, Henry walked back with her along the whole length of the walkway, from the altar steps to the west doors, out into the churchyard and into the palace.

There were cheers, fanfares and a sea of ten thousand upturned faces, all looking, it must have seemed, at him.

Henry's role as escort ceased only at the door of the bridal chamber. Beyond was not a fit place for a ten-year-old boy. But no one, curiously, was to be more concerned about what happened within. Or, depending on whom you believe, did *not* happen. The following morning Arthur boasted that it had been hot work spending the night in Spain. This does not leave much to the imagination. Catherine, on the other hand, was to swear on her immortal soul that she remained as much a virgin as when she left her mother's womb.

But that was later, much later. At the time, the fact of intercourse was simply taken for granted: 'and thus,' the recording herald wrote in his florid prose, 'these worthy persons concluded and consummate the effect and complement of the sacrament of matrimony.'

After a day's rest the royal party went in state by water to Westminster for a further round of jousting, revelling and feasting. This started on Thursday, 18 November and continued for a week. Once again Henry had a starring role – or rather made one for himself.

On the Friday night the king put on an entertainment in Westminster Hall. The walls were bright with tapestry, and a vast cupboard seven shelves high groaned with gold and silver-gilt plate. After the entertainment was over, the dancing began. Arthur led out Lady Cecily, Elizabeth of York's eldest sister; then Catherine and one of her ladies, both in Spanish costume; performed; and finally it was the turn of Henry to dance with his elder sister Margaret. He led her out by the hand and they executed their two allotted dances, which were 'bass' or slow steps.

But now Henry stepped out of the script. Finding that his heavy clothes got in the way of his fun, he 'suddenly cast off his gown' – which had been obtained at such expense – and 'danced in his jacket' with his sister. His parents looked on proudly and indulgently.

Henry was learning early that he could break the rules.

His example of uninhibited dancing was also infectious, and the poor folk who crowded into the hall had a field day snapping up the 'plates, spangles, roses and other conceits of silver and over gilt which fell from their garments both of lords and ladies and gentlemen whilst they leapt and danced'.

On Friday, 26 November the court travelled to Richmond, as the rebuilt Sheen was now known, by water.

It was like a scene from a northern Venice. The gaily dressed throng embarked at the 'bridge' or landing stage at Westminster Palace. This was 'made of timber, beset with goodly posts, with lions and dragons, and other figures and beasts and figures empainted, carven and gilt, set upon their heights and tops'. In front of it, a water-borne procession of some sixty 'right goodly covered, painted and beseen' barges formed up in order on the river. Among the flotilla, 'the duke of York's' barge stood out – though Henry himself, as part of his father's immediate suite, was not in it. Instead, he travelled with the king in the royal barge, leaving his own to bring his servants and attendants. When he arrived at Richmond he also found that he had his own suite of specially built rooms, alongside those of his father, mother, grandmother and elder brother and sister-in-law.

At Richmond the round of entertainment continued, with hunting in the park and tours of the lavishly rebuilt palace, conducted by the king himself. But there was also serious business to be done.

The issue was the status of Arthur and Catherine's marriage. Should they continue to reside at court, each in their own separate suite? Or should they take up residence at Arthur's princely capital of Ludlow, there to live as man and wife? The former had been the original intention. But that had been based on the assumption that they would be marrying when Arthur was barely fourteen. In the event, the delays in Catherine's departure from Spain meant that he was a good year older.

And that, it was decided after some soul-searching, was quite old enough to begin proper married life. So to Ludlow they went, leaving Richmond a few days before Christmas and spending the feast itself at Woodstock.

Henry never saw his brother again.

CHAPTER 9

THE LAST PRETENDER

De Puebla had spoken too soon when he gloated in January 1500 that not 'a drop of doubtful Royal blood' remained in England. Warbeck and Warwick might indeed be dead, but within two years another pretender had arisen to replace them: Edmund de la Pole, earl of Suffolk.

Just as Henry's childhood had been overshadowed by Warbeck, so his youth was to be equally affected by Suffolk. Suffolk indeed probably touched him more keenly: Perkin was an impostor and a puppet; but Suffolk was the real Yorkist thing. As son of John de la Pole, second duke of Suffolk, and Elizabeth Plantagenet, sister of Henry's maternal grandfather, Edward IV, Suffolk descended – unimpeachably – from the main Yorkist line. His royal blood meant that he was one of Henry's closest living relations, and a familiar figure at his parents' court. Henry had even been conceived under Duke John's roof, at his palatial house at Ewelme in Oxfordshire, where Henry's parents had spent a long, lazy month in the late autumn of 1490.

★   ★   ★

But what probably made the most impression on Henry was the fact that Suffolk was the star jouster of the English court. As such, he had played a prominent part in the tournaments to celebrate Henry's own creation as duke of York. He was the first of the four 'noblemen and . . . gentlemen' of the king's court who had issued the challenge for the joust; he had worn Henry's own colours of tawney and blue; and on the second day of the tournament he had been awarded the prize of 'a ring of gold with a diamond'.

Even more characteristic was Suffolk's performance on the third and final day in the tourney, or sword-fight on horseback, when his encounter with Sir Edward Burgh had all the excitement of a heavy weight boxing match. First 'the earl gave such a stroke' to his opponent that he almost knocked his sword 'out of his hand and bruised his gauntlet'. Burgh tried to change his sword to his bridle hand, but lost control of his horse during the manoeuvre. The horse turned away from Suffolk, and many thought that Burgh's hand had been 'stonied' or paralysed. But then Burgh regained both his hold on his sword and control of his horse, and hit Suffolk 'a light stroke' over the head. This unexpected, insolent tap enraged Suffolk, and 'the earl would furiously go against' his opponent until they were forcibly separated.

Henry, we can imagine, watched enthralled.

* * *

Nor was Suffolk's brawling temperament confined to the tilt-yard. According to Polydore Vergil, he was 'bold, impetuous and readily roused to anger'. This, it should be said in Suffolk's defence, was a pretty typical disposition for a young nobleman, especially one as highly born as he – which is why he was so popular among members of his own order.

Nevertheless, his character was singularly unsuited to the awkward circumstances in which he and his family found themselves. We have already seen something of these. Suffolk's eldest brother John, earl of Lincoln, had played a leading part in the first Yorkist rebellion against Henry VII in 1487, when he was killed at the battle of Stoke and attainted as a traitor. But the full consequences were only visited on the remainder of the family after the death of Duke John in 1492. Duke John had settled much of his property on Lincoln as his eldest son in his own lifetime. Lincoln's attainder meant that this was forfeit to the crown. Which meant in turn that when Suffolk inherited as the next surviving brother, the reduced family estate was not sufficient to maintain a dukedom.

Instead, when Suffolk came of age the following year, Henry VII imposed a compromise: Suffolk agreed to accept the lesser title of earl; in return he was allowed to reclaim some of Lincoln's estates, though subject to a fine of £5,000, payable in yearly instalments of £200.

★   ★   ★

The compromise was characteristically harsh but fair. It was also very similar in spirit to the settlement imposed on Surrey after the Howards' near-disastrous error in supporting Richard III. Surrey, with his coldly ambitious temperament, accepted the arrangement and used it to rebuild his fortunes. At first it seemed as though Earl Edmund would follow the same route, and for the next five years he was a prominent figure at court, in the lists and on the battlefield. He was also particularly close to his first cousin, Henry's mother, Elizabeth of York.

But, as we have seen, he had inherited more than his fair share of the Plantagenet temper. For such a personality the compact of 1493, with its double blow to his prestige and his purse, rankled deeply. And it was his temper which brought things to a head. He committed a murder, and was indicted in the court of King's Bench for the crime. The matter was smoothed over. But not Suffolk's ruffled feelings. In July 1499 he decamped first to Guisnes, one of the flanking fortresses of Calais, and thence to St Omer, in the Netherlands. There, like so many Yorkist agitators before him, he hoped to get help from his aunt, the Dowager Duchess Margaret.

The appeal for Burgundian assistance was ominous. But a combination of diplomatic pressure on the Archduke Philip and fair words from a high-level delegation, led by Suffolk's friend Sir Richard Guildford, secured his return. Once again there was both stick and carrot: Suffolk was fined another £1,000, but he was also restored to favour and the heart of the royal family. On 5 May 1500, when the court was at Canterbury en route to the Calais meeting with the Archduke Philip, Suffolk witnessed the final ratification of the treaty for the marriage of Catherine of Aragon and Henry's elder brother Arthur, and he joined Henry's parents at the Calais meeting itself.

Indeed, in his role as star jouster, he was destined to play a key part in it. The forthcoming marriage of Arthur and Catherine would set the seal on the arrival of the Tudors as one of the premier dynasties of Europe, and Henry's father was determined to celebrate it in style. At the heart of the celebrations was to be a tournament, which was planned as an international event of a type that had not been seen in England since the days of Edward IV.

The meeting between Henry VII and the Archduke Philip provided the perfect opportunity to launch the event. At the head of Philip's train was Antoine, the *grand bâtard* ('great bastard') of Burgundy (1421–1502). He had been the Burgundian champion in the last great Anglo-Burgundian tournament held in 1467, and the intervening decades had only reinforced his authority as an arbiter of chivalry. Jousters were equally prominent in Henry VII's entourage, which included, as well as Suffolk, the duke of

Buckingham, the earl of Essex, Lord Harrington, Lord William Courtenay and Sir John Peche.

While the king and the archduke discussed politics, it seems pretty safe to assume that their courtiers talked about the finer points of the tilt. The results of their deliberations were incorporated into the challenge for the wedding joust, which was issued in Calais and widely distributed. A copy in French was sent to the king of France. The Spanish ambassador got sight of this, copied it and sent it to Spain. Versions in English were also sent to the king of Scots and given to the archduke. The challenge was issued in the name of Suffolk, as the chief challenger, and five others: Essex, Harrington, Courtenay, Peche and Sir Guillaume de la Riviere, all six of whom were present in person.

Those answering the challenge were to write their name on specially prepared lists; they were also to supply a shield of their arms to be hung on a tree of arms at Westminster. In keeping with the international tone of the event, special arrangements were made to facilitate the participation of 'gentlemen strangers of whatever nation it be'.

All of this looked back to the high noon of Anglo-Burgundian chivalry under Edward IV: the tree of arms was taken from the spectacular tournament, known as the Golden Tree, which the grand bastard had organized in 1468 for the wedding of Margaret of York and Charles the Bold, while the rules of combat were copied from the regulations for tournaments drawn up by the earl of Worcester, constable to Edward IV.

But the splendour of the revival of Yorkist chivalry was suddenly dimmed by the reality of Yorkist politics. For in August 1501, just over a year after his return from the Calais meeting, Suffolk fled abroad once more with his second brother, Richard, to seek refuge with Maximilian, Philip's father and king of the Romans, in the Tyrol.

Suffolk's mind had been made up by the report he had received from Sir Robert Curzon, Suffolk's fellow challenger in the joust for Henry's creation in 1494. Curzon had been licensed by Henry VII to join Maximilian's service to fight the Turks. But it turned out that his enemy was as much Henry Tudor as the Infidel. He told Maximilian of Henry's 'murders and tyrannies' on the one hand, and Suffolk's 'propos' to recover his rights on the other. Maximilian answered sympathetically: if he might have 'one of King Edward's blood in his hands he would help him to recover the crown of England and be revenged' on Henry.

Throughout Curzon's report, Henry VII is referred to as 'H'. It is the language of the spy throughout the ages. Later on, Curzon was 'turned' and became a double agent. Or he might have been one all along.

The timing of Suffolk's flight, with Catherine of Aragon already on her way to England, caused

163

exquisite embarrassment and forced a hasty rejigging of the personnel of the marriage joust. It also threatened to bring about the final *Götterdämmerung* of the house of York; even, perhaps, to transform Henry's own destiny in life from that of a royal duke into a prince of the church.

For Suffolk was at the centre of a close-knit web of family connexions. This was brought uncomfortably into the lime-light by his movements in the days before his flight. He 'banquetted privily' in London with Lord Harrington (soon to succeed his father as marquess of Dorset), the earl of Essex and Lord William Courtenay. A 'banquet' was an entertainment at which sweetmeats, fruits and wines were served. It was elegant, fashionable and light: the perfect background for innocent conversation, or, equally, the quick, whispered words of conspiracy. Heavier fare would have been on offer when Suffolk dined with the earl of Devon, Lord William's father, in his house in Warwick Lane, which ran between Paternoster Row and Newgate Street, just to the north-west of St Paul's. Devon had come to the 'outer gate' to receive him – a gesture of unusual politeness which had set tongues wagging.

All this might mean something – or nothing. Suffolk himself hotly denied that any of his table companions had been forewarned of his flight. Others certainly knew of it, however. William Hussey was consulted by someone who was considering joining Suffolk. He advised him to see an astrologer to determine Suffolk's chance of success. William Hussey also belonged to the smart set at court: he was son of Sir John Hussey, the brother-in-law of the earl of Kent, who in turn was half-brother to the earl of Essex through their mother, Anne Woodville.

This, as far as Henry VII was concerned, was the problem: Suffolk's circle of intimates looked like a Yorkist family convention: Dorset was Queen Elizabeth of York's nephew, Essex was her first cousin and William Courtenay her brother-in-law. They banqueted and dined together. They fought together in the tournament.

Would they also fight together against the upstart Tudors?

In these circumstances the king as usual struck first, and most of the surviving males of the house of York were rounded up and charged with participating in Suffolk's treason. William Courtenay and William de la Pole, Suffolk's youngest brother, were arrested in February 1502 and sent to the Tower. De la Pole was to die there almost forty years later, and it looked as though Courtenay's fate would be the same – or worse. His wife and children were taken into the queen's protection (if indeed she had not been looking after them before), and Courtenay himself was attainted in 1504.

For the time being Thomas Grey, marquess of Dorset, the biggest fish apart from Suffolk himself to fall under suspicion, kept his freedom and his dignities. He acted as the king's lieutenant (or deputy) at the Garter feast at Windsor, and preened himself, magnificently dressed and mounted, in the reception of foreign visitors. But these were the flowers strewing the abyss, and in 1506 he too was sent to the Tower. The following year Dorset and his fellow Yorkist prisoner, Courtenay, were despatched under escort across the Channel and re-imprisoned in the castle of Calais on 18 October 1507. There, according to the chronicler of Calais, 'they were kept prisoners . . . as long as King Henry the Seventh lived, and should have been put to death, if he had lived longer'.

Where did all this leave Henry? Dorset and Courtenay were indeed 'both of kin to . . . Queen Elizabeth and of her blood', as the chronicler of Calais described them. So, and most of all, was Henry. He even bore the title of duke of York.

I am not suggesting that Henry VII's suspicions about Yorkist conspiracy, even at their darkest and most universal, extended to his second son. But it may be that this last spasm of Yorkist sentiment does help explain his father's apparently contradictory intentions for the boy.

What *was* Henry to be when his elder brother Arthur succeeded as king? Duke of York and the premier noble of England? Or, as one authority claims, archbishop of Canterbury and prince of the church?

* * *

At first sight, there seems little doubt: his father had not only created Henry duke of York, but had also given him a substantial landed endowment as such. And he was adding to this as late as 21 July 1501, when the king finally reached agreement with Lord Grey's executors for the purchase of Codnor Castle. Six months earlier, Lady Margaret Beaufort – who was privy to the king her son's inmost thoughts – showed herself similarly confident about Henry's long-term future as a great landed magnate. Her tenants in the north-west, she suggested to the king, should all be made 'retainers' – that is, sworn followers in peace and war – to 'my lord of York, your fair sweet son'.

'The which,' she added, 'shall not after be long undone.'

But did the coincidence of Suffolk's flight and Arthur's marriage force Henry VII to rethink, perhaps even to change his mind? Was it really wise, he may have wondered, to saddle the future King Arthur with Henry, duke of York? After all, the duke would be rich in land and men; Yorkist blood flowed in his veins; he bore the magic name; he even, as was already clear, *looked* Yorkist. Why, Henry VII may have concluded, spend twenty bitter years suppressing the ancient enmity of Lancaster and York only to sow the seeds of its revival in the next generation by his own voluntary act?

★　★　★

All this is possible – though there is not a scrap of direct contemporary evidence that Henry VII harboured any such doubts. But there *is* the otherwise strange assertion of Henry VIII's first, seventeenth-century biographer, Edward, Lord Herbert of Cherbury, that Henry was 'destined to the archbishopric of Canterbury, during the life of his elder brother Prince Arthur'. Their father, Henry VII's supposed intention was twofold: to save money and to get control of the church for the crown, on the one hand, and on the other to leave his second son scope to carve out a great career for himself in a sphere where he would complement, rather than rival, his elder brother.

Herbert's statement has been repeated, more or less respectfully, by almost all subsequent writers. But what is the evidence for it? Herbert himself describes his source as 'a credible author', whom he cites in the first edition of 1649 by a heavily abbreviated marginal note: 'Concil. Trid. I i'. This, it turns out, is a reference to Paolo Sarpi's sensational, anti-papalist *Historia del Concilio Tridentino* (History of the Council of Trent), which was first published in 1619 in London and dedicated to James I and VI. An English translation appeared the following year, in which the relevant passage, in Volume 1 Chapter 1, was rendered as follows:

Amongst the most famous contradictors, which the doctrine of Luther found, was Henry VIII, king of England, who not being born the king's eldest son, had been destinated by his father to be archbishop of Canterbury, and therefore in his youth was made to study.

Herbert, it is clear, has merely glossed and elaborated Sarpi. But where did Sarpi, an Italian who was born five years after Henry's death and never left Italy, get his information from? As he cites no reference, we cannot be sure. But we can guess.

The link, I suspect, was a fellow Italian. His name was anglicised as William Parron, and for many years he acted as Henry VII's semi-official astrologer.

Parron operated both at court and in the marketplace. Every 24 December (to catch the Christmas market) he published a cheaply printed 'prognostication' or almanack for the forthcoming year; and on the ensuing 1 January he presented the king with a more esoteric manuscript treatise as a New Year's Day gift for his personal enlightenment.

One of these royal gifts was entitled *Liber de optimo fato Henrici Eboraci ducis* ('Book of the good fortune of Henry, duke of York'). In the form that it has come down to us, it was compiled between April 1502 and February 1503. But it incorporates material which seems to have been written earlier, probably in late 1501.

This reused material, it has been pointed out, places 'frequent emphasis on the religious qualities of . . . si Henry's future career'. One remark in particular stands out. '*Indubitanter*,' Parron claims, '*devotus erit et bonus ecclesiasticus*.' 'Undoubtedly [Henry] will be devout and a good cleric [*ecclesiasticus*].' There is, it is true, a slight ambiguity in *ecclesiasticus*, since it could, at a pinch, mean 'churchman' in the sense of 'a supporter of the church'. But 'cleric' is by far the most common usage.

What did Parron know that others, including Henry's own grandmother, Lady Margaret Beaufort, did not? Here it should be noted that Parron had form. Back in 1499 he had composed an earlier treatise for presentation to Henry VII, *De astrorum vi fatali* ('Of the fatal power of the stars'). This was finished on 15 October. But it contains a transparent justification for the executions of Warbeck and Warwick, which did not take place till five and six weeks later, at the end of November:

> It is expedient that one man should die for the people and the whole nation perish not. For an insurrection cannot occur in any state without the death of a great part of the people and the destruction of many great families with their property.

Was Parron similarly jumping the gun in 1501 with fears about Henry, duke of York's role as a potential incendiary? And was he proposing his

170

consecration as a churchman as a way out of the problem?

Even, curiously, the succession to Canterbury was a topical hot potato at the time. Cardinal-archbishop Morton, Henry VII's long-serving minister and Thomas More's patron, had died in September 1500. His nominated successor was Thomas Langton. But Langton too died within three weeks of being translated from Winchester in January 1501. Finally Henry Deane, bishop of Salisbury, was promoted to the archbishopric, and took up office in the summer of 1501.

All this meant that there had been three arch-bishops in six months. And was Deane, Henry VII's 'faithful councillor', intended only to keep the throne of St Augustine warm until Henry had reached the canonical age for consecration?

It is possible. But Parron's scheme – and Parron himself – was overtaken by events.

CHAPTER 10

FUNERALS

After the departure of his brother and sister-in-law for Ludlow, Henry remained at court to spend Christmas with his parents at Richmond. The king was in an expansive mood: he had married his eldest son and inaugurated his new palace. Nothing was too good for his second son either, and he gave Henry £3.6s.8d with which 'to play at dice'.

This was a huge sum (at least £1,000 in today's money). No doubt Henry enjoyed himself, rolling the dice, calling the numbers and counting out his winnings and losses.

But he was to pay the price by developing a taste for heavy gambling.

Three weeks later, Henry was an important guest at another wedding. This was the marriage by proxy (that is, in the groom's absence) of his elder sister Margaret to James IV of Scotland. Relations between England and Scotland had come a long way since James IV's enthusiastic support for Warbeck. The Spanish, who were allies of both countries, worked hard at reconciliation; James, mercurial as ever, had lost interest in border raiding, while Henry VII was also dreaming dreams of a greater Britain. The treaties of marriage and alliance were agreed on 24 January 1502; the following day the proxy wedding was celebrated with much ceremony at Richmond.

First there was mass in the splendid new chapel royal of the palace, after which a 'notable sermon' was preached by Richard Fitzjames, bishop of Rochester, in the presence of 'the king and queen with their noble children, except the prince'. The party then processed to the queen's great chamber for the proxy wedding, with Henry 'duke of York, the king's second son' heading the list of the distinguished company.

Immediately after the ceremony Queen Elizabeth took her daughter 'by the hand'. It was a gesture of motherly affection; it was also a recognition of the fact that Margaret, as queen of Scots, was now her equal in status. The two dined at the same table, eating from the same dishes and both having covered cups as a mark of their sovereign status.

But there was as yet no question of sending Margaret to Scotland. She was deemed to be too young – and too under-developed for her age – for the reality of marriage with a bridegroom who was more than double her age, and notoriously fond of the ladies. Instead the treaties provided for a year-and-a-half delay, specifying that she should be handed over to her husband-to-be no later than 1 September 1503.

Meanwhile Henry's brother and new sister-in-law had arrived at the great marcher castle of Ludlow. There they were intended to gain experience in the business of government and in the equally serious business of living with each other and getting a family. Arthur apparently took to his marital duties with gusto. One of his most intimate body servants, William Thomas, later testified: '[I] made the said prince ready to bed and with other conducted him clad in his night-gown unto the princess's bed-chamber door often and sundry times whereinto he entered and there continued all night.'

Indeed, Arthur's enthusiasm for sex alarmed some of his household. Maurice St John told an unknown informant that 'Arthur, after he had lain with the Lady Catherine, at Shrovetide after his marriage, began to decay . . . which St John said was because he lay with the Lady Catherine'.

Shrove (Pancake) Tuesday fell on 8 February in 1502; on Saturday, 2 April, Arthur was dead.

The information reached the court three days later, on the night of the fourth. The council decided to break the terrible news to the king through his father confessor. Henry VII's first thought was to send for Elizabeth of York, so they could 'take the painful sorrows together'. The

174

queen comforted her grief-stricken husband 'with full great and constant comfortable words', before returning to her own apartments and breaking down in turn.

Both parents probably felt guilt as well as grief: Henry for inducting his beloved son too early into life as a married man; Elizabeth of York for having seen so very little of him since the moment she had parted from him as a baby at Farnham.

Now she would never see him again – not even the body, for Arthur, married in the heart of the kingdom at St Paul's, was buried on its fringes in a plague-ridden Worcester.

No one can read the account of the reaction of Arthur's parents to his death and doubt for a moment the reality of their feelings. But, even as they plumbed the depths, the dynastic imperative was not forgotten. 'God,' Elizabeth of York reminded her husband, 'had lent them yet a fair goodly prince; two fair princesses; and that ever God is where he was.'

And that 'fair goodly prince', Henry, was now heir.

Or rather, he was heir providing Catherine was not carrying Arthur's child. Catherine, her parents learned later, was 'suffering' – from what is unclear. It could have been grief, or physical illness, or depression brought on by the weather of that wretched marcher spring. Or it could have been a symptom of pregnancy.

Best to take no risks. Catherine was brought back from Ludlow to London by easy stages in a black velvet horse-litter provided by the queen. By late May she had reached Croydon, where Elizabeth of York sent one of the pages of her chamber to her. We do not know the nature of his message. But one thing at least was now clear: Catherine was *not* pregnant; Henry was indeed the heir. And on 22 June, as 'Henry, prince of Wales', he was given the office of keeper and chief justice of Galtres Forest, where a few years before his tutor, John Skelton, had been invested – yet again – with the garland of laurel by the ladies of the household of Thomas Howard, earl of Surrey.

But was Henry enough? As Arthur's wholly unlooked-for death had shown, it was dangerous to leave the future of the Tudor dynasty hanging by a single life – even of a boy as healthy as Henry. It was also unnecessary. For, as Elizabeth of York had reminded her husband at the climax of their grief, 'we [are] both young enough' to have more children.

The couple were prompt to act, and Elizabeth became pregnant within a couple of months of Arthur's death. On the occasion of her most recent pregnancy, when she had carried her short-lived son Edmund, there had been fears for her life. They were renewed this time. Her prayers on the feast of the conception of the Blessed Virgin, when she made offerings on both the eve of the feast and the feast day itself, 8 December, were likely to have been especially fervent. On the thirteenth, she rewarded a monk who brought 'Our Lady['s] girdle to the queen'. This was the relic, kept at Westminster Abbey, 'which women with child were wont to girdle with' to help them through the travails of pregnancy.

Her confinement was due to take place in the Tower. The queen went there to inspect the arrangements, which featured 'a rich bed' made for the occasion and trimmed with red and white roses and clouds. The embroiderers had laboured at it seven weeks, often working by candlelight to get it finished in time. She then travelled by boat to Richmond for the Christmas festivities. On Christmas Day she heard a new setting of a carol by William Cornish, the leading composer of the chapel royal; and on New Year's Day she gave and received the accustomed gifts, including one from Lady Margaret Beaufort.

One of the more brazen gifts presented at court that day came from the Italian William Parron, Henry VII's semi-official astrologer.

This was the worked-up version of his *Liber de optimo fato Henrici Eboraci ducis*. It had been written, Parron complains, against the clock, and indeed it shows signs of haste and last-minute revision. The first section, which pointed to an ecclesiastical career for Henry, remained. But new sections offered an astrological explanation for Arthur's death, declared that Henry would enjoy a triumphant reign and father many sons, and finally predicted that his mother, Elizabeth of York, would live until she was eighty.

Parron was so proud of his work that he had a second copy made, complete with a new dedication to 'Prince Henry' and a careful explanation for the boy of the illustrated frontispiece, which showed: 'First a picture of the sky at the creation of the world with the signs and planets in their houses and positions following the opinion of prophets, astrologers and theologians . . .' It was only the second work to be dedicated to Henry, and one imagines that he devoured it eagerly.

More's the pity.

A month after Parron's confident prophecy, Elizabeth of York 'took to her chamber' in the Tower on 26 January. Only days later, on the night of 2 February, the feast of the purification of the Blessed Virgin, to whom she had prayed so fervently, 'the queen travailed of a child suddenly'. The queen's midwife, Alice Massy, who seems to have assisted at the births of all her children, beginning with Prince Arthur and including Henry himself, successfully handled the emergency and delivered a baby girl. She was christened Catherine, after her aunt, the wife of Lord William Courtenay, and perhaps after Catherine of Aragon also. Ten days later, on 12 February, four yards of flannel were bought for the baby.

Elizabeth was frequently ill after labour. But this time her condition deteriorated alarmingly, and the king sent James Nattrass post-haste to fetch a physician, Dr Halesworth, from Kent. He travelled day and night. But neither Halesworth, if he arrived in time, nor the queen's 'dry nurse' could save her, and on the morning of Saturday, 11 February 1503, 'died that most gracious and virtuous princess the queen'.

It was her thirty-seventh birthday. And Henry, her surviving son, was not yet twelve.

The funeral took place on 23 February, when the funeral sermon was preached, once again, by Fitzjames, bishop of Rochester. He took his text from the Book of Job: 'Have pity upon me, have pity upon me, O ye my friends, for the hand of God hath touched me.' He spake these words,' the reporting herald writes, 'in the name of England.'

England was indeed mourning a popular and beloved queen. But there was more: death had walked abroad in the land. Prince Arthur had died, and then the queen, and while the queen was still lying in state in the Tower, Henry Deane, the newly appointed archbishop of Canterbury, died too.

The unspoken questions in the Abbey must have been: 'Who next?' and 'What next?'

★ ★ ★

Henry was not present at Fitzjames's sermon. Nor had he walked, a white-faced boy, among the throngs of black-robed mourners in his mother's funeral procession. For at that time royalty did not see death, even of its nearest and dearest.

But did Henry feel it?

We know nothing of his reaction to Arthur's death. But it is unlikely to have been profound, as the two brothers had never been close enough physically to become close emotionally. His mother's death was a different matter. News of 'the death of my dearest mother', Henry wrote some years later to Erasmus, had been 'hateful intelligence'. This seems clear enough. But the letter was in Latin, in reply to one in the same language from Erasmus. And, as was usual with such Latin compositions (at least in hands less suavely expert than those of Erasmus), Henry had not much to say and said it very well.

Still, I am inclined to take this phrase at least at face value. Henry had been close to his mother as a child. She had taught him to read, supervised his upbringing and come to the rescue when danger threatened. More recently, after her unusually long absence on progress to Wales in the late summer and autumn of 1502, Henry had sent a messenger to her on her return.

We can guess what he felt about her permanent absence.

★　　★　　★

Perhaps once again it was Henry's friend Thomas More, writing this time in English, who came nearest to expressing Henry's real feelings. Soon after the event, More wrote *A Rueful Lamentation of the Death of Queen Elizabeth*. It takes the conventional form of 'a dramatic soliloquy by the dead queen, bidding farewell to all her earthly belongings' – her children, her palaces, everything. But if the form is conventional, the tone is not. Instead, More offers a warmly sympathetic and sharply observed portrait of a woman whom he had known well and to whom he was deeply attached.

He also gives vent to his (and no doubt Henry's) indignation at Parron's bungled prophecy:

Yet was I late promised otherwise,
This year to live in wealth and delice [delight].

How true is for this year thy prophecy.
The year yet lasteth, and lo now here I lie.

But the central verse of the *Lamentation* deals with the queen's feelings about her 'own dear spouse'. She bids farewell to

The faithful love that did us both combine
In marriage and peaceable concord.

And begs her husband to bestow all his love on their children:

Erst were you father, and now must ye supply
The mother's part also.

It is not a role that comes easily to most men,
and Henry VII was no exception.

CHAPTER 11

RE-EDUCATION

The year or two following Arthur's death were a sort of limbo for Henry: everything changed and nothing changed.

He was now heir apparent and prince of Wales (though he had not yet been formally created as such). Otherwise, his life continued much as before. His separate household remained in being, save that it was now the household of the prince of Wales rather than the duke of York's. Commissions to purvey victuals and other necessaries for it were issued under this new title between November 1502 and February 1504; in February 1503 its members were also listed as 'my lord princes household' at the time of his mother's funeral.

This latter list only reinforces the impression of continuity. Henry, prince though he had become and growing up though he rapidly was, continued to live with his two sisters. This meant that there was still a powerful female presence in his establishment. Thirteen 'gentlewomen' head the list of his household and they include individuals who had been with Henry since birth or earliest boyhood.

These included his former rocker, Frideswide Puttenham; his sister Margaret's rocker, Margery Gower; and other former attendants in the nursery at Eltham like Jane Chace, Elizabeth Bailey, and Avice Skidmore.

But there are a few pointers to the future too. One of the gentlewomen of the household was Mary Reading, who was Charles Brandon's aunt, while Henry Guildford, who was to be one of Henry's closest friends and associates for the first two decades of his reign, had become one of the 'carvers, cupbearers and waiters', who did him honorific service at table.

Henry's education continued too. But here the household list points to real change, since it shows that Henry's long-serving tutor, John Skelton, had been dismissed and replaced by a highly qualified professional teacher (who just happened to be Thomas More's friend and correspondent), John Holt.

With the change – to exaggerate a little, but not much – Henry had stepped from the middle ages into the renaissance.

The exact timing is unclear. But almost certainly it came in the hectic months which followed Arthur's marriage and untimely death. Arthur's own educational establishment had been broken up on the eve of his marriage, when he had assumed adult status; his death also seems to have provoked a great coming-and-going among the surviving royal tutors.

On 29 April 1502, 40 shillings was paid 'to the duke of York's schoolmaster', probably to sweeten Skelton's departure for rural exile (as he certainly saw it) among disputatious East Anglian peasants as rector of Diss in Norfolk. Skelton may well have been followed by a bridging appointment in the person of an unknown Scotsman 'schoolmaster to the prince'. But by late 1502 or early 1503 John Holt was definitely in post, receiving, as 'Master Holt, schoolmaster', mourning cloth to walk in the funeral procession of Henry's mother, Queen Elizabeth of York.

It would be hard to think of a greater contrast to the mercurial, self-opinionated Skelton: Holt was solid, well-thought-of and had advanced step by step up the ladder of professional school-mastering.

The son of a prosperous citizen of Chichester, he probably studied at the cathedral school there, where he was later briefly master himself. He went up to Oxford, and in 1490 became a junior fellow of Waynflete's foundation of Magdalen College, which specialized in the new approaches to Latin. He shone and became usher, or assistant master, of Magdalen College School in the mid-1490s. Thence he was poached to become schoolmaster to the boys in Cardinal Morton's household at the archbishop's palace at Lambeth, for whom he wrote his innovative Latin grammar, *Lac Puerorum* ('Schoolboys' Milk'). Illustrated with woodcuts to help pupils remember the case-endings of Latin words, it was the latest thing, and would certainly have been used by Henry himself.

Holt's career path could have brought him into contact with Thomas More, who was a year or two younger, at several points: through Morton and his household, where More himself had been a pupil as a boy and with whom he remained on intimate terms; at Oxford; or in advanced intellectual circles in London. In any case the two became close, and More wrote the introductory and concluding verses to *Lac Puerorum*.

In 1500 Cardinal Morton died. Holt's career, however, continued with scarcely a blip. The following year he was appointed as master at his old school at Chichester, and he had just taken up the job when More wrote him the letter describing – in grossly unflattering terms – Catherine of Aragon's entourage on her *entrée* into London. Five months later came the bombshell of Arthur's death and Henry's succession as heir apparent.

It was, therefore, almost certainly, More's recommendation which got Holt his position as Henry's tutor. But More, as a twenty-odd-year-old law student (however brilliant), could not have secured such a plum item of patronage himself. Another, bigger figure must have come into play. Everything points to William Blount, Lord Mountjoy, Henry's *socius studiorum*.

William Blount had been born with a silver spoon in his mouth – or rather, bearing in mind the complexities of latemedieval family structure which followed from frequent remarriages – a whole canteen of cutlery. His grandfather Walter, the first baron and real founder of the family's fortunes, was an intimate of Edward IV, and of his wife's family, the Woodvilles, in particular. William's uncle James, who had sprung the earl of Oxford from imprisonment under Richard III, was equally close to Henry VII; while William's second stepfather, James Butler, earl of Ormond, was lord chamberlain to Henry's mother, Queen Elizabeth of York.

Any one of these multiple connexions could have placed Blount in Henry's household. But, bearing in mind Elizabeth of York's dominant role in Henry's upbringing, Blount's stepfather Ormond was probably the key.

Blount was born in about 1478, which made him a more-or-less exact contemporary of that other great figure in Henry's youth, Thomas More. He was a promising boy, good-looking and intelligent, and turned out to have a real gift for friendship (with men) and love (with women). He also showed an interest in formal learning that was unusual, though not unprecedented, for one of his high rank.

He seems to have gone to Queens' College, Cambridge, where Queen Elizabeth Woodville, Henry's maternal grandmother, was second foundress, and was tutored by Ralph Whitford, fellow of the college. There is no record of Blount's having taken his Cambridge degree. But, accompanied by Whitford, he certainly moved on to Paris to complete his studies. There the pair soon encountered Erasmus, to whom William had been given introduction.

The attraction was mutual and immediate. In Erasmus, William found a teacher who was both learned and urbane; while in Mountjoy, who was both bright and rich, Erasmus had his ideal pupil. Gratefully casting off the dust of collegiate life, with its unvarying diet of bad eggs and stinking fish, Erasmus moved in with Mountjoy and Whitford and shared lodgings with them in the house of an English gentleman. They studied rhetoric together, and Mountjoy polished his prose under the guidance of Europe's greatest Latin stylist.

Mountjoy, who had already interrupted his studies in 1497 when he came home to get married, returned to England for good in 1499. This time, he brought Erasmus with him for an extended visit. Erasmus spent two months at Oxford in the autumn or Michaelmas term; otherwise he was Mountjoy's guest, either in his London house in Knightrider Street, just to the south of St Paul's, or at Sayes Court near Greenwich.

In Oxford, Erasmus heard John Colet's revolutionary lectures on the Epistles of St Paul; in London, he became fast friends with Thomas More, who was studying law at Lincoln's Inn; and at Eltham he met the young Henry.

He also met Henry's then tutor, John Skelton, and the two, as we have seen, exchanged fulsome compliments. Nevertheless, Skelton's days as royal tutor were numbered from that moment. He was a practitioner of the florid Latin which had been fashionable for most of the fifteenth century; Erasmus was a pioneer of the new, easy style, and abominated everything that Skelton stood for. Erasmus also had powerful allies: Mountjoy was his most aristocratic disciple, while More was already a distinguished practitioner of the new style himself.

The trio must have decided to rescue Henry as soon as practicable. Two years later, Arthur's death and the ensuing transformation in Henry's status offered the opportunity. They seized it with both hands. Skelton was packed off to Diss, and (to judge from his former pupil's indifference) his name and scholarship were blackguarded behind his back.

The donkeywork in retraining Henry was undertaken by the professional John Holt, and after Holt's early death in 1504 by his successor and lookalike, William Hone, who had trodden in Holt's footsteps at each stage of his career: at Magdalen, in Morton's household and at Chichester.

But the dominant influence was Mountjoy. And behind Mountjoy, Erasmus himself. Mountjoy, studying with Erasmus, had got the new Latin from the horse's mouth; Henry was to get it second-hand from Erasmus's works, which Mountjoy – 'once my pupil', as Erasmus notes with a teacher's pride – now encouraged Henry to study intently.

The result was that, in time, Henry developed a style which had echoes of Erasmus's own. One later letter from Henry to Erasmus was so well-written, indeed, that Erasmus, like Latin teachers throughout the ages, suspected a crib. When he was next in England he put his doubts to Mountjoy. Mountjoy reassured him, but Erasmus was still doubtful. To settle the matter, Mountjoy showed him a bundle of drafts of Henry's correspondence, written in his own hand and including the letter addressed to Erasmus. The draft was obviously the result of much labour, as it was corrected and re-corrected; but it was in one hand throughout, and was evidently the work of a single mind.

In one important respect, however, there was continuity. Skelton had particularly emphasized the importance of history, and history remained a principal field of study for Henry and Mountjoy. This was because history, as Erasmus wrote later to Mountjoy's son Charles, was 'especially regarded by that wise and judicious king', Henry VII. But the focus would have shifted from the English and French chronicles, which had formed a staple of Skelton's teaching, to the great classical historians who had figured largely in Andre's syllabus for Arthur.

Modern languages, especially French, were not forgotten. Skelton had probably laid the foundations by reading with Henry an exciting old French chronicle describing the derring-do of Richard Coeur de Lion in the Crusades. Here, too, Skelton's departure was followed by professionalization, as a native French speaker, Giles Duwes, took over Henry's instruction by February 1503 at the latest.

Duwes, who was probably born in Normandy, had an extraordinarily long career in the Tudor service: he began as tutor in French to Henry's elder brother Prince Arthur; in 1506 he became librarian at Richmond of the largely French collection that had been built up by Edward IV and Henry VII; and he died, still in harness, in 1535, as French teacher to Henry's own daughter, Princess Mary.

He was evidently a skilled and imaginative linguist, and the manual he wrote for Mary is a model of its kind. Instead of the usual stilted dialogue, the conversational exercises are sharply observed and even funny. It is easy to see how, with a teacher like this. Henry acquired the 'clear and perfect a sight' in the language, to which John Palsgrave, author of another teach-yourself-French book, paid lavish tribute.

* * *

Duwes, who doubled as a musician as well as a linguist, was also responsible for teaching Henry the lute. He first appears in Henry's household in this capacity in 1501. But Henry, who had been bought a lute by his father in 1498, had begun to play the instrument long before. He may even, in view of his natural musical abilities, have been largely self-taught – though receiving a polish from Duwes's professional hand. In addition, Henry had a 'schoolmaster at pipes', a certain 'Guillam', who coached him in wind instruments and, to judge from his name, was similarly French or Walloon.

Finally, to make sure that his physical development was not forgotten, the twelve-year-old Henry also had a 'master at arms [or perhaps "axes"]'.

Despite the truly 'Renaissance' breadth and diversity of Henry's curriculum, however, Latin remained predominant and in pride of place. And here, after 1502 at least, there was a distinct intellectual tone. The temptation is to label it 'Erasmian', and draw the obvious conclusion: 'in fixing Henry's attention upon the writings of Erasmus, Mountjoy was unconsciously preparing his mind for the reception of the principles of the Reformation'.

The trouble is that even the Erasmus of these early years was not 'Erasmian'. He was an innovative Latin stylist, neither less nor much more either. In other words, he had not yet developed the characteristic set of attitudes that we think of as Erasmian: that the text – and particularly the

Scriptural text – speaks directly to the mind, and still more to the emotions, of the reader; that the literal meaning of the Scriptures is the proper one; that we determine the meaning of the text by considering its context, and so on.

These attitudes were closely associated with Erasmus's stylistic reforms. But he himself developed them sequentially, not simultaneously, and it always remained possible to separate the two, so that, for example, both the cases for and against the reform of the church could be (and were) argued in Latin that was Erasmian in form, however unErasmian it might be in spirit.

And if Erasmus himself was not yet Erasmian, nor perforce were the other members of the circle. Thomas More became Erasmian at roughly the same time as Erasmus himself (say by about 1513), and was a principal influence on Erasmus's own development.

But in the last decade of Henry VII's reign More's values too seem to have belonged to an earlier world.

The nature of that world is best explored through the central member of the group, Lord Mountjoy. He was not, nor ever became, Erasmian. Despite his pupilage, his close and continuing friendship with Erasmus, his sustained patronage of his old teacher and his substantial technical mastery of 'Erasmian' Latin, Mountjoy remained at home in the values of his class and society – values which both More and Erasmus came to challenge frontally.

The reason, probably, is social. Mountjoy was a gentleman before he was a scholar, and fought more naturally with the sword than with the pen. This is shown by the simplest analysis of his biography. Intellectual leanings he may have had, but he remained true to his family's military and courtly traditions: he held office in Calais; fought the French and captained Tournai, Henry VIII's short-lived trophy conquest in France; he also succeeded his stepfather Ormond as queen's lord chamberlain.

And Henry's trajectory, it is clear, was much nearer to Mountjoy's than More's. Nevertheless, his Latin teachers did their work well:

> To have educated Henry VIII, the first self-consciously latinate king for over three hundred years, was itself no mean achievement. And if Henry had not been a latinate king, would his monarchy and the Henrician Reformation have developed in the ways that they did?

Would they indeed have happened at all?

CHAPTER 12

TO COURT

Henry's twenty-four months of betwixt and between ended in 1504. He was created prince of Wales, he was married and as quickly unmarried, he went to court, and he began to make his first impression on the political nation. There is no sign that it was particularly favourable.

Parliament – incidentally the last of Henry VII's reign – met on 15 January 1504. One of its first acts was formally to strip Henry of his title of duke of York and all the estates that had gone with it. Instead, on 23 February he was created prince of Wales. The heralds received their usual fee for proclaiming his new style, and, as was customary, knights of the Bath were dubbed. Otherwise, nothing is known of the event.

Henry's creation as prince of Wales was followed by a much bigger change. The authority of the last commission to purvey for his household expired on 20 July 1504. A few weeks earlier Henry had joined his father at Richmond. He was left behind when Henry VII went to Westminster for a meeting of the council on 9 July. But the prince rejoined the king at Greenwich at the end of the month, and accompanied him on the summer progress into Kent and Sussex.

A threshold had been crossed. Henry had celebrated his birthday on 28 June. He was now in his fourteenth year – the age of maturity for a royal prince. For his elder brother Arthur his fourteenth year had seen the despatch of his bride-to-be to England; for Henry it marked his move to court – his father's court.

The Spanish ambassador was quick to notice the change. On 10 August he wrote home: 'The prince of Wales is with the king. Formerly the king did not like to take the prince of Wales with him, in order not to interrupt his studies.' The king, who was an accomplished ham actor, had put up an impressive display of paternal affection. 'It is quite wonderful,' the ambassador gushed, 'how much the king likes the prince of Wales.' 'He has good reason too,' he added, 'for the prince deserves all love.'

It would be more interesting to know how much, if at all, Henry liked his father. For the king, unlike his ebullient second son, was not an immediately likeable man.

Heredity and harsh experience had seen to that. In 1504 Henry's father was still only forty-seven. But he looked much older. The turning point seems to have come five years previously, in 1499, as he was screwing up his resolve to execute

Warbeck and Warwick. 'Henry [VII],' the Spanish ambassador noted, 'has aged so much during the last two weeks that he seems to be twenty years older.' Then had followed the still greater traumas of the deaths, in quick succession, of his elder son and his wife.

The signs are plain in Michiel Sittow's portrait of the king, painted in 1505. He still holds himself upright, with the remains of the athletic strength noticed by Polydore Vergil: 'his body was slender, but well built and strong; his height above average'. But in the face the slimness is turning to emaciation: the flesh falls away from his cheek-bones and shrinks round his jaw. The lips are also tightly pinched together. This is probably because he is trying to conceal the fact that – as Vergil again noted – 'his teeth were few, poor and blackish'.

As the rest of the face shrinks, the nose, which is long and somewhat hooked, looms large and questioning. But it is the eyes which really strike. Polydore describes them as 'small and blue'. Here they are hooded, like his mother, Lady Margaret Beaufort's; there also seems to be a cast or squint (though the irregularity could simply be the result of painterly incompetence).

Sittow's is, in short, the face of the Henry VII of legend: shrewd, suspicious, and above all mean. But there was another Henry, which Polydore also knew. The face would light up and the words would flow. Then, says Polydore, 'his appearance was remarkably attractive and his face was cheerful, especially when speaking'. And what words! His eloquence was Welsh, or even French, in its extravagance. Sometimes it had the obvious insincerity of diplomatic hyperbole. But equally this was the king who could arouse passionate loyalty – so passionate that it could endure even rebuff and reproof.

This was also the king who 'knew well how to maintain his royal majesty and all which appertains to kingship in every time and in every place'. This is, in short, the king who, despite all the probable tensions and even antipathies between them, was recognizably Henry's father.

And when he summoned Prince Henry to court in 1504 it was to play the father in deed: to train and mould his son into his future role as king. That at least was the view of the Spanish ambassador:

> But it is not only from love that the king takes the prince with him; he wishes to improve him. Certainly there could be no better school in the world than the society of such a father as Henry VII. He is so wise and so attentive to everything; nothing escapes his attention. There is no doubt the prince has an excellent governor and steward in his father. If he lives ten years longer he will leave the prince furnished

with good habits, and with immense riches, and in as happy circumstances as man can be.

As it happened, Henry VII had less than half that span allotted to him. But that was not the only reason that the results of his training of his son were more mixed than the ambassador's hyperbolic forecast. Nevertheless, and this is what matters here, it is clear that the attempt was made. Henry was not to come to the throne untrained and untested, as the conventional wisdom assumes; instead he was more conscientiously prepared for kingship than most of his predecessors.

Above all, his father had decided to train him *differently* from Arthur. Arthur had been sent away, to learn to rule experimentally, as it were, by governing his own principality and the Welsh Marches; Henry was to be kept by his father's side to learn by imitation and example.

The first and central step was thus his presence at court, where he now shadowed his father in public and in private. In 1505, for example, the Garter celebrations were unusual in both splendour and publicity. They were held in St Paul's Cathedral, which was turned into a vast chapel royal for the occasion. On St George's Eve, the king and his knights heard evensong; on St George's Day itself, they went in procession in their robes, with a relic of the saint's leg – newly sent by Maximilian, king of the Romans – borne in front of them in its case of parcel-gilt silver.

The prince walked in the procession immediately after his father, and he was in turn to become a most attentive sovereign of the order.

Henry was also at his father's side in July 1506 at Richmond. At about 11 o'clock one evening the king and the prince had taken a late summer's night stroll in a newly built gallery near the king's bedroom; less than an hour later, at about midnight, the gallery 'fell suddenly'. Miraculously, bearing in mind its position at the heart of the palace, no one was hurt. 'But the master carpenter that framed it was punished by imprisonment many days after.'

But the greatest difference with Arthur was in the matter of marriage. Arthur had been married and bedded as quickly as possible – with, some were convinced, fatal consequences. Henry VII was not to make that mistake again, even though his surviving son's destined bride was also to be Catherine of Aragon.

As soon as was decent after Prince Arthur's death (indeed rather before), negotiations had begun for another English marriage for Catherine of Aragon. In the interim, Queen Elizabeth of York had died, and Henry VII's first thought was that he should marry Catherine himself. Isabella reacted with horror; it was 'a very evil thing – one never before seen, the mere mention of which offends the ears'.

In the face of this reaction, Henry VII looked elsewhere for a bride for himself, and instead opened discussions on marrying Catherine to his second son, Prince Henry. At first everything proceeded smoothly: the marriage treaty was signed on 23 June 1503, and two days later the couple were betrothed with some ceremony at the town palace of the bishop of Salisbury, which lay on the south side of Fleet Street, next to St Bride's.

But of course Catherine's first marriage, whether or not it had been consummated, established close ties of 'affinity' – or relationship by marriage – between her and Henry. This meant that their marriage could only take place if the affinity were 'dispensed with' or legally set aside by the pope. The treaty specified that both England and Spain would use their influence with Rome to obtain the dispensation, after which the couple would undergo a preliminary form of marriage. The solemnization of matrimony proper was to take place before Henry's fifteenth birthday.

Here again all began well. On 6 July 1504 the pope indicated his willingness to grant the dispensation, and Henry VII decided to proceed immediately. The couple were formally married at some time in the late summer or autumn – though the 'very solemn' ceremony which the king promised seems to have left no mark in the records. The dispensation reached Isabella in November 1504. But on the twenty-sixth she was dead.

★   ★   ★

201

All now threatened to unravel. For Catherine the daughter of Ferdinand of Aragon was a much less attractive proposition as a daughter-in-law than Catherine the daughter of the Catholic kings of Spain.

This was because Isabella's heir in law as sovereign of Castile was not her husband, Ferdinand, but her eldest surviving daughter, Juana, who was married to the Archduke Philip of Burgundy. It was now an open question as to who would succeed in Castile: Ferdinand by the fact of possession, or Philip in legal right of his wife.

Henry VII decided to sit out the forthcoming struggle and disengage his son from the Spanish marriage. On 27 June 1505, the eve of his fourteenth birthday, Prince Henry duly repudiated – as he was entitled to – the marriage he had entered into as a boy. His real feelings about the matter are unknown. The guess must be that he had agreed to marry Catherine because his father told him to, and that he reneged on his promise for the same reason. It was the last time that he was to be so meekly obedient in matrimony.

The other person most interested in the matter. Catherine of Aragon, was not even informed that her marriage had been repudiated; instead the intention seems to have been to hold Henry's 'protestation', as it was called, as a reserve weapon.

At the same time, Henry VII also turned the the financial screws on Catherine. Only the first half of her dowry had been paid before Arthur's death, which meant that she was not entitled to her dower income as princess. In its absence she was wholly dependent on the English king for funds to maintain her substantial household at Durham House.

In late 1505 Henry VII cut them off. He suggested that it would be much more sensible for Catherine to economize by living at court, rather than maintaining her own household. So to court Catherine came as well.

There her position was intensely difficult. She was widow of one prince of Wales, and bride-to-be (or perhaps not-to-be) of another. But she was rarely allowed to see Henry, much less to live with him. For Catherine of Aragon, proud of her royalty and convinced as she was, and was always to be, of her wedded state, it was humiliating beyond measure. For Henry VII it was the perfect arrangement, as he told her himself. 'He regards me,' she reported, 'as bound and his son as free. [Prince Henry] is not so old that delay is disagreeable.'

'Thus mine,' Catherine concluded miserably, 'is always the worst part.'

In retrospect, the tragi-comedy of Henry's on-off marriage to Catherine of Aragon looks like the dominant event of these years. At the time, however, as Henry VII's coolly cynical behaviour shows, it was the merest sideshow.

Instead, as always, Henry VII's principal concern was security – and increasingly for his heir, Henry, as much as for himself. For on Henry now depended the whole future of his father's achievement: everything that he had fought for, prayed for and lied for; the hundreds he had sent to the scaffold, the thousands he had had killed in battle and the millions of money he had extorted – at God alone knows at what cost to his immortal soul – from his subjects. All this would be in vain if his son did not succeed to the crown – that heavy, bejewelled crown that Henry VII had commissioned in 1487 to celebrate his victory at Stoke over the first pretender to challenge him.

And all this too was realized by the latest and in some ways the most dangerous pretender of the reign, Edmund de la Pole, earl of Suffolk. Suffolk, now in exile at Aachen (Aix-la-Chapelle) on the borders of the Netherlands and the Holy Roman Empire, was following events in England with an émigré's feverish attention. He rejoiced at the news of Arthur's death, and a month later, on 12 May 1502, instructed his agent at Maximilian's court to set out its consequences to his patron, the king of the Romans. Everything, he was to explain, now hung on Henry's life.

> If the second son of Henry [VII] were dead [Suffolk's agent was to tell Maximilian] there would be no doubt of the title of my lord [Suffolk]. And therefore if [Suffolk] stays out of that side of the sea until the

death of the said Henry [VII], who cannot live much longer. his younger son can on no account prevail against [Suffolk].

Still worse, from Henry VII's point of view, his own intelligence confirmed Suffolk's optimism about his chances of success. For, early in 1506 – that is, just eighteen months after Henry's move to court – information reached the king on the state of opinion among the English elite.

It made grim reading.

The information took the form of an informer's report of a series of conversations among the senior officers of the Calais garrison which had taken place the previous September. Like Suffolk, the report claimed, these leading officials took for granted that the king's death was only a matter of time: 'For the king's grace,' one had said, 'is but a weak man and sickly, not likely to be no long lived man.' And, like Suffolk again, with the king's death imminent, they looked to the future – and, in some cases, to Suffolk himself.

Most blatant in her allegiance to the pretender was Lucy, Lady Browne. As the daughter of John, marquess of Montague, she was a Neville and 'a proud, high-minded woman, [who] loveth not the king's grace'. Instead, she prized her kinship to Suffolk, 'to whom . . . she will do all the pleasure and help she can do in the world'. What made her really dangerous was the fact that her husband,

Sir Anthony Browne, was the lieutenant of Calais castle. This was the key to the town's defences. And it was a key which Lady Browne was fully determined to hand over to the pretender: 'If anything should come to your grace other than well,' the informer claimed, 'she would let [Suffolk in] by the postern of the castle to the destruction of us all.'

Lady Browne's overt partisanship was unique. What was more usual, and more insidious, was a smug fence-sitting. Both Lady Browne's husband, Sir Anthony, and Sir Nicholas Vaux, the lieutenant of the flanking fortress of Guisnes, had boasted of their ability to weather any dynastic storm. 'They had two good holds to resort to, the which they said,' the informer reported, 'should be sure to make their peace, how so ever the world turn.' In other words, because they were in charge of two key fortresses, they would be able to negotiate satisfactory terms with the new regime, whatever its nature might be and whoever might be its king.

This kind of opportunism was scarcely admirable. But it was not very culpable either, and it had become the way in which most of the political nation had survived the ups and downs of the Wars of the Roses. But what if it went to the very heart of the Tudor regime? That was the informer's most sensational charge, when he raised doubts about the loyalty of Giles, Lord Daubeney, lord chamberlain, captain of the guard and governor of

Calais. 'Put it that he be true as any man living to the king's grace now,' he insinuated, 'yet change of worlds hath caused change of men's minds, and that hath been seen many times.'

Would Daubeney prove a turncoat with the rest?

The revelation which touched Henry most directly was already old news. Back in May 1501 – when Arthur was still very much alive and Henry himself merely duke of York – Henry VII had fallen seriously ill at Wanstead, a hunting lodge in Essex on the edge of Epping Forest that was a favourite of his. For a time, it would seem, his life had been despaired of, and talk naturally turned to the succession: 'what world should be if his grace [Henry VII] departed and who should have rule in England then'. One of the Calais officials chanced to have been present during these conversations, when 'many divers and great personages' had considered the possibilities. Some, the informer reported, had put forward the claims of the duke of Buckingham, 'saying that he was a noble man and would be a royal ruler'. Others supported Suffolk, 'and so gave him great praise . . . likewise'.

'But none of them,' the informer stated flatly, 'spake of my lord prince [Arthur].'

Arthur was then fourteen, the same age as Henry had reached in 1505. If Henry VII – as seemed increasingly likely – were to die in the next year or two, would Henry's claims be as comprehensively disregarded as Arthur's had been in 1501? And was there anything that Henry VII could do about it? Come to that, was there anything that Henry himself could do about it either?

CHAPTER 13

RELIGION

Henry's most valuable piece of jewellery as prince of Wales – indeed probably his most precious single possession – was 'a cross set with a table diamond and three good pearls, given by the queen'. Valued at £13.6s.8d, it was worth over three times as much as 'the proper ring, gold enamelled red and black with a fair pointed diamond' which had been given to Henry by Edmund Dudley in a vain attempt to win his favour and was promptly lost by Henry at Langley near Woodstock when he was staying there with his father in September 1507.

As both a luxury item and a religious symbol, Henry's jewelled cross would have reminded him of his mother twice over. For Elizabeth of York was as pious as she was fond of the finer things in life. Probably, when she was near to term with Henry, she had sent to Westminster Abbey for the miraculous girdle of the Blessed Virgin Mary, 'which women with child were wont to girdle with. Certainly she did for her last, fatal pregnancy in 1503. In 1497, as Henry's father prepared for the final show-down with Perkin Warbeck, she had sought both solace and safety by going on pilgrimage to Walsingham in Norfolk. And she had taken Henry with her. When she could not go on pilgrimage herself, she paid others to perform the pious deed on her behalf. In March 1502, for instance, she gave a certain Richard Milner 10 pence a day to go on pilgrimage to seventeen shrines in London and the south-east, and a similar amount to another priest to make her offerings at eighteen more holy sites, stretching from Windsor in the west to – once more – Walsingham in East Anglia.

All this initiated Henry into the magical, mysterious, many-coloured world of late medieval piety, with its sounds, smells, miracle-working images and extravagant devotions. For several decades, indeed, he was an enthusiastic participant. He went on pilgrimage at least three times as king: to Our Lady of Walsingham in Norfolk in 1511 and to the shrine of Master John Schorne at North Marston in Buckingham in July 1511, and again a decade later in May 1521. As late as Good Friday 1539, he crawled to the cross, 'his own person kneeling upon his grace's knees', while his will, as well as invoking the aid of the Virgin and 'all the Holy Company of Heaven', also made abundant provisions for intercessory prayers for his soul in purgatory.

In short, with all the future gyrations of his religious belief, Henry never entirely escaped the pious practices of his youth.

★ ★ ★

We can enter these best, however, through another figure of Henry's earlier life: William Thomas, groom of his privy chamber. Thomas, as we have already seen, had served Arthur in a similar capacity. He did not transfer to Henry's service immediately on Arthur's death, and does not appear in the list of his household in February 1503. But, probably with Henry's move to court in July 1504. Thomas was recalled and sworn as his servant. Thereafter, with the head-start of his three years' experience in Arthur's princely household, he prospered exceedingly and became one of the key figures in Henry's personal service.

The two evidently became personally close as well – close enough, indeed, to exchange prayers. 'William Thomas,' wrote Henry in a 'bede' or prayer roll, 'I pray you pray for me, your loving master: Prince Henry.'

The roll is a long, narrow strip of parchment, about eleven feet long and five inches wide, with a series of illuminations of sacred subjects interspersed with prayers and other aids to devotion. The strange shape is designed to make the roll readily portable, for it was not only to be read but *used*: as an aid to devotion indeed, but also as a magical charm or amulet.

Henry's royal badges – two Tudor roses, the ostrich plume of the prince of Wales, and his 'wife' Catherine of Aragon's emblem of a sheaf of arrows – stand at the head, on either side of a washed-out and unfortunately unidentifiable coat of arms, which may belong to the original donor. Then comes the first illumination of the Trinity, with a thirty-line long Latin prayer for victory over enemies. Next is an illumination of the crucifixion, with Christ hanging between the two thieves.

Here there is a marked change of tone. The Trinity might be the central theological doctrine of Christianity. But the crucifixion, with the image of the suffering Christ, was its burning, emotional heart. And so it is here. 'If ye be in sin or tribulation,' the rubric – which indeed is written in red ink – reads, 'kneel down upon your knees before the rood [cross], and pray God to have mercy on you, and that He will forgive you your sins, and to grant your petition as He granted paradise to the thief, desire your petition rightfully.'

Then the supplicating Christian is taught how to use each and every part of the image in the illumination to increase the fervour – and hence the efficacy – of his prayers. First he must look at Christ's feet, pierced and bleeding with the nails; next at His side, laid open and gushing from the *coup de grâce* of the centurion's lance, and so on through each of the Five Wounds. And as he looks, he must feel and pray. 'Devotedly,' the rubric continues, 'behold the feet [of Christ] and say, *Adoramus te Jhesu Christe, et benedicimus tibi, quia per sanctam crucem redemisti mundum, misere nobis* ['We worship you Jesus Christ and bless you, since by the holy cross you have redeemed the world, have mercy upon us']. Then say this psalm . . . And then say this anthem . . . And then say *Pater Noster* ['Our Father'] and *Ave Maria* ['Hail Mary'].' Next the worshipper should 'steadfastly behold the sides . . . And so behold the hands . . . And then behold the head', gashed and bloody with the crown of thorns pressed into the sacred, suffering flesh. And with each lingering, pitiful scrutiny, the rubric directs, the prayers and petitions are to be repeated in full.

Only then can the suppliant venture to contemplate the image in its full, awful entirety: 'And so, with a whole mind to all the body, say *Adoramus . . .*'

Credo in Deum ('I believe in God'), the cycle of prayer ends.

Under this, Henry wrote his inscription, with its plea for Thomas's prayers. Did they pray together, prince and groom, prostrating themselves before the image, reciting the prayers and each feeding the other's fervour?

It seems almost certain.

If so, they performed what is known as a 'spiritual exercise'. Like modern physical exercise, it involved endless repetition, and with the similar purpose of improving tone, endurance and strength – but of the mind and spirit, not of the body and muscles.

And – just as with weightlifting – there were rewards and prizes.

★   ★   ★

213

Some of these are spelled out – and in great detail – in the inscription accompanying the next illumination, which shows Christ in the sepulchre. He sits, rather than reclines, and blood spouts from the sacred wounds in the side, hands, feet and head.

Once more the English rubric directs how the image is to be used and with what effect:

> To all them that before this image of pity devotedly say *5 Pater Noster, 5 Ave Maria and 1 Credo* ['I believe', that is, the Creed], shall have 52,712 years and 40 days of pardon granted to them by St Gregory and other holy men.

The '52,712 years and 40 days of pardon' was the reduction in the amount of time to be spent in 'purgatory' that would result from fulfilling the rubric. 'Purgatory' was the name given by the medieval church to the intermediate state between heaven and hell. Like hell, it was a place of suffering. But, unlike hell, the suffering was for a specific time, and not for eternity; and it was aimed not to punish the soul, as in hell, but to cleanse or 'purge' it to fit it eventually for entry into heaven.

Purgatory, in short, was the natural destination of Everyman: the ordinary fallible human being who had sinned too much to be immediately received into heaven, but not so grievously as to

214

be condemned to hell. This meant that reducing the time to be spent in purgatory became one of the central concerns of late-medieval piety. Two of the means available appear in the rubric. The first was the performance of specific acts of piety or 'good works', like the contemplation of the holy image and the recital of the prayers; the other was the invocation of saints, in this case, St Gregory.

We shall come across many more, including those that could be performed even after Everyman was dead and his soul already in purgatory.

The fourth image also shows Christ on the cross, but alone and with two angels beneath holding a cloth on which drops the blood from His wounds. 'This cross,' the rubric declares, '15 times moten [moved or multiplied] is the length of our Lord Jesus Christ.' Here we change gear again: the sacred becomes magical, and the image turns into a charm, whose mighty powers are listed by the rubric:

> And that day ye bear it upon you there shall no evil spirit have any power of you on land nor on water, nor with thunder nor lightning be hurt, nor die in deadly sin without confession, nor with fire be brent [burned], nor water be drowned; and it shall break your enemies' power and increase your worldly goods.

It would also work its magic for women who, unlike Henry's mother, were unable to borrow the Westminster relic of the Virgin's girdle:

> And if a woman be in travail of child, lay this on her body and she shall be delivered without peril, the child christendom and the mother purification [that is, the child shall be christened and the mother purified].

Another, even more powerful, image/charm appears beneath in the form of the three nails of the passion. They are about four inches long, the two outer nails impaling the hands and feet, while the centre nail bears the wounded heart. 'Pope Innocent,' the rubric states, 'hath granted to every man and woman that beareth upon them the length of these nails, saying daily *5 Pater Noster, 5 Ave Maria,* and 1 *Credo,* shall have seven gifts.' These too are enumerated:

- The first is that he shall not die no sudden death.
- The second is that he shall not be slain with no sword nor knife.
- The third is that he shall not be poisoned.
- The fourth, his enemies shall not overcome him.
- The fifth is he shall have sufficient goods to his life's end.

- The sixth is he shall not die without all the sacraments of holy church.
- The seventh is that he shall be defended from all evil spirits, pestilence, fevers, and all other infirmities on land and on water.

There follows an image of the Virgin and Child; then six more illuminations of saints, each with his proper anthems and invocations: St Michael, St George. St Erasmus, St Christopher, St Anthony and St Armagil of Brittany.

With this last we come back once more to Henry and his own family circle. The 'life and legend [of St Armagil]'. the rubric explains, 'was brought out of Brittany at the instance of the king our sovereign lord, Henry VII.' For long ago, back in his years of exile, Henry's father had nearly been shipwrecked by storms off the coast of Brittany. He had prayed to St Armagil and had been saved. In gratitude, when he became king, he introduced the saint's cult into England. His feast day of 16 August was added to the calendar of the English church in 1498; his image, which shows him, as on Prince Henry's roll, leading a dragon by a stole wrapped round its neck, was painted on the reredos of the altar at Romsey Abbey; and statues of him were carved in Henry VII's chapel at Westminster Abbey and on John Morton's tomb at Canterbury.

Morton, cardinal, archbishop and lord chancellor, was the coolest head among the English statesmen of the age. If Morton subscribed to the cult of saints, with their lives and legends, their gruesome martyr-doms, their miracles and wonder-working powers, what could not be allowed to an impressionable teenage boy like Henry?

But what, equally, might Henry's reaction be if his belief in their magic – so abundantly testified to by this bede-roll – faded?

CHAPTER 14

PHILIP

Henry, thanks to his wide reading of history and chronicles, in which he had been encouraged by all his teachers, was familiar with many different styles of kingship. But they were in the past. As far as the present was concerned, he had seen only one contemporary monarch in action: his own father, Henry VII.

At the beginning of 1506, however, chance introduced Henry to another ruler, the Archduke Philip of Burgundy. Philip presented the greatest possible contrast to Henry's father: he was young, dashing and sports-mad.

Henry found Philip immensely attractive. He became a sort of elder brother to him, and in time a model for his own kingship.

Philip's involuntary visit to England was another consequence of the revolution in foreign affairs which had followed the death of Catherine of Aragon's mother, Queen Isabella of Castile. Immediately after her death, Philip claimed Castile in the right of his wife Juana, and proclaimed himself king. Then, in January 1506, he set sail from the

Netherlands, with virtually his whole court, to go to Spain and make his claim good.

The voyage began well, making record time down the Channel with favourable winds. It was a royal progress by sea: passing 'before Calais by night, shooting guns, having great torches lit . . . trumpets and minstrels playing and singing'. But as the Burgundians cleared the Channel, the pomp and pageantry turned to near-tragedy. The fleet was suddenly becalmed, and then hit by a furious storm that drove the ships back towards England, scattering them as they went. Most put in at Falmouth in Cornwall, but the king and queen were carried further to the east, and made land at Melcombe Regis in the lee of the Isle of Portland.

Once ashore, the royal party was lured further inland, on the pretext that supplies would be more plentiful there. Philip, understanding that he was effectively a prisoner, decided to put a brave face on things (as indeed he had during the storm), and sent his secretary to Henry VII to announce his arrival and request that he and his wife might be allowed to visit him. Henry welcomed him with open arms: never has a spider invited a fly to step into a more gilded parlour.

In all the lavish hospitality, Prince Henry acted as co-host with his father. It was a training in outward graciousness; it might also have been a lesson in how to make sure that the bill was paid – promptly and in full. For Henry VII was determined to exact a heavy price for Philip's entertainment.

It was decided that the meeting between the two kings would take place at Windsor. Sir Thomas Brandon, the master of the horse, was sent to the west country with horses and litters to act as Philip's escort. En route, the party stopped at Winchester, where Philip was entertained by the bishop, Richard Foxe, who was also lord privy seal and the king's principal minister.

That same evening, Henry himself arrived, 'with a large and noble company'. The prince and king greeted each other warmly, so much so that 'on seeing them together you would have thought that they were brother and good friends'. Brothers, or at least brothers-in-law, they were indeed formally, in view of Henry's on-off marriage to Catherine of Aragon, Juana's sister. And they may well have become friends too, in the course of the visit.

The following day Philip and Henry left for Windsor, where on 31 January they were met over a mile outside the town by Henry VII himself. He welcomed Philip in his perfect, if rather over-enthusiastic, French, protesting that he was as dear to him 'as my own son who is here present'. There then followed a competition in elaborate courtesy. It was resolved by all three riding abreast, with Philip in the middle between Henry senior on his right hand and Henry junior on his left. In the castle Philip was lodged in King Henry's own apartments, while the king stayed in the inter-communicating set of rooms which had belonged to Queen Elizabeth of York.

Sessions of hard negotiation now alternated with entertainment. This ranged from the savagery of horse-baiting to the almost Victorian domesticity of the late-afternoon entertainment laid on by Catherine of Aragon and her sister-in-law, Princess Mary. First Catherine and one of her ladies, both in Spanish dress, danced, and then Mary and one of her English attendants. The atmosphere turned suddenly sour when Catherine asked Philip, who was engrossed in conversation with Henry VII, to dance. He excused himself. When she pressed him he replied brusquely that he was a mariner, 'And yet ye would cause me to dance' – and continued talking to the king. Mary offered Catherine sisterly consolation by going to sit with her on the edge of the carpet under the cloth of estate. Finally Mary took the floor with a display of the Tudor musical talent, playing on the lute and the clavichord. 'Who played very well, and she was of all folks there greatly praised that of her youth [she was not yet ten] in everything she behaved herself so well.'

On 9 February the seal was set on the visit with the formal signing of a peace treaty and an exchange of orders of chivalry: Philip was made a knight of the Garter, and Prince Henry a knight of the Golden Fleece. Henry VII put the Garter round Philip's leg, and Prince Henry 'buckled it and made it fast'. Then the treaties were signed, the *Te Deum* was sung and the trumpets blew. Finally, Philip, having changed into the robes of his own order, made Prince Henry a knight of the Golden Fleece. The Prince read the oath 'himself in French'.

On returning from mass, the two kings and the prince dined together 'in a little chamber, because they did not want to have many witnesses'. The room was in fact the secret or inmost chamber of the suite assigned to Philip. There Henry VII spoke freely of his feelings at the day's events. 'You have seen at Winchester,' he said to Philip, 'the Round Table hanging in the Church.' That was a subject of romance and history, because it was supposedly King Arthur's. 'But I hope,' the king continued, 'that people will also talk of this table, and that they will say, long after our deaths, that at this table was sealed the true and perpetual friendship between the empire of Rome, the kingdom of Castile, Flanders, Brabant and the kingdom of England.' The table would, he promised, be put on display, inscribed with the date and the noble company that had eaten on it.

Henry VII's place in history was one of his central concerns; his other was to guarantee the survival of his dynasty. And that meant ensuring the succession of his son, Prince Henry. The king now turned to his son and spoke to him bluntly:

'My son of Wales, you see that I am old; soon you will have need of your good friends.'

And Philip was to be the foremost, whose interests he was to put before his own.

It was Prince Henry's first summit conference, and it established a lasting taste for the genre – as well it might, for the sense of occasion was overpowering: the pageantry, the food and wine, his father's words, now heady now solemn, and above all the fact that he was sitting as an equal with two kings and disposing of the fate of Europe. For the occasion was not only designed to cement the friendship of the Habsburgs and the Tudors, it would also, as Henry VII put it with a delicious, intimate bluntness, 'hardly please our enemies'.

'Our enemies' were the French.

The conversation continued far into the evening. Even as they talked, word came of the arrival of a French embassy. The entertainment of the ambassador was left to the prince. It would be an opportunity to show what he felt. Among other pastimes, Henry showed off his skills with the bow: he killed a deer and drew several other good shots, on which the ambassador congratulated him. The prince replied, with studied ambiguity, that 'They were good for a Frenchman.'

His meaning was that he would like to have had a Frenchman as his target; his guest, happily, understood him to say that he had shot well enough to be compared with the best French archers.

On Tuesday, 10 February this clubby atmosphere of male bonding and competition was interrupted by a disturbing female presence: Queen Juana arrived at Windsor. History knows her as 'the Mad'. It would be fairer to say at this stage that she was neurotic. The principal symptom was a jealous possessiveness about her husband. A year previously she had dismissed most of her women, retaining only a single elderly lady. On this voyage she tried, with sulks and tantrums, to force the removal of even this improbable source of temptation.

The threat of shipwreck had been an opportunity for another extravagant show of passion. As her husband sat lamenting that he was to be the occasion of such loss of life, she had crouched between his legs, twining herself about him so that death itself should not part them. But safe on land the old tensions had surfaced, and they had made their separate ways to Windsor, his fast, hers slow. Fearful perhaps of embarrassments, the English royal family received her privately: not at the public entrance to the king's apartments, but at the privy or back stairs which gave on to the park. There she was greeted by Henry VII, her sister Catherine of Aragon, and Princess Mary.

The three women seem to have spent the rest of the day together. The following day Catherine and Mary went to Richmond. There they were soon joined by King Henry, who was anxious to make sure that his new palace looked its best for his royal visitors. Meantime, Philip and Juana remained at Windsor until the weekend. Then they separated again. Philip rode to Richmond, hunting and hawking on the way, while Juana made straight for the west country to rejoin her ships. The pains of the journey – and of the separation from her husband – were eased by the loan of the late Queen Elizabeth's 'rich litters and chairs'.

Later, Catherine of Aragon recalled her joy at meeting the sister she had last seen ten years previously and would never see again – and 'the distress which filled my heart, a few hours afterwards, on account of your hasty and sudden departure'. Henry VII allegedly shared Catherine's feelings, but decided that it was unwise to interfere between husband and wife. But Catherine herself was probably the real reason for Juana's enforced departure. Philip seems to have feared that she might encourage her sister to take a more independent line about her inheritance – which is why he had snubbed Catherine a few days before, and curtailed her meeting with Juana now.

Whatever feelings she aroused, neither Juana's arrival nor her sudden departure was allowed to spoil things. Philip, who was as good a guest as Henry VII was a host, was now approaching Richmond. Even before he was met by the king, he stopped to admire the fantastic silhouette of the new palace, with its clustering onion-domed turrets rising straight from the Thames. If he ever returned to Brussels, he said, Richmond 'should be a pattern unto him'.

It was the ultimate accolade for the upstart Tudors. Richmond, architectural historians argue, was modelled on the continental castle-palaces that Henry VII had seen on his travels. Now the owner of some of Europe's most sumptuous residences was proclaiming that Richmond would be a model for his future building. No wonder that Henry too would be a great builder.

At this point, both the contemporary narratives of the visit seem to have suffered from a surfeit of splendour: the Burgundian gives up, and the English turns into a series of jotted notes.

The probability is that Henry VII took his visitor over the palace himself – just as he had Catherine and her entourage when she was the newly-wedded wife of his eldest son Arthur. Then he showed off the gardens and pleasure grounds, with their facilities for every form of sport and amusement; the chapel, with its images of the sainted kings of England; the library, 'with many goodly pleasant books of works full delightful, sage, merry and also right cunning, both in Latin and in English'; and above all the hall.

Like the chapel, the hall was decorated with statues of kings. But these were the warriors, not the saints. Here were Brute and Arthur, Hengist the Dane, and Normans and Plantagenets: William, Richard, Edward, Henry 'and many other of that name'. They were shown armed and in armour, and underneath each there was a written account of their 'deeds and acts' as set out in the chronicles. But one stood out:

> Among this number of famous kings, in the higher part, on the left hand, is the seemly picture and personage of our most excellent and high sovereign . . . King Henry the Seventh, as worthy that room and place with those glorious princes as any king that ever reigned in this land.

Henry VII had given himself pride of place.

King Henry's son listened and watched. It was a familiar story. Skelton had made sure he had read the chronicles as a boy. And Skelton and almost everybody else had dinned into him that his father was the very model of a modern monarch. But Prince Henry now had two models in front of him: his father and his father's guest. King Henry was old (or at least rapidly ageing), and perhaps too polite, too garrulous, too obviously cunning; King Philip, on the other hand, was not yet thirty, and was called 'the Fair'.

According to Polydore Vergil, who was probably an eyewitness of his English visit, he more than lived up to his sobriquet: 'He was of medium height, handsome of face, and heavily built; he was talented, generous and gentlemanly.' Save for his middling stature, it could have been a description of the young man Henry was soon to be.

The contrast with his father was as much a matter of behaviour as appearance: King Henry (it must have seemed to his son's critical gaze) just talked; King Philip did. For instance, a few days previously the two kings had gone to watch a tennis match. Cloth-of-gold cushions were placed for them, and the viewing gallery hung with tapestry. But Philip quickly tired of being a spectator. He stripped off his heavy, rich outer garments and played with the marquess of Dorset, 'the king looking on them'.

It had been the same back home in the Netherlands. Shortly before his departure, Philip had held a tournament in Brussels in honour of his father, Maximilian. It took place indoors by torchlight. Not only did Philip take part, his father could not resist joining in as well. Maximilian rode incognito and tilted with his son. 'And each shivered three spears so adroitly that for address and everything else they proved themselves superior to all their competitors.'

The contrast with the round of spectator sports Philip was offered in England could not have been greater.

★   ★   ★

It remained only for Philip to pay the bill. He did so with a good grace. On the morning of Sunday, 15 February he offered to hand over the pretender, Edmund de la Pole, earl of Suffolk, 'unasked'. It was a grand public gesture, and worthy of a prince of Burgundy. But behind it lay weeks of intense private negotiation in which the parties had tried to reconcile Henry VII's determination to get his hands on Suffolk with Philip's promise to protect and aid him.

Suffolk himself had joined in on 28 January, when he gave a set of instructions to his agents. In them he sought a peace with honour with Henry VII: the king would restore him to favour, to his dukedom and to his ancestral lands; he, for his part, would become the king's 'true subject and liegeman' and, after his death, would remain faithful 'to my lord prince the king's son'. Prince Henry, as well as the king, would ratify whatever agreement was reached. Finally, Suffolk's brother William, and all others who were 'in prison for the said duke's sake or cause', were to be released and restored to their property.

The Burgundians believed, or professed to believe, that Henry VII had agreed to something like these terms, and Suffolk seems to have believed so too. His reception in Calais should have disabused him. He was handed over on 16 March. Eight days later, on the twenty-fourth, he was shipped to Dover with an escort of forty soldiers of the garrison, all in armour. In Dover he was met by the formidable Sir Thomas Lovell and taken to the Tower. But so long as Philip remained on English soil, Henry – out of regard for his guest's feelings – maintained the fiction that Suffolk's imprisonment was an 'honourable' one, pending the outcome of successful negotiations.

Meanwhile, after a final round of entertainment, Philip finally took his leave of his hosts. The parting was itself a long-drawn-out affair. They said their farewells before dinner on Monday, 2 March. After dining, Philip was booted and spurred and ready to leave when the king and prince, also booted and spurred, appeared and announced that they would accompany him on the first stage of his journey. A mile or so from Windsor, the last farewells were made. Henry VII's final words were to entrust his son to Philip's care, beseeching him to be his 'father, protector and friend'. Immediately after leaving Windsor, Philip became feverish – 'partly because of the Lenten fare and partly because of the weather, which was severe' – and lay sick for eight or nine days at Reading Abbey. Having resumed his journey, he met Juana at Exeter and reached Falmouth on 26 March. But it was another three weeks before the winds turned favourable.

With Philip's final departure from Falmouth on 16 April, the pretence of Suffolk's honourable treatment was abandoned. He was 'exhaustively interrogated'; two more of his associates, George Neville, Lord Abergavenny and Sir Thomas

Green, were arrested, and Suffolk himself disappeared into the recesses of the Tower, from which he was to emerge – years later – only for his execution.

Meanwhile Henry wrote to Philip. The letter, dated at Greenwich, 9 April 1506, is the first of Henry's to survive. It is written in French, as so many of his later letters were to be, including much of his correspondence with Anne Boleyn. The composition could have been the work of the king's secretary in the French tongue, John Meautis, whose job it was to draft royal correspondence in French. But the signs are that, with his thorough grounding in the language, Henry scarcely needed his help.

But if, as seems likely, he composed the letter himself, he did so by dictation. For it is written in a fine, regular clerk's script. Only the subscription and signature – 'Vostre Humble cosyn, Henry Prynce de galles' – are in Henry's own hand. Yet even these seven words are instantly recognizable. Henry is the graphologist's dream: the writing is the man; it is big, bold and rather square. All that will happen as Henry gets older is that the hand will loosen up: the strokes will become more varied, the letters wider, and the spaces between them bigger.

The content of the letter, like the penmanship of the body of the text, is fairly formal. It is a request to Philip to show his favour to Catherine of Aragon's chamberlain, who had business in Spain. This is probably Don Pedro Manrique, who was the husband of Catherine's former duenna, Doña Elvira Manuel. In making the request on behalf of Catherine's household official, Henry gives Catherine her full title of 'my most dear and well-beloved consort the princess my wife'.

More interesting, though, is the way in which Henry addresses Philip himself. Calling him 'most high, most excellent, and mighty prince', he begs him that he will 'apprise me from time to time and let me know of your good health and prosperity'. In return, he assures Philip, 'whenever I can find a fitting messenger I am determined to do the like to you'. The terms are formal, but the request for a correspondence is unusually direct: bearing in mind Henry's age, it is almost as though he were asking the king-archduke to be his penpal.

But this auspicious beginning went nowhere. Within six months of his arrival in Spain, Philip was dead. The news of his death spread throughout Europe. Towards the end of the year, Erasmus picked it up and wrote to condole Henry. The fact that he did so is interesting. It shows the scholar's determination to keep up the acquaintance which had begun in 1499. It also suggests that he had heard that Henry and Philip had got on famously during the days they had spent together at the beginning of the year.

It was 17 January 1507 before Henry got round

to replying. This, his second surviving letter, is in Latin rather than French; it is also in his own hand. We know this from an endorsement which Erasmus wrote on a copy of the letter: 'the whole of the letter enclosed he wrote when a youth in his own hand'. Henry gave Erasmus elaborate thanks for his sympathy on the news of Philip's death, 'for never, since the death of my dearest mother, hath there come to me more hateful intelligence'. We have already discussed whether the phrase was a true reflection of his feelings about his mother and decided that it was; it was almost certainly sincerely meant about Philip as well.

It remained only for Henry to put his feelings about Philip into practice.

CHAPTER 15

JOUSTING

P hilip's influence took almost immediate effect, and helped shape one of the dominant traits of Henry's character: his obsessive dedication to sport. The sports changed with time – beginning with the active and dangerous games of his youth, which burned off his surplus energies in a self-imposed martyrdom, and ending with the gentle, old man's pastime of hawking.

But in his teens one sport involved Henry to the exclusion of everything else. Nowadays young men get obsessed with football; Henry ate, slept and drank jousting.

The jousting mania struck Henry in the eighteen months following Philip's visit. The court had consoled itself for the king-archduke's departure with a week-long tournament in honour of the lady of the May on 14–21 May 1506. A year later, in 1507, the May – that celebration of renewal and young love, in which youths went into the green-wood to gather boughs of May blossom for their true loves – was again marked by a joust.

The joust took place at Kennington, two miles

to the south of London Bridge, and it is unclear whether Henry was a spectator – though as Kennington was the old suburban residence of the prince of Wales, it seems more than likely.

What is certain, however, is that the joust provoked unusual criticism. This stung the organizers into a reply in the form of a follow-up joust and tourney in June; they also commissioned a verse pamphlet to set out their case in print. The use of print suggests a real attempt to win over public opinion; but the jousters also had a narrower and more important target audience – Henry, who (the pamphlet boasts) had been sitting on the edge of his seat throughout the June tournament, and behind Henry, his father the king.

The verse pamphlet summarizes the criticism of jousting in the vaguest and most generalized terms.

> Some reprehende
> Suche as entende
> To condiscende
> To chyualry
>
> God then amende
> And grace them sende
> Not to offende
> More till they deye.

It is easy to read between the lines. For the treason of Suffolk and his jousting companions had given the whole sport a bad name: jousters were politically unreliable at best, and down-right Yorkists and traitors at worst.

What, wiser heads no doubt asked, was the heir to the Tudor throne doing spending day in, day out in the company of such men?

There was also a practical as well as a presentational problem. Suffolk's treason and the ensuing arrests had seriously depleted the number of skilled jousters at the English court. Henry VII's solution was to create the post of spear in the summer of 1504, a few months after Henry had come to court. A small of group of young men of good birth were given a generous stipend – for themselves and for a custrell, a page and two archers each. A knight with these auxiliaries formed the basic fighting unit of the day. But the numbers involved were too small to make any serious military contribution.

They *were* enough, however, thoroughly to rejuvenate the tournament, and one of the spears, Charles Brandon, was among the four challengers in the May joust of 1507; he was also one of the two principal challengers in the June tournament.

The trouble was that the distinction between the newly minted young spears and the old Adam of Suffolk's cronies was by no means clear-cut. William Hussey, also one of the four challengers in the May joust, had, as we have seen, been up to his neck in the Suffolk affair. And Hussey was brother-in-law of the young earl of Kent, who was Brandon's fellow challenger in the June tournament.

Nor was it only a matter of past transgressions. Kent, for instance, who had succeeded to his earldom in 1503, was so headstrong and improvident that he took only four years to get himself almost irretrievably into debt – partly to moneylenders, but principally to the king. By the summer of 1507, indeed, his situation was so bad that Henry VII imposed an extraordinary settlement on him. This treated Kent as though he were *non compos mentis*: he surrendered control of his estates, gave up the management of his own household and agreed to reside permanently at court.

Here, presumably, the king felt he could keep an eye on him. In fact the young reprobate seems to have spent most of his time inducting the king's admirably brought-up son into the finer points of knightly biffing and bashing. Kent even gave Henry a symbolic present of a silver image of a knight – 'a man armed on horseback' – to keep his devotion to chivalry up to scratch.

Did Henry's father know? Did he care?

There was one apparent shining exception to all this. Charles Brandon, who was to become Henry's closest friend and eventual brother-in-law, had, as son of Sir William Brandon, Henry VII's standard-bearer who had fallen heroically at Bosworth, an impeccable lineage of Lancastrian loyalism.

But Brandon, too, kept some strange company. He was master of the horse to Henry Bourchier, earl of Essex. He lived in the earl's house in Knightrider Street, where he was a neighbour of Henry's high-minded *socius studiorum*, Lord Mountjoy. And he was in the middle of a messy, on-off affair with another member of the earl's household, Anne Browne. After premarital sex, the birth of a bastard, Charles's betrayal and brief marriage to Anne's elderly aunt, the couple eloped and were married first privately and then publicly – just to make sure.

Anne also brought her own political baggage, as she was the daughter of Sir Anthony Browne of Calais and his wife Lucy, who had both taken such a cavalier view of their allegiance to the Tudors. As for that matter did Essex, Brandon's noble patron. Essex, who descended himself from two of Edward III's sons and was half-brother to the earl of Kent, had been one of the select group who had banqueted with Suffolk on the eve of his flight into exile. And he was the only one still out of gaol. 'Quite why,' his latest biographer observes, 'is hard to say.'

In view of all this, it is not surprising that the jousters tried to use their second tournament in June to present themselves and their sport as whiter than white. Literally so, as the challengers wore a white enamelled heart between the letters 'R' and 'H' on a blue ground. White betokened a pure, unspotted heart, 'R H' stood for 'Roy Henry', while blue was the colour of constancy.

The resulting message was spelled out by the author of the descriptive poem:

> Theyr hertes whyte and pure in euery houre
> Shall truely reste for ony storme or shoure
> And to serue euer truely to theyr powre
> Our kynge royall.

And Henry VII must have believed – or at least affected to believe – them. He permitted his daughter and Henry's younger sister, Mary, who 'hath to fader Kynge and Emperoure alone', to act as lady of the June joust. He honoured them with his own presence.

Above all, he gave 'our yonge prince Henry' free rein as an enthusiastic spectator.

It was, nevertheless, a role that Henry visibly chafed at. Later that year the Spanish ambassador commented on his unusual stature: 'There is no finer youth in the world than the prince of Wales,' De Puebla reported; 'he is already taller than his father, and his limbs are of gigantic size.' The verse-chronicler of the tournament was similarly struck:

> Notwithstondynge his yonge and tender aege
> He is moost comly of his parsonage

Size and strength were the two basic physical quali-
fications for the successful jouster, and Henry was
eager to put his natural advantages to the test:

> Syth our prynce moost comly of stature
> Is desyrous to the moost knyghtly vre
> Of armes to whiche marcyall auenture
> Is his courage.

Meantime, he was eager for jousting talk, and was
willing to bend the rules of etiquette to get it:

> And though a prynce/and kynges sone be he
> It pleaseth hym of his benygnyte
> To suffre gentylmen of lowe degre
> In his presence
> To speke of armes and of other defence
> Without doynge vnto his grace offence.

By the following year, Henry had come off the
terraces and on to the pitch – or rather the tilt-yard.
We even have the dates of the fixtures, thanks to
the remarkable Latin *Annales* which the royal historian, Bernard André, composed for the twenty-third
regnal year of Henry VII (1507–08).

The *Annales* is one of a series of yearly narratives which André intended as a continuation of
his *Life* of the king. Only two of these continu-
ations survive, for 1504–05 and 1507–08. The
former, like most of André's work, is full of high-
flown generalization; but the latter is a sort of

241

diary. It seems to have been written in the heat of the moment, and events tumble over each other in all the vivid disorder of real life: extraordinary weather, the deaths of friends in high and low places, and – above all – Prince Henry's sudden sporting prowess.

News of this first came to André's ears in mid-May 1508. The king was convalescing from his most recent bout of severe illness at Eltham, Henry's boyhood home; meanwhile Henry was undergoing one of the rites of passage into manhood next door in the tilt-yard at Greenwich. 'Daily' he was running at the ring 'with his companions in arms'. This was not the first time, as André refers to Henry's exercising himself 'previously as well as at this time'.

The daily training paid off, and at the next joust, held at Greenwich on 15 June 1508, Henry was triumphant. 'The jousting at Greenwich in the presence of the nobility,' André noted, 'was very heavily attended on account of the excellence of the young armed prince, supported round about with very famous nobles on all sides.' Henry had a similar triumph in July, at another joust held at Richmond. This time the king himself watched his son compete: 'very many men fought with him but he was superior to all of them'.

It is, however, important to be clear what André was saying. His grandiose phraseology of heroes and renown conjures up daring deeds of derring-do. The reality was rather more modest. To understand it we need to disentangle more carefully the terms used to describe the different forms of chivalric mock-combat. As we have already begun to see, 'tournament' or 'joust' was the name of the whole meeting, in which a variety of specific events were often combined. These might include the 'joust' proper, in which the combatants rode against each other, one to one, with lances, and the 'tourney', in which the combatants fought, again on horseback and one to one, with swords. The tournament of June 1507, for instance, began with the joust and continued with the tourney. This became the usual English pattern.

In the case of both the joust and the tourney the practice had developed of dividing the contestants by a barrier known as the 'tilt'. This stopped the horses and riders from colliding directly with each other; it also required the blows with the lance to be oblique. With such blows the impact was reduced, and the lance was more likely to shiver. The tilt, in short, was an important safety measure, though it only reduced rather than eliminated the risk of an inherently dangerous activity. Another type of wooden safety fence, known as the 'barriers', gave its name to a form of foot combat in which the contestants, singly or in groups, fought over the barrier with swords or battle-axes.

★   ★   ★

243

Henry took part in none of these. André is quite specific about the fact, and on each occasion describes Henry as competing only in the *'hastiludia ad anulum'*, or running at the ring. This is defined by one authority as follows: 'the object of this sport was to catch a suspended ring on the point of one's lance. It was far safer than jousting, and hence often preferred. It was also a way of practising for jousting.'

Henry, in short, was still very much in the junior team: he had yet to graduate to the real and often dangerous business of the joust and tourney.

André himself spelled out the distinction on the occasion of the tournament on 15 June 1508. 'In these games,' he commented, 'the key thing worth watching was that remarkable sight where the tilting ring is sought by the lances.' 'Then afterwards,' he added, 'and without the prince, the stronger exercised in hand-to-hand combat.' And when the stronger got to work in earnest, more than sparks flew: in 1507 the verse-chronicler had described how

Pyeces of harneys [armour] flewe in to the place
Theyr swerdes brake they smote thycke and a pace

One challenger was 'hurt in dede'.
Limiting Henry to riding at the ring was an

obvious precaution against similar injuries – or worse. Even so, dangers remained, and at the end of June 1508 one of Henry's principal mentors in martial sports, the earl of Kent, broke his arm 'while fighting [*inter duellandum*] with the prince'. Here for once André's Latin is ambiguous: if '*duellan-dum*' has a specific sense it probably means tourneying with swords, but it is impossible to be sure.

With this trifling exception, André's evidence seems clearcut. Yet almost all Henry's modern biographers assert that he jousted – in the full sense – as a youth. They do so on the basis of the despatches of the Spanish ambassador Fuensalida. He arrived in England in the spring of 1508, which means that his statements can be checked against André's narrative. The results are instructive. Shortly after his arrival, Fuensalida was invited to Richmond to watch a tournament that had been organized in honour of Princess Mary's betrothal and for the entertainment of the ambassadors at the English court. During his visit he had an audience with the king, who waxed lyrical about his children, Mary and Henry, and their intended spouses.

One historian imagines his praise of Henry taking on a fresh edge as the proud father glimpsed his son on the tiltyard, shining and erect like a young god. The joust, which took place on 5, 6 and 7 March, was also mentioned by André.

In view of the diplomatic importance of the event there had been lengthy preparations. The tournament had been proclaimed in January, and Lord Henry Stafford, the brother of the duke of Buckingham, and other lords had been practising daily at Kennington. At the end of February there was a sort of dress rehearsal, again at Kennington, '*vultibus occlusis*' – with closed visors – which allowed the participants to practise the most difficult and highly-scoring manoeuvre of breaking a lance on their opponent's helmet.

Finally came the joust itself: the magnificence of the spectacle, André claimed, was in everyone's mouth, and the knights, led by Stafford and the earl of Kent, had fought 'hotly backwards and forwards'.

Only one thing was missing: the involvement of Prince Henry. André's failure to mention his name proves conclusively that he did not take part – and, to be fair, Fuensalida nowhere states that he did. Fuensalida's actual references to Henry's martial activities is more modest. 'Since Easter', he noted, the prince had been running at the ring (*correr la sortija*) and tourneying, and the king had watched. This, clearly, is a synopsis of the events in May, June and July which are described more fully by André: Fuensalida is vague and generalized, André precise and detailed.

And above all, André is clear that Henry only 'rode at the ring'.

★　　★　　★

It has always seemed strange that Henry VII, who so jealously guarded the person of his only surviving heir, should have allowed Henry to submit himself to the uncontrollable hazards of the tilt. Now it is clear that he did not. But running at the ring, for all its circumscribed quality, was an earnest of things to come.

Henry would joust just as soon as there was no one to say nay.

It seems almost as strange, however, that Henry VII allowed his son to keep the kind of company he did: with a rake like Brandon, a wastrel like Kent and the assorted aristocratic misfits and ne'er-do-wells who now crowded into the tiltyard to catch the eye of their future king.

Did he worry about their possible influence on his son? That they would corrupt him and make him as giddy, extravagant and mindlessly violent as they were?

And what of the whiff of Yorkist sentiment which, in spite of everything, clung to the jousting fraternity? Henry VII had spent his whole life nipping Yorkist conspiracy in the bud.

Would Henry?

Or was there perhaps method in the ageing king's madness? For Henry VII, it is clear, had never been fully accepted by the nobility. They tolerated him, respected him and, latterly, feared him. But they did not love him. Did Henry VII want his second son to be different? And did he realize that the rough camaraderie of jousting was the most effective means to that end?

It is possible. And it seems certain that Henry himself – despite his youth – knew exactly what he was doing.

CHAPTER 16

DYING

Henry's father was dying: slowly and by fits and starts. The fact was obvious to nearly everybody else, though till almost the end he himself talked confidently of recovery.

Meanwhile, Henry continued at court, getting bigger, stronger and better-known as his father dwindled and declined. There is no sing that he was reaching out for the crown. But, cautiously and almost imperceptibly, courtiers and councillors began to adjust to the ending of the old reign and the beginning of the new.

At least, most of them did. For some, it is clear, found the prince a much more receptive audience than others. Jousters, clearly, were welcome. As were scholars and their patrons. But what of the lawyers and financial experts who were the powerhouse of Henry VII's government in its latter phase? Would they too have the ear of the prince?

Or would they be out in the cold – or worse?

The downward spiral in the king's health began in the spring of 1507. A 'quinsy' or severe throat infection left him unable to eat or drink for some six days, and 'his life was despaired of.' But he survived and commenced a slow recovery. By the autumn, indeed, he seemed to be in rude health: he was exercising daily, with hunting or hawking; he was even, De Puebla noted with surprise, 'growing stout'.

Early the following year, however, in February 1508, he fell grievously ill once more, this time with *articulari morbo* ('a disease of the joints'). This has been glossed as 'gout'. But it seems to have been more like an acute rheumatic fever. A month later there had been little or no improvement, and the worst was evidently feared.

Lady Margaret Beaufort came to court to be at her son's side, and took charge. The king was moved by water by easy stages from Richmond to the supposedly healthier Greenwich. And there, on 15 March 1508, Henry stood in for his father, invisible in his sick-room, and dined in public in the king's chamber: 'the prince, in place of the king, that day dined as was customary with certain lords in the king's chamber'.

Henry had sat in his father's seat; probably he and everybody else expected that he would shortly be wearing his crown.

But, once again, Henry VII cheated death – though at a great cost. For the next three months he suffered from chronic fatigue, a loss of appetite and bouts of depression. There were moments when he seemed to be recovering. But they proved to be false dawns, and it was not until early July that his malaise – mental and physical – really lifted. André dated the moment to about 10 July, when, 'thanks to the relaxed state of his mind', Henry rode the ten or a dozen miles from Hanworth to Langley Park and began a great circuit through the hunting country between Windsor and Richmond. For 'previously', André noted, 'a long illness had depressed him for much of the time with tiredness and weight-loss'.

The combination was profoundly debilitating, and must have rendered the hustle and bustle and hubbub of court life almost intolerable. The king did the essentials: he gave audience to ambassadors, watched Henry joust at Richmond and transacted business. But whenever he could, he escaped: on 11 May 'he withdrew privately . . . to Eltham in order to refresh his health'; on 3 July 'he retreated' to Hanworth; 'then he went along the river to Fulham to hunt there with a small retinue' and 'retired' to Hanworth once more.

Meanwhile, 'at Greenwich the king's household and the royal family, observed in their magnificence, were waiting for the king himself'.

The result was an aberration: there was a court without a king, and a king without a court. There was also a capital without a monarch, as months now passed without the king deigning to step foot in London. Instead, royal life focused on the two great suburban palace-complexes of Richmond

251

and Greenwich. The former lay some ten miles to the west of the City; the latter five miles to the east. They were linked by the great highway of Tudor London: the Thames. Every few months the king took his 'new barge', freshly painted and with 'a dragon . . . stand[ing] in the foreship', and moved from Richmond to Greenwich or back again. Normally he took two days over the journey, with an overnight stop in or near the City. But he avoided his own palaces of Westminster and the Tower, preferring instead to stay privately at the bishop of Bath's opulent town-house which lay to the west of the Middle Temple, and, with its gardens and appurtenances, occupied the whole space between The Strand and the river.

This meant that all London saw of its king was a glimpse of his great barge and its escort as it swept up- or down-stream. But even this, in a city starved of the oxygen of royalty, was enough to set off demonstrations of loyalty. 'It is scarcely possible to say,' noted André of one such river-transit, 'how much joy gripped this city at [the king's] approach.'

Nor, for that matter, was the king much more generally visible in his 'house[s] of honour', as André called them, at Richmond or Greenwich. Some fifteen years earlier, in 1493 or '94, Henry VII had broken with tradition and set up a new department of the royal household. Historically there were two of these: the lord steward's department, which provided food and drink; and the lord chamberlain's department, which dealt with both ceremony and the king's personal service. To these Henry VII added a third: the secret or privy chamber. This took over responsibility for the king's body service; it was also used, as its name indicates, to enforce a much more rigorous separation between the king's public and private lives.

In this, the secret chamber reflected the moment of its genesis. It was a product of the security scare triggered by the Perkin Warbeck affair, when treason, as we have seen, had reached into the very heart of the royal court and implicated both head officers of the traditional household: the lord steward and the lord chamberlain himself. But the new emphasis on privacy was also conditioned by Henry VII's unique character and experience. He was foreign to England and English ways; and he was never really at home with the English elite, nor was he ever fully accepted by them.

In these circumstances, the protection of a door, a guard and a wall of etiquette became a matter of necessity as well as personal preference.

Naturally, the king's taste for privacy was also translated into bricks and mortar. Both in his new buildings – like Richmond and Greenwich – and in his adaptations of existing structures – like Windsor Castle – Henry VII created a honeycomb of private rooms for himself and his family: his mother, wife and children. Towards the end, even this was not enough, and he acquired *maisons de retraite* in the vicinity of his two favourite palaces – Hanworth near Richmond and Wanstead near Greenwich – and laid out considerable sums on them. Hanworth was valued especially for its gardens and Wanstead for its park. But, above all, it was their seclusion that mattered: they were, in effect, free-standing privy lodgings.

It was into this secretive, private world that Henry now found himself plunged. The evidence lies in the accounts of the royal household for 1507–08, where there is a special section for 'payments for the expenses of the most noble lord Henry, prince of Wales residing in the court with our lord the king'. These show that he accompanied his father step by step in his shuttlecock movements between Richmond and Greenwich and back again, joined his private hunting parties and, as the sweating sickness took hold once more in high summer, sought refuge with him in the houses of favoured courtiers that had escaped the blight of infection.

No doubt this perpetual proximity to his ailing father sometimes became irksome to Henry. But did it really crush his personality and development in the fashion suggested by the new Spanish ambassador, Gutierre Gomez de Fuensalida, knight-commander of Membrilla, in a well-known despatch? The prince, Fuensalida reported a few months after his arrival in England in the spring of 1508, was kept in closer seclusion than a nubile girl back home in Spain:

> He was never permitted to go out of the palace, except for exercise through a private door leading into the park. At these times he was surrounded by the persons specially appointed by the king as his tutors and companions, and no one else dared, on his life, to approach him. He took his meals alone, and spent most of his day in his own room, which had no other entrance than through the king's bedchamber. He was in complete subjection to his father and his grandmother and never opened his mouth in public except to answer a question from one of them.

Perhaps. But the ambassador, remember, was not an impartial reporter; instead, he was writing to justify his own failure to gain access to Henry to put the case directly for the conclusion of the prince's on-off marriage to Catherine of Aragon. Moreover, there is plenty of evidence which points in a different direction. Take, for instance. Henry's behaviour in the tilt-yard. Whether as a spectator or competitor, his uninhibited enthusiasm hardly looks like the product of shyness or repression. Nor does his willingness to talk jousting to all and sundry suggest any fear – on his part or on that of his interlocutors – about engaging in conversation. But what most undermines Fuensalida's reliability as a witness is something else: it is his conviction that Henry would turn out to be much like his father.

Instead, of course, explaining how he came to be so different is the real challenge. And this in turn suggests another reading of the events of the last year of Henry VII's life. Father and son were indeed living cheek-by-jowl in the privy lodgings and, still more, in the *maisons de retraite* at Hanworth and Wanstead. But, despite their proximity, they were leading surprisingly separate and different lives. This is exemplified in two of the leading attendants of their respective households: Henry's *socius studiorum*, Lord Mountjoy, and his father's principal private servant, known as the groom of the stool, Hugh Denys.

It would be hard to think of two more different men – or two more distinctive careers.

We have already met William Blount, Lord Mountjoy, as the dominant influence on Henry's later formal education. This had ended, as was customary, in Henry's fourteenth year. At about the same time, Mountjoy had been appointed as lieutenant of Hammes Castle in the pale (or outlying territories) of Calais. This was a position which was more or less hereditary in his family. But neither event severed Mountjoy's connexion with his young charge. Instead, much of the time, he discharged his responsibilities at Hammes through a deputy and remained resident at court. In 1507–08, indeed, he was in daily attendance on the prince. This is shown by the prince of Wales section of the royal household accounts for this year, which contain a regular entry for the carriage of *estuffamentum domini Mountjoye* ('Lord Mountjoy's stuff') *per totum itinerum predictum* ('through the whole of the foresaid journey').

The role of attendant lord was one to which Mountjoy was ideally suited. The point, as so often, was caught by his former teacher Erasmus, who described his pupil as 'the most learned of the noble and the noblest of the learned'. As a gentleman, Mountjoy happily took part in all the usual diversions of the court, from hunting to music and dancing. But as a scholar, he continued to work with Henry to polish his understanding of Latin. They read selected works together; Mountjoy also encouraged the prince to keep up his Latin correspondence with figures like Erasmus himself.

And Erasmus was, of course, a window for Henry into the whole world of European culture – a world, moreover, that Erasmus had himself begun to transform. The transformation really got under way in 1505–06 when Erasmus returned to England, probably at Mountjoy's invitation, and stayed with his friend – and Henry's acquaintance – Thomas More in his house in Bucklersbury. There More and Erasmus spent their time translating the dialogues of the Greek poet Lucian into Latin.

The exercise helped them perfect their knowledge of Greek; but it also laid the foundations for their critique of contemporary culture. Tradition and custom, they began to consider – whether in the church, in chivalry or in ordinary human relations – were the great obstacle to reason and reform. Only, they concluded, if mankind managed to break the bonds of tradition could humanity rediscover itself – and God.

The resulting collection of translations from Lucian was printed in 1506, and became all the rage. Probably it went over Henry's head at this stage. But Erasmus, who was worldly enough to be a supremely effective self-propagandist, had made sure that it would be widely noted in England by dedicating the constituent essays to leading members of the English political establishment. The dedicatees included the man who had christened Henry, Richard Foxe, now bishop of Winchester and lord privy seal, Thomas Ruthall, the king's secretary, and William Warham, who had succeeded as archbishop of Canterbury and lord chancellor in 1503. These men – the *crème de la crème* of Oxford canon lawyers – were Henry VII's leading clerical ministers and the weightiest members of the royal council.

Did they reflect that Erasmus's flattering letters of dedication also gave them a link to Mountjoy, and through him to the heir to the throne and their master-to-be?

★ ★ ★

Next door, in the king's private apartments, it was a very different story. If Hugh Denys knew of Henry and Mountjoy's labours over Erasmian Latin, and – still more abstruse – Erasmian ideas, he would have dismissed them as sublime mysticism and nonsense. For Denys was a practical man who had risen from a modest West Country gentry background by getting his hands dirty. Indeed, it might be said he had got them very dirty, since, as groom of the stool, he had charge of the royal close-stool or commode, and assisted the king when he relieved himself on it.

The establishment of the secret chamber greatly expanded both the groom's importance and his portfolio. Denys became the head officer of the new department. He controlled access to the king. He assumed responsibility for the everyday necessities and the little luxuries that eased the royal burden – for Henry's father, despite his soldier's toughness, was a sensitive soul and loved his creature comforts. Finally, Denys became the king's personal treasurer, running an account that later became known as the privy purse.

And this was most important of all, since Henry VII loved his money even more than his personal comfort.

Henry VII's tight-fistedness was a family trait which he inherited from his mother, Lady Margaret Beaufort, who was as grasping as she was pious. It was intensified by the penury of exile.

And it was a wholly justified reaction to the chaos and inefficiency of the royal finances at the beginning of his reign, when, it may be recalled, he had had to plead with his own exchequer for the few tens of pounds needed to induct Henry into the Garter in proper style.

But in the last few years of his reign, avarice was erected into a policy. Polydore Vergil, the sophisticated Italian whom Henry VII himself commissioned to write a new-style history of England, dated the change, like so much else, to the earl of Suffolk's bid for the throne. The bid had failed resoundingly. But, even in its failure, it showed how shallow was Henry VII's hold on the loyalties of the elite. The king drew an obvious conclusion: he had repeatedly tried and failed to win loyalty by fair means; now he would compel it by foul.

The result was a reign of fiscal terror.

The means employed were two financial instruments known as 'bonds' and 'recognizances'. Bonds and recognizances (the differences between them are technical and need not concern us here) are agreements with a penalty clause for non-compliance. They were used in a variety of ways. Some of these – such as to guarantee payment of a debt to the king or ensure the proper performance of an office – were more or less legitimate. Others were not. Most characteristic and objectionable was Henry VII's practice of linking them to the imposition of fines. Individuals were fined, often astronomic amounts, for offences real or imaginary. A portion of the fine was levied immediately, and the remainder suspended. The victim was then required to acknowledge his indebtedness to the king for the full amount, and to enter into bonds to pay it if he broke whatever conditions the king or his agents might impose.

Thenceforward he was at the king's mercy, and faced financial ruin if he stepped out of line.

These arrangements were assessed and enforced by a sub-committee or 'by-court' of the king's council called the council-learned-at-law, whose dominant members were Sir Richard Empson, chancellor of the duchy of Lancaster, and Edmund Dudley, who became the first president of the council. Denys, whose intimate attendance on the king meant that he knew better than most which way the wind was blowing, had been an early associate of the two lawyers: they plucked plums of patronage together and picked up cheap the property of those who had been forced to sell by the king's policies.

But in the autumn of 1508, Denys himself moved centre-stage. By this time, Henry VII had made an apparently full recovery from his serious illness of the spring; he had also, by a policy of rigorous quarantine, escaped the newly rampant sweating sickness. Rejuvenated by all this, he threw himself into the business of government with fresh enthusiasm. According to André, at this time 'the king totally devoted himself to the approaching betrothal' of Henry's little sister Mary to Charles, son and heir of the Archduke Philip, and bought 'many precious goods from Italian merchants'. In fact Henry VII had other, much more serious, matters on his mind, as he had decided on a wholesale extension of his policy of fiscal terrorism.

Hitherto, the objectives of his policy had been as much political as financial. This meant that his victims had largely been limited to the elite, who had the capacity to make trouble: they were, Vergil notes, 'not the poor but the wealthy, churchmen, rich magnates, even the intimates of the king himself'. Now Henry VII decided to cast his net much wider. The post of surveyor of the king's prerogative was created, and charged with the rigorous, universal enforcement of the king's rights as head of the feudal system. To make sure this happened, local commissioners were appointed under the surveyor, Edward Belknap, to enforce the policy on a county-by-county basis.

All the elements of an alternative system of taxation – permanent, nation-wide and exempt from either parliamentary authority or scrutiny – were now in place.

But what is most interesting is the fate of Belknap's profits. The terms of his appointment are silent on this, but it soon became clear that they were to be paid over directly to Hugh Denys as a kind of private royal slush fund. Where they were paid is interesting too. Some were handed over at Greenwich or Richmond. But the private *maisons de retraite*, Wanstead and Hanworth, figure largely too. And it was at either Wanstead or Greenwich that Henry's mentor, Lord Mountjoy, found himself caught up in the toils of Hugh Denys and the surveyor of the prerogative when he was required to enter into bonds for £320 to repay an old debt to the king. The bonds were for more than double the original amount, which in any case Mountjoy had not borrowed from the king but from a third party who had subsequently been outlawed.

Belknap handed over a further tranche of 'fines assessed by the king's highness' to Denys at Hanworth at an unknown date in February 1509. Then, suddenly, his account book breaks off, unfinished and incomplete.

This time Henry VII *was* dying. And he knew it.

CHAPTER 17

END

The extended Christmas celebrations of 1508 marked a high-water mark for the Tudor dynasty, with the proxy marriage of Henry's sister Mary, aged twelve, to the Archduke Philip's nine-year-old son, Charles. The union, according to the printed English account rushed out by the royal printer, Richard Pynson, was 'the most notable alliance and greatest marriage of Christendom'.

For once propaganda spoke no more than the truth, as Charles was heir to the greatest agglomeration of territories since his namesake, Charlemagne: from his grandfather Maximilian he would inherit the Holy Roman Empire and Austria; from his grandmother Mary, daughter of Charles the Bold, would come Burgundy and the Netherlands; while through his Spanish grandparents, Ferdinand and Isabella, he was destined to rule not only Castile and Aragon, but also a rapidly growing empire in the New World.

'If God send him life', as the pamphlet noted with proper caution. It would also require something of a political miracle as well to bring such diverse and distant regions, each with its own distinct identity and traditions, to accept a common sovereign.

But for Henry VII the mere prospect was enough, and – with Prince Henry as the ever-dutiful son at his side – he pulled out all the stops to make the celebrations worthy of the event.

The festivities were divided, like the whole royal itinerary at this time, between Greenwich and Richmond. They began at Greenwich in early December, when the Burgundian ambassadors were splendidly received in formal audience. The king sat under a canopy of cloth-of-gold, with Prince Henry on his left hand at the head of the lay nobility. Complimentary speeches were exchanged; then the final terms were hammered out. There followed a few days' interval as the court moved to Richmond for the proxy wedding. This took place on the seventeenth. Mary, schooled with the same teachers as her brother Henry, acquitted herself well, speaking her lengthy vows 'perfectly and distinctly in the French tongue . . . without any bashing of countenance, stop or interruption'.

It was a performance which surprised many and – we are told – reduced not a few to tears. Then rings were exchanged and fanfares blown.

Three days of jousting followed, after which the court returned once more to Greenwich to celebrate Christmas. But pleasure had lasted long enough. There was work to be done; fines to be levied and money to be lovingly counted and bagged. Above all, perhaps, there was Belknap and his new account. As soon as the twelve days of Christmas were over, the royal barge took Henry VII upstream once more. He stayed a day or two at Richmond, and then gratefully sought the privacy of Hanworth. And there, on 27 January 1509, Belknap handed over another instalment of 'fines before assessed by the king's highness' to his colleague Hugh Denys. The king checked the figures and the cash and made a marginal note: 'In hand paid '£125 11 shillings 8 pence.' Then he put his sign manual: 'HR'.

All was well.

A week or two later illness struck the king again. At first he tried to continue as usual. He remained at Hanworth. He assessed more fines. And once more Belknap handed over the bulk of the cash to Denys.

But the king did not countersign. He was getting worse. And worse.

Ash Wednesday fell on 21 February in 1509. For the faithful, it was a day of solemn reflection which marks the beginning of Lent and its preparation for Easter. Henry VII had always been punctilious about the externals of religion. But now there was real, fearful urgency. His confessor was summoned and the king made confession 'with all diligence and great repentance'. Then, fresh from the sacrament of absolution, he made three solemn promises. First, he promised to make 'a true reformation' of all who administered justice, 'that justice from henceforward truly and indifferently might be executed in all causes'. Second, he swore to give promotions in the church only to those who were 'virtuous and well learned'. And third, he undertook to give a general pardon to his people.

The king had felt the hand of death, and feared that God would judge him as harshly as he had judged others.

But his confessor comforted him and assured him that it was not too late – with the church's help – to make amends. The king's devotions now became more and more extravagant – almost indeed with an edge of desperation. When he undertook penance, 'he wept and sobbed by the space of three quarters of an hour'. When he took communion, he removed his hat, knelt and crawled to receive it. And when he was beyond swallowing, he kissed the very foot of the monstrance in which the consecrated wafer lay, 'with so many knockings and beatings of his breast'.

Evidently, he felt he had much to repent.

He also vowed, as he had not quite given up on this world, to turn over a new leaf. He moved from Hanworth, with its associations of covert jiggery-pokery, back to Richmond. He said repeatedly to 'his secret servants . . . that if it please God to send him life they should see him a new changed man'. And, as an earnest, he began to detach himself from some of his most notorious agents of extortion. Denys, for instance, suddenly found himself frozen out: his funds dried up and his accounts stuttered to a halt. He might even have been suspended from his post as groom of the stool.

Instead, Richard Weston appears to have taken over as acting head of the secret chamber. He was well known to Prince Henry, having, frequently borne his father's gifts to him. He was an enemy of Empson – or at least could be relied on to try to frustrate his schemes – and a friend of Warham, Foxe and 'Mr Guildford' – that is, most likely, Henry Guildford, who was one of the carvers and cupbearers in Henry's princely household.

Were these alignments a portent of things to come?

The king's final agony lasted – it was reported with grim precision – 'by the space of twenty-seven hours together'. It started at about 10 p.m. on Friday, 20 April. As soon as 'he well perceived that he began utterly to fail', Henry VII summoned his confessor once more to administer the last rites. Slowly and painfully, 'as he might for weakness', he offered every part of his body to the saving touch of the holy oils. He heard the mass of the Blessed Virgin, 'to whom always . . . he had a . . . special devotion'. He adored the crucifix, embracing it and kissing it. Finally, overcome with pain and fear, 'with all his might and power, he called upon the name of Our Lord'.

At some point, he also summoned Henry. 'He . . . gave him fatherly and godly exhortation, committing unto him the laborious governance of this realm.' No doubt. But reports of the specifics of what Henry VII said to his son vary – especially in the matter of Catherine of Aragon. Or rather they directly contradict each other. Two members of the council informed the Spanish ambassador that 'on his deathbed Henry VII had assured his son that he was free to marry whom he chose'. However, Henry himself tells the opposite story. He 'was charged', he informed Margaret of Savoy in June 1509, 'by [his father], on his death bed, among other good counsels, to fulfil the old treaty with Ferdinand and Isabella of Spain by taking their daughter Catherine in marriage'.

Whom to believe?

In one sense, it does not matter. For Henry VII's power, which alone gave force to his words, was almost over. 'At 11 o'clock in the night', and after a final struggle, he died on Saturday, 21 April.

From that moment, Henry was king. At least, he would have been if anyone outside the inmost circle of the court and council had been told that his father was dead.

Instead, the death was kept a profound secret for the next two days. During this time, the rituals of the court continued as though nothing had happened. On 23 April, St George's Day, the heralds cried the customary 'largesse' in the name of 'King Henry VII', while Henry went to even-song and supper, 'all which time he was served and named as prince and not as king'.

Such secrecy was possible, of course, only because of the establishment of the 'secret' or privy chamber. This had created an inner world in which the king might live – or die – unobserved by all but the select few. This also meant that the staff of the privy chamber had a crucial role to play in events – as was shown by the extraordinary charade enacted in the early afternoon of St George's Day in the king's presence chamber at Richmond.

This starred Richard Weston, groom of the privy chamber and probably its acting head. The door of the privy chamber opened and Weston came out. 'With a smiling countenance' he summoned William Warham, the archbishop of Canterbury and lord chancellor, and certain other lords 'to come to sp[eak] to the king'. They entered as requested and 'remained in the king's secret chamber a good pause'. Then they emerged, also 'with good countenance . . . showing no great manner of mourning that men might perceive'.

★   ★   ★

What was going on? Thomas Wriothesley, Garter king of arms and author of this account of Henry VII's death and funeral, states that the delay in announcing the king's death was to allow time for the leading councillors to gather – for 'the substance of the lords [to be] assembled'. That was part of the story, no doubt. But it can hardly be the whole truth. Instead, it seems certain that the king's deathbed had also turned in to a fight to the death among the king's councillors.

Within the next few hours, the issue was decided. Barely had Henry finished eating his supper as prince of Wales than his father's death was 'published' at court. Immediately, preparations for the king's funeral began. They were supervised by a high-powered team of councillors headed by Lady Margaret Beaufort, who had hurried to court as soon as it was clear that her son was failing, while Wriothesley supplied the necessary expertise and knowledge of precedents.

The following day, Tuesday, 24 April, the ordinary forms of the ending of one reign and the beginning of the next were gone through with. Henry was proclaimed King Henry VIII in London in the morning, and after dinner at Richmond (that is, about noon) he left for the capital to take up residence in the Tower of London.

There was no need to use the royal barge, as

had been the practice under the invalid Henry VII. Instead, in the bloom of youth and energy, Henry rode the dozen or so miles to take possession of the Tower – and his kingdom.

But not everything had changed. Residence in the Tower was indeed traditional at the start of a reign. But it could also provide cover, as it had done so often under Henry VII, to trap an over-mighty subject or a suspected traitor.

And it did so once more. 'By a politick mean', according to one account, or by an 'early in the morning' arrest, according to another, Empson and Dudley were brought to the Tower, where they were imprisoned on charges of treason.

The coup round Henry VII's deathbed had achieved its first aim.

CHAPTER 18

KING

He was king. Henry had been a knight before he was four; now, aged seventeen years and ten months, he was king. King! The word – even across the great gulf fixed by revolution, republicanism and modernity – still resonates. Then, in a king-centred world, it was a be-all and end-all of imagination and fact. Kings were the heroes and villains of knightly romance. Their deeds filled the chronicles which Henry had read so assiduously with Skelton and Mountjoy. Kings, good and bad, were just as prominent in the Bible, while God himself was King of Kings and Lord of Lords. The laws were the king's, as was the public peace, the coinage and the very highway. Church and court alike conspired to elevate the king's person and make it sacred to the point of idolatry. The trumpets and the heralds' cry had proclaimed his name, number and titles and wished him long life:

May the king live forever!

Three or four days into his reign, however, Henry had experienced little if any of the glamour or

273

romance of kingship. Instead, his accession had been as hole-in-the-corner as anything under his father. And – it is clear – with *his* connivance. Henry, who had been present at his father's deathbed, must have been a willing actor in the strange game of concealment which was played out at Richmond in the following forty-eight hours. He must likewise have acquiesced at least in its prime aim of bringing down Empson and Dudley.

Nor did things alter much when, three days after his father's death, he took up residence in the Tower on 24 April. The earl of Oxford, who was also constable of the Tower, resumed his role as military strongman of the regime. Under Oxford's command, the Tower itself was put under heavy guard; strict watch was kept throughout all the wards of the City of London, while Henry himself remained 'closely and secret' within the fortress.

Was it an accession? Or a *coup d'état*? Or fear of a *coup d'état*? There was certainly an element of the last. The former pretender, the earl of Suffolk, was safely in the Tower, as was his brother William. But the remaining de la Pole brother, Richard, was still at large in exile and still proclaiming himself the 'White Rose' and true inheritor of England. Also at large, and at home, was Edward Stafford, duke of Buckingham. A few years previously, political gossip in high circles had rated Buckingham appreciatively as 'a noble man' and touted him as a possible king who 'would be a royal ruler'; now, in 1509, rumours were also swirling among the servants and adherents of Buckingham's close friend and ally the earl of Northumberland that the duke would be 'lord protector of England'. The last lord protector had been Richard, duke of Gloucester. And then and previously the protectorship had been a stepping stone to the throne.

Finally, there was the real possibility of civil strife among the old king's warring councillors. 'Perceiving that [Henry VII's] illness would prove fatal,' Empson's indictment alleged, 'he resolved to seize the government of the young king and realm for himself and others of his affinity and opinion,' and to this end summoned his armed retainers to London. Dudley was also charged with the same offence of summoning retainers, and the detail of both sets of charges has been described as 'remarkably credible'.

None of this would have much surprised the young Henry, nor, I imagine, greatly disconcerted him. For he had been well prepared by both education and experience. Skelton's *Speculum* had painted an unremittingly grim picture of the likely fate of kings. And – if he required the evidence – five years of living at his father's court and in close proximity to the king in his decline had exposed him to the endless varieties of human weakness, greed and delusion. Lastly and most importantly, there were his own memories of the building where he now found himself. It was here, in the Tower, that he and his mother had taken refuge in 1497 as the Cornish rebel army skirted the city. For days, his father's throne and his own life had hung in the balance until the crushing royal victory at Blackheath.

After that, Henry – even at his youngest and callowest – had a short way with rebels.

Etiquette, as was usual in the life of kings, also played a part in the course of events. English custom, it was explained to the puzzled Fuensalida, required a king to keep a low profile until the funeral of his predecessor. Indeed, until Henry VII was buried, there were in effect *two* kings in England: the living, though largely invisible, King Henry in the Tower, and his dead father at Richmond. And it was the latter who enjoyed all the pomp and show, as his corpse was moved stage by stage from its first resting place in the closet or private oratory next to the king's bedchamber, out through the black-hung chambers and gallery to the chapel royal, where it lay in state for a week, until its departure for London and its burial at Westminster.

All this time 'there was continually kept a right sumptuous household, all lords and other officers as they did in the king's living kept their rooms [places] and better served than the ordinary custom was'. And it was not only the royal household which stayed behind with Henry VII. 'The council' too, Wriothesley noted, 'attended upon the corpse of the late king defunct' and remained at Richmond. It was headed by Henry's grand-mother, Lady Margaret Beaufort, who seems to have acted as virtual regent, while its other domin-ant members were Richard Foxe, lord privy seal, and Thomas Howard, earl of Surrey and lord treasurer.

In stark contrast, the living King Henry was accom-panied to the Tower only by his former princely household – which now became, *de facto*, the new inner royal household – and a skeleton council consisting of William Warham, archbishop of Canterbury and lord chancellor, and Thomas Ruthall, royal secretary and bishop-elect of Durham. The pair were in no position to take deci-sions independent of the parent-body at Richmond, nor did they attempt to do so. But they *did* command, with the combination of the great seal and the sign manual or signature of the new king, the means to give effect to the decisions already taken at Richmond in the frantic forty-eight hours or so of plotting and horse-trading which had followed Henry VII's death.

The most sensational decision, to arrest Empson and Dudley, had already been implemented; but the council had decided to go further, and not only make scapegoats of Henry VII's most un-popular ministers, but also to signal a sharp change of policy. The method of making this clear was to be the issuing of a general pardon, or wiping-clean of the legal slate. Henry VII, in fulfilment of his promise to his confessor to become a new man, had already issued a deathbed general pardon on 16 April. But the general pardon was not quite what it seemed. For it to be effective, individuals had to sue out pardons in their own names and to pay the necessary fees in chancery. This – such was the fear of Henry VII's regime of law enforcement – they did in droves, and at least forty-four people rushed to take it out in only a couple of days.

But Henry VII's pardon died with him. Now the triumphant faction of his councillors resolved to reissue it – but with a difference. The old king's pardon was a dry list of offences that were eligible to be excused; the new monarch's was to be a lush exercise in feel-good rhetoric. The judges, Henry was made to say, from the highest to the lowest, were to 'minister justice . . . freely, rightwisely, and indifferently to every of his subjects' – even when the king himself was a party. And if Henry or his councillors lapsed from his own high standards and tried to pressure the judges into giving the king a favourable verdict, they were to ignore the intervention, whatever the cost.

Not only justice was to be free, but trade and manufactures as well. Henry VII's relations with the City had degenerated into a cold war that threatened to break out into open resistance and rioting. Henry VIII, on the other hand, offered his royal word to 'all manner of merchants . . . clothiers, artificers, and folks of all manner of mysteries and occupations' that they could go about their business 'freely, quietly and peaceably and without any fear of forfeiture' from over-zealous officials or prying informers.

Nor, finally, were Henry's subjects left to draw their own conclusions about the differences between his father's pardon and his own. *His* pardon, the text declared, had been issued of the new king's 'good heart' and was 'much more ample, gracious and beneficial' than his father's.

In short, the text came within a whisper of turning the two pardons into a contrast between two kings: the bad old man versus the good new youth.

The text must have been brought up in draft with the royal party when it rode from Richmond to the Tower; it may even have been already written out in proper form. At any rate, shortly after Henry's arrival in the Tower, it was presented to him to sign. He did so slowly and carefully, and making sure that each letter was properly formed: 'Henry R'.

It was his first official act as king, and his first repudiation of his father.

The moment Henry had finished writing, the 'signed bill', as it was now known, was taken to

Lord Chancellor Warham and his officials to be rewritten, sealed and enrolled. This was the ancient process of authenticating and recording royal acts that stretched back to the Conquest and beyond. But new, cutting-edge technology was deployed as well, as the text was also rushed to the workshop of the king's printer, Richard Pynson, to be turned into a printed proclamation.

Bearing in mind its length, it was an all-night job for the compositors and printers. But the following morning, 25 April, it was ready. First the pardon was proclaimed in a loud voice at central points in the City; then the printed copies were posted and distributed, 'that every man might thereof have knowledge'.

The effect was instantaneous, as popular rejoicing broke out throughout the City. Over the next few days a little more red meat was thrown to the people, with the well-publicized arrests of some of the fallen ministers' most notorious agents. Henry played a direct part in this process too, since he was at the centre of the lobbying which determined just who was an extortioner and who was not (the line, after all, was a fine one, since not only Empson and Dudley but more or less the whole political elite had been involved in Henry VII's policies up to the neck). Thus, when the list of those who were to be excepted from the general pardon was presented to him for signature on the thirtieth, he added a name in his own hand.

★　　★　　★

But long before then, the verdict of public opinion was clear. 'Henry VII's death,' Fuensalida reported home on 27 April, 'is now public knowledge because Henry VIII is in the Tower and has proclaimed a general pardon. He has released many prisoners and arrested all those responsible for the bribery and tyranny of his father's reign.' 'The people,' the ambassador continued, 'are very happy and few tears are being shed for Henry VII. Instead, people are as joyful as if they had been released from prison.' And they knew whom to thank for their deliverance: 'the new king', Fuensalida's report concludes, 'has ordered the arrest of two of Henry VII's officials who were responsible for collecting the king's monies and has proclaimed that all those who feel they were wronged by either his father or his officials should present their reasons to his council so that amends can be made'.

It is also clear just how cleverly the traditional etiquette surrounding the end of one reign and the beginning of the next was exploited for current political ends. Henry's strange, secluded sojourn in the Tower allowed him to repudiate his father's most unpopular policies without quite associating himself with the unfilial act of criticising his father. Similarly, the ostentatious attendance of the council on the body of their dead master at Richmond squared another awkward circle. They, after all, had organized the coup against two of the dead king's leading ministers almost before the breath was out of his body; they had also ventriloquized his son's behaviour. That could easily be construed as the blackest ingratitude. But the separation between Richmond and London saved the day: events might have been planned at Richmond by the council, but they were put into effect miles away in London, where they were presented as the sole initiative of the new king.

Finally, and conversely, the parallel households of the dead and living kings helped make the contrast between the two regimes seem much greater than it really was. The truth was that everybody who held real power round Henry VIII had also held it round his father. That was not what public opinion wanted to hear. It wanted a clean break. But the mass attendance of the council on the corpse of the dead king on the one hand, and Henry VIII's apparently uncounselled state on the other, did indeed offer the simulacrum of a rupture.

And that, with the new king's character and appearance, was enough.

Henry VII's posthumous usefulness was now almost at an end. On Wednesday, 9 May, at about 3 p.m., the late king's funeral procession, having made its way from Richmond along the south bank, crossed London Bridge and entered the City. Headed by the sword-bearer of London and the king's messengers, riding two by two 'with their boxes at their breasts', and including the serried ranks of the church, the judiciary, the City, the foreign merchant communities resident in London, the royal household, the heralds, the peerage and the yeomen of the guard, it numbered hundreds if not thousands, all arrayed in order and clad in mourning black. Henry's personal household marched there too, with 'torches innumerable'.

But not Henry. For the king could not see death – not even the death of a father.

At the centre of the procession was the late king's coffin, surmounted by his life-size, lifelike effigy, crowned and robed and holding the orb and sceptre and carried on a funeral car drawn by seven great horses, also trapped in black. At the west doors of St Paul's, the procession halted and was received by the bishop of London in cope and mitre. Then, amid clouds of incense, the coffin with its image was removed from the car and carried inside the church 'by twelve person of the guard, because of the great weight thereof'. There it rested overnight. The following morning, three masses were sung, ending in the mass of requiem. Then Bishop Fisher of Rochester preached his 'notable sermon' with its vivid picture of its subject's last days and his struggle with death – and his conscience. 'Ah! King Henry, King Henry,' the preacher cried at the sermon's climax, 'if you wert alive again, many a one that is here present now would pretend a full great pity and tenderness upon thee.'

How many of his hearers, including in particular Fisher's fellow councillors and executors, squirmed a little at the charge of hypocrisy? If they did, the moment passed quickly – for, after all, they were politicians.

After a break for dinner, the coffin was replaced on its car and the procession re-formed for the final leg of the journey to Westminster Abbey. There the body rested overnight once more on a magnificent hearse or bier. Then, early on the morning of the eleventh came the funeral proper. Once more, three masses were sung, culminating in the requiem sung by William Warham, archbishop of Canterbury, assisted by eighteen bishops and mitred abbots.

At the offertory there took place an extraordinary scene of divestment. Throughout the procession, the coffin with its image of the king in majesty had been accompanied by knights carrying the king's armour, sword and helmet with its battle crown. Another knight, Sir Edward Howard, second son of the earl of Surrey, had ridden in the king's actual battle-armour, bearing his battle-axe reversed, with its head resting on his foot. Now the armour, sword and helmet were offered up in turn at the altar. Then Howard rode into the Abbey, dismounted and presented himself. Two monks stripped him of the king's arms and armour, revealing him as himself, clad like the others in mourning black.

After the late king's knighthood had gone the

way of all flesh, his sovereignty departed too: the image was removed from the coffin and all its royal ornaments were stripped. Finally, as a mere man, the king was lowered into the vault alongside Henry's mother, Elizabeth of York. Warham cast down earth, while Surrey as lord treasurer and the earl of Shrewsbury as lord steward of the household broke their white staves of office and threw them on the coffin too, followed by all the other head officers. Then the vault was closed and covered in cloth-of-gold.

The final scene belonged to the heralds. They took off their embroidered tabards of the royal arms and hung them on the hearse and cried 'lamentably in French': 'The noble King Henry the Seventh is dead.' Then, after a moment, they put their tabards back on and cried, also with a loud voice: '*Vive le noble roy Henry le VIIIth!*'

God send the noble king Henry the Eighth long life!

A day or so later, Henry, who had passed the time by organizing a tournament in the Tower, quit its gloomy walls for his birthplace of Greenwich – and his reign.

CHAPTER 19

FIRST STEPS

It was not only Henry who had been marking time pending his father's funeral. So had the whole operations of his government: apart from the general pardon and the fought-over exceptions to it, the only business transacted in April and early May was the formal reappointment of the judges and the law officers of the crown, the attorney- and solicitor-generals. But, with Henry VII safely interred, the floodgates of patronage opened.

Or at least they did for those who had been on the winning side.

First in the queue was Sir Henry Marney, who was made vice-chamberlain and captain of the guard on 12 May, the day after Henry VII's funeral, and, in short order thereafter, chancellor of the duchy of Lancaster, steward of the duchy of Cornwall, warden of the stannaries and, in reversion, steward of the duchy of Lancaster and the great honour of Clare.

It was an extraordinary accumulation of positions, which immediately turned Marney into one of the richest office-holders under the crown. Yet

Marney had come more or less from nowhere. That at least is what Henry himself said when, almost thirty years later, he recalled Marney and others of his council at the beginning of his reign as 'but scant well born gentlemen; and yet of no great lands till they were promoted by us and so made knights and lords'. A rather more substantial background is suggested by Polydore Vergil, who names Marney as a councillor both to Henry's father, Henry VII, and his elder brother, Arthur. But his activity in these positions – if he ever held them – has left no trace in the records. Instead, he appears only as an Essex country gentleman, who was prominent in the government of his shire, and as a member of the household of Henry as prince of Wales – perhaps indeed its head, as vice-chamberlain to the prince.

At any rate, Marney's connexion with Henry went back a long way, since he had been one of the twenty-two gentlemen who had been dubbed knights of the Bath at Henry's creation as duke of York in 1494. A William and Grace Marney, who may have been a son and daughter-in-law of Marney's, appear as members of Henry's household in 1503; Marney himself witnessed Henry's protestation against his marriage to Catherine of Aragon in 1505; while Henry gave him a New Year's Day gift in both 1508 and 1509.

All this is suggestive. But we can only guess at the qualities which led Henry to single Marney out for such accelerated promotion – or led Marney's fellow councillors to acquiesce in it. Perhaps, as a grey-beard (he had been born in about 1456–57) and a competent and conscientious administrator, he was the person closest to Henry who appeared as 'one of us' to Henry VII's surviving ministers. Perhaps, since she appointed him as one of her executors, it was Henry's grandmother, Lady Margaret Beaufort, who engineered his promotion.

But, finally, the clue to the enigma has to lie in Henry's own personal favour. A dozen or so years later, Marney was still one of the handful 'who . . . have great authority and credit with the king'. Henry also did him the rare privilege of staying with him at his house at Layer Marney in Essex, which was then abuilding. Even its architecture, with its soaring height and adventurous use of Italianate terracotta and early renaissance orna-ment, testifies to their close relationship.

Henry liked Marney, and that was that.

Marney's offices came from two sources: the chancellorship of the duchy of Lancaster was vacant since it had been held by the fallen minister Empson; but the vice-chamberlainship and captaincy of the guard were very much occupied. Indeed Thomas, Lord Darcy had been appointed to these offices barely a year previously; he also continued to discharge them throughout Henry VII's funeral ceremonies. This meant he had to be eased out to make way for Marney. But it was done with great tact and careful consideration for both

Darcy's pride and his pocket. On 18 May, at the first chapter of the Garter of Henry's reign, Darcy was chosen as one of the two new knights; Darcy also received a stream of confirmations of existing positions and new grants of office which made him the dominant force on the eastern or Northumbrian march against Scotland – and this much to the chagrin of the earl of Northumberland, who regarded the wardenship of the East March as his by right as a family perquisite.

But why were the vice-chamberlainship and the captaincy of the guard chosen for Marney? Partly, it was accidental. As the most recently appointed official of Henry VII's council, Darcy, the current vice-chamberlain, was more vulnerable than his longer-serving colleagues: it was a case of last in, first out. But there was more to it than that: the combined offices controlled the king's personal security; the vice-chamberlainship, with its requirement of more-or-less continuous attendance on the king, could also serve as the hotline between the king and his council. With a king like Henry VII, who was executive chairman of his own council, the role was scarcely necessary. But Henry, it was probably already clear, had much less appetite than his father for the hard graft of kingship.

Perhaps the older councillors hoped that Marney would coach his young master in the ways of business; perhaps, more realistically, they realized they had to find ways to mitigate Henry's indolence, and saw in Marney a mutually acceptable means.

Now that Marney was satisfied and Darcy appeased, it seems to have become something of a free for all. On 14 May, George Talbot, earl of Shrewsbury and lord steward, secured the valuable sinecure of one of the two chamberlainships of the exchequer; two days later, on 16 May, no fewer than four letters patent were issued, by which Henry confirmed his father's multitude of grants to the earl of Oxford; the same day at Greenwich Henry affixed his signature or sign manual to a similar number of signed bills for the lord chamberlain, Charles Somerset, Lord Herbert, which confirmed his existing Welsh offices and added innumerable new ones; then, on 19 May, it was the turn of Henry's own grandmother, Lady Margaret Beaufort.

The manor of Woking in Surrey, which had been the principal Home Counties residence of the Beauforts, had been recovered by Lady Margaret at the beginning of Henry VII's reign. But in 1503, in exchange for Hunsdon in Hertfordshire, she had surrendered Woking to the king her son, and Henry VII had spent considerable sums on rebuilding it. Now, faced with the softer touch of her grandson, Lady Margaret got Woking back, improvements and all.

One lesser figure stands out among these coroneted suitors: Richard Weston, formerly groom of

Henry VII's secret chamber. Weston's quick thinking and courtier's smoothness had been vital in keeping the old king's death secret; now he too had his reward, with a series of bills signed by Henry at Greenwich on 21 and 22 May. Like his betters, it was a case of something old, something new: Weston secured Henry's confirmation of his grants from Henry's father, regained the old family office of captain of Guernsey and, as the plum in the pudding, was made keeper of Hanworth, the royal *maison de retraite* near Richmond where his rival Hugh Denys had once reigned supreme in Henry VII's confidence.

By the summer, when Darcy had gone to take up his new position in the north and the dust had settled in London, the constellation of power around Henry was clear. Richard Foxe, bishop of Winchester and lord privy seal, remained, as he had been in the previous reign, the senior minister. But he had to share power – it was rumoured, probably incorrectly, unwillingly – with others: Lord Treasurer Surrey, Lord Steward Shrewsbury, Secretary Ruthall, Sir Thomas Brandon, the master of the horse – and, of course, Henry's favourite, Sir Henry Marney. There was also, if we believe Darcy himself, an even smaller inner ring, consisting of Foxe, Ruthall and – again – Marney.

These men were Henry's councillors. But, overwhelmingly, they had been chosen by his father, and were accustomed to his father's methods. On

291

the other hand, Marney's role shows that Henry, despite his youth and inexperience, was not a cipher: Marney was as much the king's voice on the council as the council's mouthpiece to the king.

And it was as his master's voice that Marney – though the most junior member of the council – carried so much weight.

These May days also showed Henry, for the first time, something of the exhilaration of kingship. He had quit the Tower for the sights and scents of Greenwich, which was, and was long to remain, his favourite residence. And there, rather like W. S. Gilbert's lord chancellor, he sat in his court all day, agiving agreeable girls – and lands and offices and titles – away. He signed his name dozens of times – more probably than in all his life so far – and each time he signed, he granted what was desired. Recipients promised eternal gratitude, and Henry basked in the pleasure he gave them – and himself.

It was intoxicating and – the council evidently feared – habit-forming. The result was that – having helped themselves and their friends to what they no doubt richly deserved – Henry's councillors moved swiftly to control the flow of patronage for everybody else.

For Henry's signature was only the first step in the making of a grant. The instrument that actually conferred the patronage was royal 'letters patent' (the plural form was always used). 'Letters patent' were a formal document, written on parchment, in Latin and with the massive, double-sided wax disc of the great seal hanging from the parchment on a strip cut partway along its bottom margin.

There were two routes to the issuing of letters patent: one long, the other short. In the short route, the 'bill' or letter signed by Henry acted as an immediate instruction or 'warrant' to Lord Chancellor Warham to have the letters patent drawn up. His office prepared and wrote out the parchment and applied the great seal, whose matrix or mould (made of precious metal) Warham held *ex officio*. In the long route, on the other hand, two other royal seals, the signet seal, held by Secretary Ruthall, and the privy seal, held by Warham's senior colleague Bishop Foxe, were interposed. This meant that the 'bill' with Henry's signature now acted as a warrant only to Ruthall. Ruthall's office then drew up another warrant, sealed it with the signet and addressed it to Foxe. Foxe's office in turn prepared yet another warrant, sealed it with the privy seal and sent it to Warham. Finally Warham's office, duly authorized, issued the letters patent in proper form.

The long route, in short, was long indeed. Viewed in one perspective, it was an extreme example of bureaucratic make-work, which cost suitors time and – since fees were payable at every stage – money. But it also had a real function, since it imposed two additional layers of scrutiny on the royal bounty. For this to work, of course, the lord privy seal and the chancellor had actually to read and note – and if need be query – what they sealed. We can guess that this was the case with Foxe, who seems to have read and remembered everything; we know it was with Warham. He 'has sped', Warham wrote to his friend Lord Darcy, 'the commissions which Darcy sent to be sealed'. Warham had 'sped' or expedited them indeed: Warham's letter was dated 25 March; the principal commission was issued under the great seal three days later, on the twenty-eighth.

In view of this kind of scrupulous oversight, all that was necessary for the control of royal patronage was for the 'course of the seals', as it was known, to be enforced. Back in 1444, and faced with the prodigal patronage of another young king, Henry VI, the council had tried to impose the long route by conciliar order. Now Henry VIII's council did the same thing – and very successfully. And even when signed bills *were* used, they tended to be counter-signed by a representative group of royal councillors.

The result was, in effect, to create a regency council behind the façade of a nominally adult monarch.

Henry, used to doing what his father told him, acquiesced – for the time being at least.

There was one item of business, however, that had not waited for Henry VII's funeral. It was too important, and touched Henry too deeply.

It was his marriage.

No one was more surprised than the Spanish ambassador, Fuensalida. Back the previous autumn, he had noted Catherine of Aragon's conviction that Henry would treat her better than his father. Fuensalida 'hopes to God that this will be the case'. But he is none too optimistic: 'because, speaking frankly, the prince is not considered to be a very genial person'.

Now this not 'very genial person' held Catherine's fate in his hands. Catherine, for her part, seems to have worked hard at maintaining contact with the youth she persisted in regarding as her husband, and she showered him with gifts of jewellery. On 1 January 1504, she gave him a gold collar enamelled with red and white roses; on 1 January 1506, a ring with a pointed diamond; and on 1 January 1507 'a goodly girdle [belt] of white satin' with a gold buckle of Spanish work. Henry gave Catherine in turn 'a ring with an emerald' on 1 January 1506, and 'a fair rose of rubies set in a rose white and green' on 1 January 1508.

At first sight, the exchanges look touching. But this alas was hardly the stuff of true love, since both of Henry's gifts to Catherine were recycled presents he had received from others. And he was just as unsentimental with Catherine's own presents, no fewer than three of which he gave to his father as *his* New Year's gift in 1507, 1508 and 1509.

★　★　★

There were apparently more substantial problems as well, and on 24 April Fuensalida reported that he had 'been told that a member of the king's council has said that [the marriage] is unlikely because from what they know of Henry it would burden his conscience to marry his brother's widow'.

In the fullness of time, these phrases – about his conscience and his brother's widow – were to become the leitmotifs of Henry's case against his first marriage. But, for almost two decades, we hear nothing more of them.

Did Henry suppress his doubts? Had he forgotten them? Did he even utter them in the first place? Or were his views invented, or at any rate glossed, by a hostile councillor?

We do not know.

Three or four days later, however, the council put out feelers to the Spanish ambassador, and negotiations reopened in earnest. Throughout, the council – which was supposed to be devoting itself to the arrangements for the interment of the dead king – was careful to keep Fuensalida at a distance and transact business through individual councillors as intermediaries.

But the ruse was transparent, and on 1 May the king's secretary Ruthall himself came to see Fuensalida. 'Their conversation concluded,' Fuensalida reported, 'the king's secretary returned to Henry VIII and his council and related the conversation back to them.' Actually, what seems to have happened was that Ruthall, who had been attending Henry in the Tower, now travelled to Richmond to join the rest of the council. That same day, along with his fellow councillors and executors, he signed a warrant authorizing the issue of another £2,000 for Henry VII's funeral expenses and led the discussion at the council board on Henry's marriage.

The outcome (probably in the absence of Archbishop Warham, who seems to have been the most doubtful of the legality of the marriage) was favourable. This led to the dispatch of an even more powerful delegation, consisting of Lord Privy Seal Foxe as well as Ruthall, both of whom turned up at Fuensalida's lodgings on 3 May. Foxe, as was his wont, took charge and cut through the fog of diplomacy. It was a new reign, he emphasized, with a new king who had none of the baggage of the old. They should take advantage of that and make a fresh start. Each side should be frank with the other; put their cards on the table and aim for a quick agreement.

At this point Foxe became confidential. Fuensalida, he told the ambassador in secret, 'should inform Ferdinand [of Aragon] that he was going to advise Henry that he should make up his mind to marry Catherine quickly and before people started to interfere in the matter and construct obstacles'. 'The king's council,' Foxe added, 'were currently in favour of the marriage.'

297

He left hanging in the air the thought that this might soon change.

Then he pressed the point home. 'If Ferdinand *did* intend to agree to the marriage', Foxe concluded, he should strike while the iron was hot.

On 8 May, just as Henry VII's funeral ceremonies got under way, agreement was reached: negotiations that had dragged on for nearly seven years were settled in almost as many days.

The inwardness of what happened will probably never be known. But the issue of Henry's adulthood must be an important part of the story. The council had taken away with one hand in the matter of patronage, where the reimposition of the old rules about signed bills treated Henry as a minor in tutelage. But, in railroading through Henry's marriage, the council gave back with the other hand. And more. For a married king – and soon, no doubt, to be the father of an heir – *was* an adult king.

Who could doubt it?

Indeed, the symmetry is such that it almost looks as though Henry's marriage was a *quid pro quo* for his acquiescence in the limitations on his patronage. Or perhaps – and what amounts to much the same thing – it was a diversionary tactic shrewdly calculated to stop Henry brooding too much on his real place in affairs of state – or the lack of it.

In either case, it's clear why Bishop Foxe made

himself the real author of the marriage, and what he thought he and his fellow councillors were going to get out of it.

In the short term at least he was not disappointed.

The inevitable delays in communications with Spain, where Ferdinand, who was normally so quick on the uptake, rather struggled to keep pace with the speed of events in England, meant that it took another month before the diplomatic niceties were complete. On 8 June Warham, whatever his private doubts, issued the necessary marriage licence. And three days later, on 11 June, Henry and Catherine were married at Greenwich. The ceremony took place in the queen's closet or oratory, and was small-scale and private. The names of only two witnesses are known – Lord Steward Shrewsbury and William Thomas, groom of the privy chamber.

Thomas had previously served Henry's elder brother Arthur in the same capacity, and had attended him when he went to sleep with Catherine.

What tales did he tell? Or did he observe a valet's discretion?

CHAPTER 20

'VIRTUE, GLORY, IMMORTALITY'

Henry was not the only one to find those May days of 1509 intoxicating. William Blount, Lord Mountjoy, Henry's companion of studies and the mentor of his teenage years, was perhaps the man who knew the young king best. He had been with him at Richmond when his father died; had accompanied him on that strange, half-secret ride to the Tower and thence, with relief, to Greenwich. He seems also to have been a party to the deadly factioneering in the last days of the old reign and the first of the new, and hinted darkly at his recent 'many occupations and other special causes which I dared not commit to writing'. He was even – at the moment that Henry was tying the knot with Catherine of Aragon – courting one of her Spanish ladies, who was shortly to become his second wife.

But now, on 27 May 1509, *ex praetorio Grenuuici* ('from the palace of Greenwich'), Mountjoy was sufficiently at leisure to write a long letter to his old teacher and friend, Erasmus, who was staying, not altogether happily, in Rome.

The letter is of course written in Latin. But an

almost boyish enthusiasm and wonderment keep bursting through the rolling, grandiloquent phrases.

For Mountjoy had witnessed an epiphany.

'*Our* prince', Mountjoy writes proprietorially, as he is sure Erasmus has heard already, has 'succeeded to his father's throne'. He is *Henricus Octavus* ('Henry the Eighth'), 'whom we may well call our *Octavius*' – that is, the first and greatest Roman emperor, who was afterwards surnamed Augustus.

Those, Mountjoy continues, like Erasmus himself, who knew Henry well, were already familiar with his 'extraordinary and almost divine character'. But even they have been surprised by 'what a hero he now shows himself, how wisely he behaves, what a lover he is of justice and goodness, what affection he bears to the learned'. 'Oh my Erasmus,' Mountjoy exclaims, 'if you could see how all the world here is rejoicing in the possession of so great a prince, how his life is all their desire, you could not contain your tears for joy.'

Finally, as if all this were not enough, Mountjoy resorts to the language of prophecy and revelation: 'The heavens laugh, the earth exults, all things are full of milk, of honey and of nectar! Avarice is expelled the country. Liberality scatters wealth with bounteous hand. Our king does not desire gold or gems or precious metals, but virtue, glory, immortality.'

★ ★ ★

301

Virtue, glory, immortality. It is easy to laugh. Or – bearing in mind what was to happen, not least to Mountjoy himself – to cry. But either reaction would be mistaken. For Mountjoy did not get Henry as wrong as all that. Henry's youthful innocence, his burning desire to be good, might fade almost as quickly as a summer flower. But the ambition, the determination to be famous, to make a mark in the world – in a word, to be *great* – never altered.

From time to time, it was frustrated and diverted. It might change form. But the driving impulse remained: *he would be famous*.

And in this at least he succeeded.

But all this was in the future. Back in 1509, Mountjoy had another, personal reason for feeling a little smug. His own father, John, the third baron, had been overwhelmed by the turmoil of the last tumultuous months of Richard III's reign and had died a bitter and disillusioned man. 'Live right-wisely,' his will had enjoined William and his younger brother, 'and never . . . take the state of baron upon them if they may lay it from them nor . . . desire to be great about princes, for it is dangerous.'

But the advice fell on deaf ears. William's galaxy of family connexions had propelled him, almost inevitably, to the court. He had become 'great' round Prince Henry. Indeed, he had helped mould him as much as any man.

Now, it seemed, he was vindicated.

★   ★   ★

'I will give you an example,' Mountjoy's letter continued, as he reported a recent conversation with the king. 'The other day [Henry] wished he was more learned. I said, "that is not what we expect of your grace, but that you will foster and encourage learned men". "Yea surely", said he, "for indeed without them we should scarcely exist at all!"'

'What more splendid saying,' Mountjoy exclaimed, 'could fall from the lips of a prince?'

Or one, he quickly added, more encouraging to Erasmus. After all, Erasmus did not simply know Henry, but was also 'intimate, having received from him (as few others have) a letter traced with his own fingers'.

'Make up your mind,' Mountjoy exhorted his old teacher, 'that the last day of your wretchedness has dawned. You will come to a prince who will say: "Accept our wealth and be our great sage!"'

Over twenty years later, Erasmus commented ruefully on his decision: 'I never made a more unlucky choice.'

At the time, however, he leapt at the opportunity and arrived in his friend Thomas More's household only two months later, in August 1509.

CHAPTER 21

CORONATION

O n 11 June, the day of Henry's wedding to
Catherine of Aragon, the formal preparations for his coronation also began with the
issuing of a commission to Surrey, Shrewsbury and
the chief justice to convene the 'court of claims' to
decide on who had the right to offer the king
honorific services at his coronation. Since the
government did not wish to be bothered with the
course of the seals for its own business, the commission was warranted by a signed bill. But, as was the
new practice, the bill was counter-signed by a
powerful trio of councillors: Privy Seal Foxe, Lord
Chamberlain Herbert, and Sir Thomas Lovell.

Did Henry reflect, a little wryly, that he could not
even initiate his coronation on his own authority?

In point of fact, the real business of organizing
the ceremony had begun some weeks earlier with
the drawing up of a briefing paper known as the
'device for the manner and order of the coronation' of King Henry VIII and Queen Catherine.
The 'device' was closely modelled on the similarly
titled paper for Henry VII's coronation in 1485

and, even more closely (since that too was a double coronation), on the 'device' for the coronation of Richard III and Queen Anne in 1483. And, like those earlier papers, Henry's 'device' provided for an entirely traditional ceremony.

The celebrations proper got under way on 21 June, when Henry came on horseback from Greenwich and entered the Tower via London Bridge and Gracechurch Street. The following night, the ceremonies of the creation of knights of the Bath began. Fifteen years earlier, Henry himself had been one of the postulant knights. Now he stood in his father's shoes. He made the sign of the cross on each knight's shoulder and kissed it. Many of the knights had close personal ties with the young king. Sir Thomas Knyvet was his jousting hero. Sir Henry Clifford, who was only two years younger than Henry, had been brought up with him as both duke of York and prince, 'which ingrafted such a love in the said prince towards him, that it continued to the very end'. But closest of all was Mountjoy.

Did Henry's kiss linger a little longer on his friend and mentor's shoulder?

The eve-of-coronation procession, from the Tower, through the City and thence to Westminster, did not set off till almost 4 o'clock on Saturday, 23 June. But no matter, for it was brilliant sunshine and the long summer evening stretched ahead. First rode the newly created knights of the Bath, in long blue gowns with white laces on their left shoulders. These they were supposed to wear until a noble lady removed them after they had undertaken a feat of arms. Edward Stafford, duke of Buckingham and the greatest and richest noble in the land, preceded the king. In 1501 he had been touted as a possible candidate for the throne. Now he wore a long gown of needlework, 'right costly and rich', and carried a little silver baton in token of the fact that he was constable of England. The duke claimed this – the most ancient and powerful surviving great office of state – by hereditary right, and never ceased to press his entitlement to it.

But letters patent conferred the office on Buckingham for a single day, and even then in carefully circumscribed terms: 'on 23 June only, viz., the day preceding the coronation'. Henry signed this bill alone: even without the counter-signature of his councillors he knew when it was dangerous to be indiscriminately generous.

Then came Henry. He wore his parliament robe of red velvet furred with ermine over a coat of cloth-of-gold, thickly set with precious stones and surmounted with a collar of great ballas rubies. His horse was trapped with cloth-of-gold and ermine, and a canopy, also of cloth-of-gold, was held over his head by four barons of the Cinque Ports.

Henry, now almost fully grown and approaching six feet in height, cut an impressive figure. And it was intensified by his dress and the magic of his royal status.

But – perhaps ominously – the London chronicler seems to have had eyes only for Buckingham.

Henry was followed by mounted attendants wearing surcoats of arms. In pride of place came the arms of England's royal saints – St Edward, St Edmund and St George – and then the arms of England and France.

Henry, who was as conventionally religious as he was royal, was, at this supreme moment, invoking the intercession of his saintly predecessors in governing England and – it soon became clear – in reclaiming France.

Then came another of Henry's boyhood heroes: Sir Thomas Brandon, the master of the horse, who had kept the torch of chivalry burning in the last years of Henry VII's reign. He led the king's richly caparisoned charger and wore 'traverse his body a great baldric of gold, great and massy', which he had been given by Henry's father a year previously as a recognition of 'his loyalty and prowess in feats of arms' (*propter fidem ac ipsius in duellando dexteritatem*).

After this triumphant display of royal chivalry, the cavalcade took on a different character with the queen's procession. Catherine of Aragon reclined alone in a horse litter. She was dressed in a 'rich mantle of cloth of tissue'; her hair, a lustrous dark auburn, was let down (as was also traditional) and hung round her shoulders, and on her head she wore a simple 'circlet of silk, gold and pearl'.

She had already won the hearts of Londoners at Arthur's wedding. Now she confirmed her hold. And – whatever the vicissitudes of her life – she never lost it.

In her train was the woman who had been the key figure in her husband's early life: Anne Luke, Henry's wet-nurse. Did Anne's heart swell with pride as she saw the child she had suckled as man and king?

Her purse certainly did, since Henry confirmed and augmented the ample grants she had received from his father.

The queen's procession had just reached The Cardinal's Hat, a well-known tavern on the north side of Lombard Street, when a sudden, violent shower broke out of a seemingly clear sky. The downpour was so heavy that it threatened to overwhelm the decorative canopy that was carried over the queen. Instead, with all her finery, she had to take shelter under the awning of a humble draper's stall.

It was the only blemish on an otherwise perfect day. And, in any case, the summer shower passed as quickly as it came and the procession, only a little ruffled, continued its stately progress to Westminster.

★ ★ ★

The next day, the twenty-fourth, was Midsummer's Day, and the day chosen for the coronation itself. It was a day of rejoicing and mystery: bonfires burned on Midsummer's Eve and the fairies were abroad. And Henry and Catherine, as they processed on foot through the great hall towards the Abbey church, seemed indeed to be another Oberon and Titania: their magic spell would knit up old wounds and end ancient hatreds, and all, *all* would live happily ever after.

Or so it seemed at eight o'clock on that brilliant summer morning as, preceded by no fewer than twenty-eight bishops in copes and mitres, the couple set out for the solemn ceremony. For hour after hour, Archbishop Warham's voice echoed round the crossing or coronation theatre of the Abbey, in solemn invocation and admonition. First he presented Henry to his people, who acclaimed him four times with cries of *Vivat, vivat rex*, Long live the king! Then Henry swore the traditional oaths of an English king. He was anointed nine-fold with the holy oils of chrism. He was invested with the regalia and crowned and acclaimed. Finally the process was repeated for Catherine.

Henry was now king indeed. Beside the magic and the mystery of the ceremony, his earlier creations, as duke of York and prince of Wales, must have faded into nothing.

Two aspects of the service in particular seem to have made a powerful impression on him: the oath-taking and the anointing. Theologically, the anointing, not the crowning, was the heart of the ritual. This is clearer in French, where the service is known as *le sacre* or 'consecration'. At its most elevated, the anointing could be seen as a sacrament – a unique eighth sacrament by which kings were called to serve God and were marked out, indelibly, from the rest of creation.

There is no doubt, it seems to me, that, with all the switchbacks of Henry's religious belief, he held firmly to this high view of the royal station. Indeed, as other certainties lapsed, *this* loomed larger and larger in his mind until it filled it with an overweening sense of his own importance and manifest destiny.

But there was more to it even than that. For the oil lay at the heart of the foundation legend of Henry's own Lancastrian dynasty. According to this, the Virgin had revealed herself to St Thomas Becket in a vision; handed him the holy oils in an *ampulla* in the form of a golden eagle; and instructed him that this was to be the coronation unction of the kings of England. 'But not those wicked ones who now reign,' she warned. 'But kings of the English,' she went on to promise, '*shall* arise who will be anointed with this oil . . . the first to be anointed with this oil . . . shall recover by force the land lost by his forefathers, that is to say, Normandy and Acquitaine.'

The *ampulla* and its mystically revealed oil had first been used for the coronation of the

Lancastrian usurper, Henry IV. And his son, Henry V, had indeed come within a whisper of fulfilling the prophecy and recovering France.

Henry, it is clear, was determined to be another, greater Henry V. And how – with the magic of the oil and the patronage of Becket – could he fail?

The oath too ground itself into Henry's mind as a foundation charter of his kingship, even as a sort of contract. It took a quasi-liturgical form of verses and responses, as Warham put a series of questions and injunctions to Henry and Henry replied to each with a brief and unequivocal commitment.

'Will ye grant,' Warham began, 'and keep to the people of England, the laws and customs to them as of old rightful and devout kings granted and the same ratify and confirm by your oath, and specially the laws, customs and liberties granted to the clergy and people by your noble predecessor and glorious king Saint Edward?'

'*I grant and promise*,' Henry replied,

'Ye shall keep,' Warham continued, 'after your strength and power, to the church of God, to the clergy, and the people, holy peace and goodly concord.'

'*I shall keep.*'

'Ye shall make to be done, after your strength and power, equal and rightful justice in all your dooms and judgments, and discretion with mercy and truth.'

'*I shall do.*'

'Do you grant the rightful laws and customs to be holden, and promise ye, after your strength and power, such laws as to the worship of God shall be chosen by your people by you to be strengthened and defended?'

'I grant and promise.'

As if all that were not enough, another assisting bishop now took over the task of interrogation and – in painstaking detail – required the king to promise to respect the particular privileges of church and churchmen and church or canon law. 'With good will and devout soul,' Henry replied, 'I shall keep the privileges of the law . . . canon and of holy church . . . and I shall . . . by God's grace defend you, and every each of you, bishops and abbots, through[out] my realm.'

'So help me God,' he concluded, *'and these holy evangelists, by me bodily touched upon this holy altar.'*

Henry, we know, like all conventional Christians at the time, believed profoundly in the force of oaths. He had sworn. And he fully intended to keep his word.

At the time.

The celebratory joust for the coronation took place at Westminster on the Tuesday and Thursday of the following week, the latter of which happened to be Henry's birthday. There was of course no question of the king taking part himself; instead, rather as he had done as an impatient teenager,

312

Henry had to sit out the sport alongside Catherine in their richly hung and decorated viewing stand.

Heaven knows what his thoughts were. For, in a curious way, the theme of the joust seems to have been intended to dramatize the tensions between the different aspects of the young king's character. Probably it was devised by William Cornish, the master of the children of the chapel royal, who was the main impresario and dramaturge of court entertainment in these years.

If so, he did his work well.

On the first day of the joust, the 'home' team of knights were presented to Henry and Catherine by a lady dressed as Pallas Athene, the Greek goddess of wisdom. She bore a crystal shield and proclaimed the knights to be her 'scholars'. Then their opponents entered and a gentleman dressed in blue and bearing Cupid's golden dart announced that they would challenge Wisdom's scholars in the name of the Love of Ladies. He also bandied some sharp words. His knights, he said, had heard that 'Dame Pallas had presented . . . her scholars to the king, but whether,' he added tartly, 'they came to learn or to teach feats of arms, they knew not.'

On the second day of the joust, Pallas's knights appeared as before. But this time they were challenged by Diana's knights, who entered with all the panoply of the hunt, including hounds and a live deer, which was promptly slaughtered by the dogs.

Wisdom, Love or Hunting? All three vied for

the young king's energies and soul. He would have to choose. Which would it be?

In the joust at least Henry showed himself as peacemaker, as the sport risked turning nasty. Diana's knights claimed the swords of Pallas's followers if they were victorious. This was perilously close to dishonouring them, so, 'fearing a grudge'. Henry limited the tourney to a few strokes each, and all went away happy.

The following day, death struck again. Henry's grandmother, Lady Margaret Beaufort, had played a leading part in the preparations for the coronation, and the council had met, under her presidency and in her chamber at court, to agree some of the arrangements. Along with Henry's sister, Princess Mary, she had witnessed the eve-of-coronation procession from a specially hired house in Cheapside, with a lattice protecting the ladies from public view. And, at the coronation itself, 'wherein she had full great joy', she rather cast a pall on things by muttering that 'some adversity would follow'. But she recovered her spirits to eat heartily at the ensuing coronation banquet in Westminster Hall.

Too heartily, perhaps. As her cupbearer at the ceremonies, Henry Parker, later Lord Morley, recalled, 'she took her infirmity with eating of a cygnet'. She lingered in increasing discomfort till the morning of 29 June, and then summoned

Bishop Fisher of Rochester to perform the last rites. 'The bishop,' Parker remembered, 'said Mass before her, and as he lift up the precious host, this worthy lady expired.'

In less than two months, Henry had lost the two dominant figures of his youth: his father and his grandmother. He was now not only king but paterfamilias and undisputed head of his family.

And all this at the age of only eighteen.

CHAPTER 22

'I SAW A NEW HEAVEN
AND A NEW EARTH...'

Among the crowds thronging the streets of
London and Westminster for the coronation was Henry's old acquaintance,
Thomas More. More seems to have shared
more or less the same vantage points as the
City chronicler; certainly he reports the same
events. But they are transmuted from hobbling
prose into the ringing encomia of Latin verse.
For More – normally so cool in his reading of
human nature, so sceptical of the motives of
those in power, especially kings, and so little
inclined to be carried away by the sweaty
emotions of the mob – responded to Henry's
coronation with an uninhibited enthusiasm that
makes Mountjoy's own outpourings look almost
staid.

It was not the first time that the advent of a
young, able, good-looking and charismatic leader
had provoked an outbreak of messianic joy. Nor
would it be the last.

Nevertheless, that Henry-mania included such

316

cheerleaders as More suggests that it had real substance.

How real, of course, only events would tell.

More's tribute to Henry consisted of five Latin poems: four short, each making a single point, and one longer and more substantial. All were written in the heat of the moment, and More intended to present them to the king immediately after the coronation festivities. But then unkind fate intervened, and the illuminator to whom More had sent them for embellishment was stricken with an attack of the gout. His legs, as More wryly noted, thus delayed the work of his hands, and risked destroying the whole purpose of More's occasional verse.

But More turned this, as he turned every other circumstance of the coronation, to compliment: since the joy at Henry's accession would be everlasting, delay – he proclaimed in the preface – added to the poems' message, rather than detracted from it.

And this was only the beginning: the sudden downpour of rain, which had threatened to drench the eve-of-coronation procession, was turned into a happy augury, as was Henry's handling of the joust, which led – uniquely, More claims – to a tournament free of bloodshed or mishap. The third of the short poems hailed Henry as the 'end of history' and the return of the golden age; while the fourth celebrated the consummation of the union of the red rose and the white in his person: 'therefore', More declares, 'if anyone loved either of these roses, let him love this one in which is found whatever he loved. But if any one is so fierce that he will not love this rose, then he will fear it, for this flower has its own thorns too.'

But, strikingly, the most extravagant language – which is taken from Chapter 21 of the Book of Revelations – is reserved for the longest and most considered of the poems. This presents Henry's accession as a second coming, and the king himself as a messiah who will 'wipe the tear from every eye and put joy in the place of our long distress'. He combines every physical and mental advantage: he is tall and handsome, with a face whose fresh beauty could belong to a young girl; his sword gives the strongest stroke, his lance hits home the hardest, his arrow always finds the target, and he has a mind to match. And, since his intelligence has been 'enhanced by a liberal education' and 'steeped in philosophy's own precepts', 'what could lie beyond [his] powers'?

And the proof is there, More insists: already, 'on his first day', he had done more than most princes in long reigns. This, undoubtedly, is a direct reference to Henry's general pardon, whose propaganda value More, as a lawyer-cum-poet, was particularly well placed to grasp. By this first act, More expansively declares, the nobility is restored to its proper status, the merchant is given back his prosperity and his freedom of trade, and, above all, the laws, previously perverted to injustice, are restored to 'their ancient force and dignity'.

More even makes explicit the reproof to Henry VII, which his son's general pardon had left tactfully unspoken. 'What if, in the hope of being kind to his people,' More asks, '[Henry] decided to retract certain provisions of the law which he knew his father had approved? In this he placed his fatherland [*patria*], as he should, before his father [*pater*].'

Indeed, More articulates the political significance of the general pardon so effectively that it almost looks as though he had had something to do with it. And it is just possible that he had. He was, after all, uniquely well placed and connected: he was a Londoner and writes proudly as such (*Londoniensis*), a lawyer, a scholar and acquainted, if not intimate, with both Henry and the inner circle of his court and government. He had also dabbled in opposition to the old king. And he was young.

Who better to suggest a fresh start and how to go about it?

And if More had not been part of things already, then he certainly aspired to be. His five congratulatory poems, written in their fashionable italic script and elegantly (if tardily) illuminated, had cost him time, effort and money. This is because he saw them as an investment, a bid for a place in the sun.

All the rest of Henry's youthful entourage were at it. Why shouldn't he be? Especially when – he could reasonably feel – he understood better than anyone else what was at stake.

For More, who would be great himself, had glimpsed the capacity for greatness in Henry. And in this at least he was right. All his specific hopes in the king were to be dashed. But greatness there would be – even if the form it took crushed More, like so many others, in its path.

All that was for the future. Now there was the unfinished business of Henry VII's reign to be dealt with. As London filled with peers for the coronation, a meeting of the great council was summoned. This was an assembly of all the peers – lay and ecclesiastical – and so in effect a parliament without the commons. The great council met in June and, almost certainly, Henry himself presided. He would have been a sympathetic chairman. He had once worn the robes of a duke and held great offices of state. Indeed, in another, not very different world, he would have been sitting, as duke of York and earl marshal of England, as the senior peer to his brother King Arthur. As it was, his experience made him comfortable with the peerage in a way that his father, brought up abroad and always a foreigner on English soil, never had been.

His friends too sat on the benches, like Mountjoy. Perhaps More had been an adviser;

certainly he was aware of the outcome of the debates, which again he reflected in his congratulatory poems. 'The nobility,' he declared, 'long since at the mercy of the dregs of the population [that is, Empson and Dudley], the nobility, whose title has too long been without meaning, now lifts its head, now rejoices in such a king, and has proper reason for rejoicing.' This account suggests that the great council had witnessed historicist arguments about the proper role of the nobility in government which Henry, with his wide reading in English chronicle history, had supported and guided into action.

The result was that the great council marked the beginnings of a vigorous reassertion of noble power. The first concrete steps were taken a few weeks later, in July, when a series of high-powered investigatory commissions, known as commissions of 'oyer and terminer' ('to hear and to determine'), were issued. The commissioners, who were a mixture of regional magnates reinforced with senior judges, were empowered to investigate every crime from treason to trespass; they were also authorized to hear complaints about infringements 'of the statute of Magna Carta concerning the liberties of England', as well as any other breaches of 'the laws and customs of our kingdom of England'.

These last provisions stood the usual purpose of a commission of oyer and terminer on its head. Normally, such commissions were issued to enable the government to investigate the sins of the subject – like treasonable involvement in rebellion. The 1509 commissions, on the other hand, were an invitation to the subject to complain to the government about its own past high-handed executive actions. Such self-criticism is rare today; it was totally extraordinary in the sixteenth century. Just as remarkable is the invocation of Magna Carta. Magna Carta had slept for most of the fifteenth century, for then the problems of English government arose from the weakness and not the strength of the monarchy. But, with Henry VII's aggressive revival of the crown's power, the traditional symbol of resistance to royal tyranny had become relevant once more.

Originally of course Magna Carta had been the work of the nobility, and they always remained its most enthusiastic proponents. So it was still. I think, in 1509.

Then, as now, politics tended to slumber in the summer. But in 1509 the momentum of change was maintained well into the long vacation. On 18 July Dudley was tried for treason in London, and Empson in Northampton on 8 August. Both were found guilty, not only of preparing an armed rising, but also of seeking 'to separate and remove all the dukes, earls, barons and other magnates of England from the favour and council of the king and to subjugate the . . . magnates of England to the governance and rule of [Empson and Dudley]'. This was the traditional charge which the medieval nobility had used to bring down over-powerful – and low-born – ministers who threatened their privileged position as the king's councillors by right of birth. That it was revived now was as significant in its way as the renewed appeal to Magna Carta. Both pointed to a recrudescence of noble power, which must have been countenanced by Henry – if not actually encouraged by him.

The nobility were also major beneficiaries of the decision to cancel many of the bonds and recognizances imposed by Henry VII – whether as an act of grace by the new king or on the grounds that they had been 'made by undue means of certain of the council learned of our . . . late father . . . contrary to law, reason and good conscience, to the manifest charge and peril of the soul of our . . . late father'. This process too got fully under way in July 1509. On the twelfth Henry gave instructions to Dr John Young, the master of the rolls, to cancel the recognizances made by Lord Dacre; and on the twenty-first he lifted the vastly more onerous obligations on Lord Abergavenny, which totalled '£100,000 or thereabouts'; he released Henry Clifford's and Lord Delaware's recognizances in October; Lords Herbert's and Mountjoy's in November; and the duke of Buckingham's in December; while in March 1510, Henry cancelled the earl of Northumberland's recognizances and pardoned the huge fine of £10,000 which Henry VII had imposed on him.

★　　★　　★

July 1509 also saw the most dramatic policy reversal of all, when on the tenth Henry sent Sir Thomas Lovell to take Thomas Grey, marquess of Dorset, out of his imprisonment in the Castle of Calais and bring him back to England.

Long and bitter experience had convinced Henry VII that members of the extended Yorkist family, like Dorset, could not be trusted. But it was their close ties of friendship, if not more, with Edmund de la Pole, earl of Suffolk, that had proved the last straw. William Courtenay, Henry's uncle by marriage, had been arrested immediately; Dorset, Henry's cousin of the half-blood, a few years later. And, as we have seen, at the time of Henry VII's death both were languishing in the Castle of Calais, where they were awaiting – it was rumoured – imminent execution.

But Henry's feeling about the house of York was very different from his father's corrosive suspicion. They were his mother's side of the family, and his own ancestors and blood relations. He was comfortable with them, and – at least as important – they were comfortable with him. Once again. More puts his finger on it in his congratulatory poems. These not only hail Henry as the true scion of both the roses, they also emphasize that he inherited the best qualities of each side of the family:

Whatever virtues your ancestors had, these are yours too . . . For you, sir, have your father's wisdom, you have your mother's kindly strength, the devout intelligence of your paternal grandmother, the noble heart of your mother's father.

And indeed when it came to appearance, Henry looked much more Yorkist than Tudor. And he looked most of all (as we have seen already) like his Yorkist grandfather, Edward IV. This, Polydore Vergil was convinced, was a major part of his appeal. 'For just as Edward,' he observes, 'was the most warmly thought of by the English people among all English kings, so this successor of his, Henry, was very like him in general appearance, in greatness of mind and generosity and for that reason was the more acclaimed and approved of all.'

Even, it seems clear, by the Tudors' erstwhile dynastic rivals. The de la Poles remained unreconciled and unreconcilable, and Henry never tried to win them over (though he did make proper provisions for Suffolk's unfortunate wife, Margaret). But, for the rest, Henry was eager to offer them an honoured place as members of a newly united royal family, and they were just as eager to accept.

The formalities of Dorset's pardon and reconciliation with the king took barely a month. And even before they were completed he seems to have been back at court as one of the select group of intimates who accompanied Henry on his first summer progress.

There were other straws in the wind. Tuesday,

31 July was the last day Henry spent at Greenwich before leaving for the progress. Among the final items of business he transacted was the signing of bills for annuities for two of his closest female relations: £100 a year for Margaret Pole and 200 marks (£133.6s.8d) for Catherine Courtenay.

Margaret Pole, née Plantagenet, was daughter of Henry's great-uncle, George, duke of Clarence, and sister of Edward, earl of Warwick. The former had been executed by Edward IV in 1478, and the latter by Henry VII in 1499. This left Margaret with her royal blood but with little else following the attainders of both her father and her brother and the forfeiture of all their possessions. Soon after the battle of Stoke in 1487, Lady Margaret Beaufort engineered Margaret's marriage to Richard Pole, her nephew of the half-blood. The marriage took place in the presence of the king and queen; in 1493 Richard was appointed chamberlain to Prince Arthur and in 1499 he became knight of the Garter. With his abilities and his marriage, he seemed destined for great things. But he died in 1504, leaving his wife and her brood of five children in straitened circumstances.

In theory, Margaret's galaxy of royal relations should have ensured that she was well looked after in her widowhood. But these were dark days for the house of York. Rather uncharacteristically, Lady Margaret Beaufort seems to have done nothing; while Henry VII did as little as possible. He helped pay for Sir Richard's funeral expenses and his widow's initial resettlement costs of board, lodging and clothing. That, bearing in mind their ties of kinship and service, was the least that was decent. But then he quickly lost interest.

A better bet for Margaret was Catherine of Aragon. The two women had become close during Catherine's brief married life at Ludlow. But Catherine too seemed a broken reed after the death of her mother, Isabella of Castile, had reduced her value in the marriage market. It may be that Margaret and Catherine remained in touch in the last, miserable years of Henry VII's reign. But all they could have offered each other was cold comfort.

Henry VIII's accession transformed Margaret's prospects, as it had done so much else. Quite why in Margaret's case is not fully clear. Since all her connexions had been with Arthur's Marcher household and not Henry's Home Counties one, their paths had crossed only rarely, and Henry can scarcely have known her. But she had a powerful advocate in Catherine of Aragon, who chose her as one of her principal attendants during the coronation. Margaret was summoned to London, lodged at the king's expense and given livery clothing as though she had been a countess.

But Catherine's advocacy can only explain so much. And it certainly cannot account for Henry's eventual decision to restore Margaret to her ancestral status and make her a countess indeed and in her own right as heiress, through her mother, of the earls of Salisbury. Reginald, Margaret's third son and later cardinal, claimed that the restoration was the result of another act of deathbed repentance by Henry VII, and was enjoined upon his son with his last breaths. It is possible. But not, I think, very likely.

Instead, Henry restored Margaret – as he did his other Yorkist relations – because he wanted to. He thought it a duty (which is perhaps where his father's wishes come in). But it was also a pleasure. Like his mother, Elizabeth of York, he had a strong sense of family and family obligation. It flattered his ego to see himself (still in his teens!) as patriarch of a spreading family tree. It enormously increased the security of the Tudor dynasty. And above all, perhaps, it pointed the contrast between his father and himself: the former uneasily grasping a crown that was his by force rather than right; the latter in secure, relaxed and supremely rightful possession.

That, Henry might feel, was worth more than the lands of a few earldoms.

Complications over her late brother Warwick's attainder and rival claims to the lands (not least Henry's) delayed Margaret's restoration until the parliament of 1512. Long before then, others had jumped the queue – not least the family of the other noble lady who was given an annuity at the same time as Margaret: Catherine Courtenay, née Plantagenet.

There was a thirteen-year gap between Catherine, the next to youngest child of Edward IV and Elizabeth Woodville, and Elizabeth of York as the eldest. Nevertheless, the two sisters were close, and the disaster of the arrest and subsequent attainder of Catherine's husband, Lord William Courtenay, only made them closer. And after Elizabeth of York's early death, it was Catherine's nephew Henry who stepped into the breach. 'My Lady Catherine' and her attendant groom lived with Henry as members of his household as prince of Wales. As such, she gave him gifts, albeit modest ones as befitted her reduced circumstances – a gold ring, and another 'little ring with a little triangle diamond'. But Henry, as was his regular practice, gave them away again to other members of his entourage.

Nothing, however, should be read into this: Catherine was already a fixture in Henry's circle while he was still prince. And she and hers would benefit correspondingly when he became king: she appeared as the principal attendant on Henry's sister Mary for their father's funeral; she kept her place at court and she received a £40 reward while Henry was still at Greenwich in July 1509. But, above all, with the grant of her annuity came formal recognition as 'the king's aunt'.

Sorting out the position of her husband, Lord William Courtenay, took much longer, however, since he found himself in a legal minefield. Following his involvement in the Suffolk affair, he had been attainted by act of parliament in 1504. The act acknowledged that his father Edward Courtenay, earl of Devon, was 'not privy or partner to the offences of his son', and therefore guaranteed the earl his property for life. But, the act declared, in view of William's treason, 'it were not reason he should inherit'; instead, it provided that 'immediately after [the earl's] death' all his possessions should 'revert to the king'. A final clause, reflecting the uncertainties of the time, also gave Henry VII the power to reverse William's attainder by 'pardon of treason by the king's letters patent under his great seal made'.

William now found himself caught between these several provisions of the act as between the upper and nether millstones. And they threatened to grind him as fine. His father had died on 29 May 1509. This immediately gave effect to the forfeiture of the earldom and its lands. But Henry VII had also died a month earlier. And this, unfortunately for William, meant that the king's power to reverse the attainder by letters patent had died with him.

This was a challenge to Henry as much as to William. Henry now had to learn another lesson: not even he could abrogate an act of parliament; only another act of another parliament could do that.

But if Henry could not repeal the act, he could evade it. And that is what he now proceeded to do. William was still in custody in Calais in September 1509. There, despite his imprisonment, he was evidently living in some style, since his gaoler complained of 'his great charge' in keeping him. Then, at some point in the next few months, he was released and brought back to England. And by 1 June 1510 he was slugging it out in a tourney with his old friend and sparring partner, Sir Thomas Knyvet. It was as though the seven years which had elapsed since his arrest in 1502 had vanished like a bad dream.

Not quite, however. William might be back at court and in favour. But he was still in legal limbo. Finally, and no doubt many hours of lawyers' time later, a solution was come up with. On 9 May 1511 Henry reversed William's attainder by letters patent 'as much as is legally in our power' (*quantum in nobis est*). Then, the following day, on 10 May, he created him earl of Devon by royal charter. It remained only for Henry formally to invest him with the earldom by girding on a sword and his restoration would be complete.

But, only a month later, and before the ceremony could be carried out, William, who had survived so many legal threats to his life, died of a sudden attack of pleurisy on 9 June. His body lay 'in his chamber in the court' at Greenwich, before being taken by river for burial at the Black Friars. His old jousting companions, like Sir Thomas Knyvet and Sir Edward Howard, acted as his mourners.

And Henry, able to make full reparation at last, ordered him to be buried with the honours due to an earl.

This was not quite the new heaven and new earth of More's messianic verses. But it did represent a genuine fresh start in politics. It was also a renewal of the hope of dynastic reconciliation which had been offered long ago by the marriage of Henry's parents and then so quickly dashed.

Undoubtedly, Henry had help and advice. More himself might have come in useful, for there is a strikingly 'Yorkist' vein running through his early works. We have already seen something of this in his 'Rueful Lamentation' for Henry's mother, Elizabeth of York; even more striking is the measured, stately opening of his *History of King Richard III*, which he wrote three or four years after Henry's accession. This lists Edward IV's 'much fair issue', beginning with the two princes and ending with a delightful thumbnail sketch of Catherine, wife of William Courtenay:

> [She], long time tossed in either fortune, sometime in wealth, oft in adversity, at the last, if this be the last, for yet she liveth, is by the benignity of her nephew, King Henry VIII, in very prosperous estate, and worthy of her birth and virtue.

And More, he could reflect with satisfaction, had helped bring about this happy ending: he acted as one of her legal advisers in her final settlement with Henry; he had also, we can be sure, put in a good word behind the scenes.

But More's 'Yorkist' sympathies only mattered because they were shared by Henry. They also formed part of a wider pattern, in which Henry, despite his reaction against his father, showed himself very much a chip off the old block. Henry the elder had kept the English elites in fear by the recognizances he had imposed; Henry the younger would bind them to him with gratitude for the recognizances he had cancelled.

But he was just as careful to record the facts. A list of the cancelled recognizances was drawn up, carefully noting the name of the recognizors and the nature, cause and amount of each obligation. It was prefaced with an elaborate heading, written in Henry's name, and certainly expressing his sentiments. He may even have dictated it word for word.

Hereafter ensue divers recognizances . . . drawn by our special commandment out of divers books signed with the hand of our dearest father, to rest of remembrance in this present book, to the intent it may appear to us hereafter how favourable and benevolent sovereign lord we have been unto divers our nobles and other our subjects, in discharge and pardoning of many and sundry . . . weighty causes.

There, alongside dozens of lesser fry, were the names of Northumberland and Dorset, Dacre and Darcy, and Dorset's mother, the dowager marchioness. But the book was not only to record Henry's generosity, it was also to serve as a reminder to the recipients of what they owed him in turn – not in money, as to his father, but in something more precious: gratitude. They had been spared much: 'whereby they stand the more especially bounden unto us, and therefore truly and faithfully to serve us . . . when and as oft as the case . . . shall require'.

And Henry already knew the circumstances in which he would call in these debts of gratitude: it was war.

CHAPTER 23

BREAKING FREE:
WILLIAM COMPTON

Henry decided to spend his first Christmas as king at Richmond, his father's great palace to the west of London, with its clustering onion-domes, its galleries, gardens and parks.

But first, en route from Greenwich, he stopped off at the Tower on 12–14 December 1509. The Tower was not only palace and prison, it was also the principal arsenal of the kingdom and a working fortress with a massive complement of heavy cannon. All this was irresistible to Henry, for whom fortifications and ordnance were a lifelong passion. No doubt he had used his residence in the Tower in the first few weeks of his reign to familiarize himself with the set-up and in July he issued an 'ordnance' to regulate the yeomen of the guard on garrison duty there. Now this flying visit gave the gunners of the Tower the opportunity to nobble *him*. Headed by Richard Falconer, the master gunner, they approached Henry in a body on 14 December and got him to sign the 'bills' for the letters patent for their wages. All but Falconer have foreign names and one, Blasius Billard, is explicitly described as 'Sowecher' or 'Swiss'.

Making England less dependent on imports and foreign expertise in munitions would be one of Henry's great aims – and achievements.

Henry arrived at Richmond on the twenty-third and the familiar round of Christmas festivities began. On Christmas Day he heard mass and took communion (though only the consecrated wafer) in the chapel royal and the choir sang *Gloria in excelsis Deo*; there were plays in the hall on Thursday the twenty-seventh and Sunday the thirtieth; on New Year's Day he gave and received gifts and rewarded the heralds when they proclaimed his titles (he really was king!) and cried 'Largesse!'; and on Twelfth Night he watched another play in the hall.

It was the same as the Christmases of his childhood and youth. Yet it was different too because he, not his father, was king. But, he perhaps found himself wondering, just *how* different?

Still the great armed image of his father as the prince of warrior kings looked down on him from the roof of the hall. Still there were the memories of the endless plots and pretenders of his father's reign. He had tried to lay to rest as many of these ghosts as possible. But some remained obstinately unexorcised, as he had just been reminded when he paid out the £200 half-yearly instalment of the vast annuity of £400 which his father had given Sir

Robert Curzon as his reward for betraying Edmund de la Pole, earl of Suffolk. And still Suffolk and his youngest brother William languished in the Tower, where he too had so recently stayed.

And still, above all, the council – *his* council – was dominated by his father's ministers who acted towards him, he must often have felt, as a sort of collective father: their favourite word too was 'no'.

Even his wife Catherine of Aragon, of whom he was genuinely fond, constantly reminded him that he still had a father in Ferdinand of Aragon, to whom he likewise owed a duty of filial obedience:

> As to the king my lord [she wrote to *her* father Ferdinand a month after her marriage] amongst the reasons that oblige me to love him much more than myself, the one most strong . . . is his being so true a son of your highness, with desire of greater obedience and love to serve you than ever son had to his father.

Was there no escape from fathers?

One who *had* escaped early from his own father was William Compton, William Thomas's colleague as groom of the privy chamber to Henry as prince of Wales. Compton's father Edmund, a modest Warwickshire gentleman, had died on 21 April 1493 – sixteen years to the day before Henry VII – leaving as his heir his son William, aged 'eleven years old and more'. We do not know when or by whose patronage William joined Prince Henry's household. But by the end of Henry VII's reign he was one of Henry's closest attendants. Along with William Royt, who acted as Henry's usher, Compton was trusted to ride ahead and prepare Henry's chambers in the next residence the court was due to use.

Henry, as princes of Wales tend to be, was fussy about such things. Compton was gaining valuable experience in what his master wanted and how to deliver it.

He would have plenty of opportunity to use it when Henry became king.

For then his rise was meteoric. By the time of the coronation on 24 June Compton was already, along with Thomas, the leading member of the new king's privy or secret chamber. He is not formally described as groom of the stool till almost a year later, in April 1510, but almost certainly he had stepped into Hugh Denys's shoes within weeks or even days of Henry's accession. And soon he was handling much greater sums of money than his predecessor ever had.

Denys had dealt in the dribs and drabs wrung out of Henry VII's subjects by the surveyor of the king's prerogative; Compton, by contrast, found himself the recipient of the riches which, para-doxically, descended on the new king as a result of his own generosity. Henry (in so far as he had

338

been allowed to) had dealt out largesse with an open hand – whether as straightforward patronage, cancelled bonds and recognizances, or his 'much more ample, gracious and beneficial' general pardon. But all needed royal letters patent to put them into effect. And letters patent, as we have seen, needed to be paid for.

The resulting cash windfall was collected in the first instance by the financial officer of the chancery, known as the clerk of the hanaper. In the first twelve weeks of the reign, the money – some £2,000 – was handed over directly to the king. Thereafter, as was to become the practice in so many instances, great and small, Compton acted on Henry's behalf and received the money instead: £1,040 on 1 December (which no doubt came in handy for Christmas), £607 on 1 March 1510, £400 in both June and July, and £340 in November. Nor was this all. At the same time, Compton received other large sums from the king's consolidated land revenues: £2,328 in 1509–10, £1,406 in 1510–11, and £812 in 1511–12.

In all of this Compton was simply a proxy for Henry: he was receiving large sums because Henry wished to spend large sums on his personal pleasures and amusements and his everyday living. For Henry's attitude to money was both like and very unlike his father's. Both were fond of money and both needed lots of it. But there the resemblance ended. Henry's father, at least towards the end of his reign, came to see the accumulation of money as an end in itself, which is why he left so much of it. For Henry, on the other hand, money was only a means to an end, be it honour, glory, immortality – or simply having a good time.

In a nutshell, the father was a saver; the son, a spender.

Which is why, having spent several fortunes in the course of his reign, Henry died almost as heavily in debt as his father had been in credit.

Compton's financial role at the beginning of the reign was the perfect epitome of this: the privy purse, as his account became known, was a purely spending agency. And it was the only one in which Henry showed any direct interest or involvement.

Compton would have been at the king's side throughout the Christmas and New Year festivities. But it was also his job to be the king's eyes and ears. And it was no doubt through Compton that Henry heard 'secretly' that 'diverse gentlemen' had organized a joust at Richmond for 12 January 1510.

This was both a challenge and an opportunity. Henry, to his mounting frustration, had been held to his father's veto on participation in tournaments: 'the king ran never openly before', as the chronicler Edward Hall observes in his account of the affair.

But, Henry quickly decided, this tournament, relatively low-key and well away from the glare of publicity in London, might provide just the opportunity he had been waiting for to challenge – or at least evade – the ban on his taking part in jousting. And he turned to Compton to find the means. For Compton had yet another job. It was the same as other confidential servants' throughout the ages, in literature as in life: Sancho Panza for his master, Don Quixote; Figaro for his, Count Almaviva; Jeeves for his, the ineffable Bertie Wooster. So it was for Compton and Henry. Master and man were a team, a pantomime horse, in which Compton – like his fictional counterparts – had, simultaneously, to play the rear legs and be the brains of the enterprise.

Between the two of them, it was decided that Henry should take part in the joust. But he would do so incognito, 'unknown to all persons and unlooked for'. This more or less squared the circle. Henry would have his fun, without openly defying the ban on his taking part. Compton would ride as Henry's aide or assistant, just like Sancho Panza with Don Quixote, and he would sort out the practical details.

This he did with his accustomed efficiency. Arms, armour and horses were prepared and the two of them were 'secretly armed in the little park of Richmond'.

Then they entered the lists. 'Stranger' knights, with visors closed and without identifying coats of arms, were stock figures of chivalric fiction. Henry was now taking part in one of the knightly romances that were a staple of his teenage reading. And, as with most parts, he played it well. So did Compton. 'There were broken many staves', Hall reports, 'and great praise [was] given to the two strangers.'

But then near disaster struck and wrecked the scheme. Compton's next opponent was Sir Edward Neville. Neville, the younger brother of Lord Abergavenny, was one of the original 'spears' appointed under Henry's father. As such, he was a more-or-less professional jouster. He also shared Henry's own height and physique; indeed, when they were masked in a court revel, it was easy to mix them up. This combination was too much for Compton: Neville 'hurt him sore, and [Compton] was likely to die'.

The play was now in danger of turning into a tragedy. It was time to bring down the curtain. 'One person there was that knew the king, and cried "God save the king!"' But that only made matters worse. Was the badly injured stranger-knight the king? Was it accident or treason? 'With that', Hall reports, 'all the people were astonished.'

It was left to Henry to save the day, which he did in a single dramatic gesture. 'Then the king disclosed himself, to the great comfort of all the people.'

Henry, as was to become a habit, got away with it. Compton, too, made a good recovery from his accident and soon resumed his place as the king's right-hand man.

Henry had broken the ban on participation, but not flagrantly. And he continued to tread warily. There was of course no question of going back to his seat in the royal box. Instead, he decided that his next outing would be in a running at the ring. For who could object at that? Even his father had allowed him to do it and had actually watched him perform.

Now there was no father, but there were his father-in-law Ferdinand's ambassadors to impress and patronize. They 'had never seen the king in harness [armour]' and were eager to do so. Henry was only too happy to oblige. The competition was set for 17 March and Henry captained one of the two teams. Over their armour, both he and his horse were magnificently attired in purple velvet, cut in letter shapes and backed in cloth-of-gold, so that it looked as though it had been embroidered with various mottoes. There was also a thick scattering of hundreds of sheaves of arrows (for Aragon) and castles (for Castile). These were made of pure gold and came from the stores of treasure that Compton had already begun to accumulate.

Then came the contest. Everybody ran twelve courses. Henry, who carried the ring off five times and touched it thrice, did best and was awarded the prize. The ambassadors crowded round to congratulate him. Could they have some of the badges?, they asked. Grandly, Henry agreed and they helped themselves. Hall xenophobically suggests that they 'took all or the more part'. The accounts of Richard Gibson, the master of the revels, tell a different story. 'Given by the king', they note, 'to the lords of Spain that beheld the king's running at the ring: 10 pieces.'

After the show was over, the outfits of the king and his horse were handed back over to Henry, who promptly passed them on to 'Mr Compton'.

Next time, Henry and Compton decided, Henry's public was ready for him to take part in a real joust. Or at least some of them were. For, according to Hall, there was a clear division of opinion between young and old. 'All young persons highly praised' Henry's decision to ride in the lists, he writes, 'but the ancient fathers much doubted'. Then he elaborates: the latter 'consider [ed] the tender youth of the king, and divers chances of horse and armour: in so much that it was openly spoken, that steel was not so strong, but that it might be broken, nor no horse could be so sure of foot, but he may fall'.

Henry had had enough of fathers, ancient or otherwise, and he carried on regardless: 'yet, for all these doubts, the lusty prince proceeded to his challenge'. And to the next. And the next.

There was no stopping him now.

★　★　★

Compton's rise quickly attracted attention. 'I have written to you . . . the credit that one named Compton has with the king of England,' the French ambassador informed his government back home. 'It is he of this kingdom who has the most [credit] for the moment and to whom [Henry] speaks the most about his affair[s].' Others were less sure. Indeed, Lord Herbert of Cherbury, a seventeenth-century scholar-nobleman and Henry's first biographer, saw him as rising without trace. Compton, he notes, was next in the king's favour to the two giants of the council, Foxe and Surrey. But, he claims, he could be discounted since he was 'more attentive to his profit than public affairs'. That is not quite, however, what Herbert's source, Polydore Vergil, says:

> And admitted to the same wrestling-school [of politics], the third man [after Foxe and Surrey] was William Compton, the first minister of the royal bedchamber, *but since he concerned himself more with things of an intimate nature rather than matters of state [or 'power'],* he gave no cause for suspicion.

Vergil, as usual, gets it about right. But, in a personal monarchy, 'things of an intimate nature' are not unimportant. Compton's role, as Jeeves to Henry's Wooster, helped the boy to begin to find himself as a man and a king. Most important was their incognito appearance in the Richmond tournament. It might look like a schoolboy prank, but it was also Henry's first challenge to the near paternal authority of his council. And it would not have happened without Compton.

Moreover, once tasted, Henry found that getting his own way became addictive. And there would be others – more forceful and ambitious than Compton – who realized this and determined to give him what he wanted.

They were not, of course, altruistic. For giving Henry his head would also give them what *they* wanted: power.

CHAPTER 24

MARRIED LIFE

'Choose a wife for yourself and always love her only,' Skelton had advised his young charge eight years previously in the *Speculum principis* which he had presented to Henry at Eltham in 1501. Eight years are a long time in the life of a young man – long enough, indeed, to forget not only the advice but its giver. And that, evidently, is what Skelton feared had happened. He had written and despatched a set of congratulatory verses on Henry's accession, entitled 'A laud and praise made for our sovereign lord the king':

> The rose both white and red
> In one rose now doth grow;
> Grace the seed did sow.
> England now gather flowers,
> Exclude now all dolours.

But no messenger had arrived to summon him back to court from his fenny exile in Diss. So he tried again. This time he sought to revive youthful memories of those days at Eltham by sending

347

Henry a second copy of his *Speculum*, topped and tailed by other occasional verses and ending with a passionate complaint about the way Henry was neglecting his old tutor:

> Shall I blame this notable failure of with-drawn generosity on so great and so munificent a king? May God avert it! . . . Farewell, my prince [he ends], easily prince of all princes. Know that you are the king: that you rule, and are not ruled. Hear Samuel; read Daniel: remove Ishmael, remove him, remove him!

For the time being, however, Henry remained impervious to his pleas.

But if Henry had apparently forgotten Skelton, he had taken his advice to heart. For Henry really does seem to have chosen Catherine for himself. And he was – or at least he persuaded himself that he was – seriously in love with her. 'As for that entire love which we bear to [Catherine]', he wrote to her father, Ferdinand of Aragon, it is such that 'even if we were still free, it is she . . . we would choose for our wife before all other'. That was in July 1509, a month after their wedding and in the first flush marital happiness.

But would he love her 'always' as Skelton enjoined? Would he even love her very long?

★　★　★

Such thoughts were far from everyone's mind when another Anglo–Spanish marriage took place, between Henry's old mentor, Lord Mountjoy, and Ines de Veñegas, one of Catherine's Spanish ladies. This was the second Spanish marriage in the Mountjoy family. A century previously, one of Mountjoy's ancestors had married a lady-in-waiting of Constance of Castile, second wife to John of Gaunt, duke of Lancaster, and Mountjoy bore in his arms the two wolves sable of the house of Ayala to prove it. This second marriage, in strikingly similar circumstances to the first, had Henry's enthusiastic backing. '[He] thinks', he wrote to his father-in-law, Ferdinand of Aragon, 'it very desirable that Spanish and English families should be united by family ties.' Henry warmly endorsed Mountjoy himself as 'one of his barons, whom he holds in high esteem', and he sought Ferdinand's support for the new Lady Mountjoy's attempts to recover money she was owed in Spain.

And Henry did all this in a letter, written in Latin and in his own hand – which, as he hated the business of writing, was always a sign of real commitment.

A day or two after writing the letter on 30 July, Henry and Catherine set out on their first summer progress. It took the form of a complete circuit round London, through the parks and pleasure grounds that then ringed the capital. Many were familiar to Henry from his childhood and youth:

Woking, which death had redelivered him from the grasping hands of his grandmother; Farnham, where his deceased brother Arthur had spent the first months of his short life; and Hanworth and Wanstead, his father's *maisons de retraite*, where Henry had lived in enforced proximity to the old king in the last years of his reign. En route, Henry diverted himself, as he informed Ferdinand, with 'birding, hunting, and other innocent and honest pastimes, also in visiting different parts of his kingdom'. He 'does not', Henry added hastily, 'on that account neglect affairs of state'.

Perhaps. But, then as now, there was rarely much going on in the summer months. Instead, Henry and Catherine were free to begin to discover England – and each other. It is clear they liked what they found.

The progress ended in late October at Greenwich. This was Henry's own birthplace, Henry and Catherine had been married there, and, they decided, it would be where their first child was born as well.

For Catherine was pregnant. Henry informed Ferdinand of the news at the beginning of November. 'Your daughter', he wrote, 'with the favour of heaven has conceived in her womb a living child, and is right heavy herewith, which we signify to your majesty for the great joy thereof that we take and the exultation of our whole realm.'

★　★　★

By then, if the later calculations about the date of the delivery are to be believed, Catherine was about five months pregnant. The fact cast Henry's behaviour over Christmas in a darker light. With his wife 'right heavy', the schoolboy antics of riding incognito in the joust on 12 January now look like wilful self-indulgence. And worse was to come. On 18 January, 'suddenly in a morning', Henry and twelve companions burst into the queen's chamber, all dressed in Kendal Green like Robin Hood and his Merry Men, and complete with a woman got up as Maid Marian.

It was supposed to be done 'for a gladness to the queen's grace'. In fact it seems to have given her a nasty surprise: 'the queen', Hall reports, 'the ladies and all other there were abashed, as well for the strange sight, as also for their sudden coming'. A few perfunctory steps were danced, then Henry and his fellow revellers withdrew – perhaps a little abashed in their turn.

Was Henry's boisterous adolescent behaviour starting to become a strain for Catherine? Or was it all part of the charm?

Whatever Catherine's feelings about her husband, all at least seemed to be going well with her pregnancy. The couple paid a brief visit to Greenwich in mid-January to get the preparations for her lying-in under way. The court then returned to Westminster for Henry's first parliament.

And at Westminster on the morning of 31 January Catherine suddenly miscarried of a baby girl. According to her confessor, she had experienced no discomfort or other symptoms, 'except that one knee pained her the night before'. The miscarriage was kept secret, the confessor continued, so that 'no one knew about it . . . except the king . . . two Spanish women, a physician and I'. Instead of diminishing, however, Catherine's belly remained swollen and, if anything, got bigger. This was probably the result of infection, but her physician persuaded himself that she remained pregnant with a second foetus. And, despite Catherine's own doubts and the fact that her periods resumed, he was believed.

The ceremonious machinery of a royal birth now moved inexorably into gear. In mid-February the Venetian ambassador 'congratulated the king on the queen's pregnancy' and on the twenty-sixth a warrant was issued for the materials needed to refurbish 'our nursery, God willing'. This was probably the very nursery in which Henry himself had been suckled. The 'cradle of estate', where he had once lain, was to be re-covered in crimson cloth-of-gold and the royal arms 'amended if need be'. The customary generous supplies of pillows, sheets, counterpanes and swaddling bands were to be provided, together with beds for the wet-nurse and the two rockers, and hangings for the chamber of the lady mistress.

Even the lady mistress was the same Elizabeth Denton who had ruled Henry's infancy with a rod of iron – always tempered, it would seem, for her beguiling charge. For Henry retained the fondest memories of her. Many people from Henry's youth had done well out of his accession, including his wet-nurse, Anne Lock. But few did as well as Mrs Denton. In quick succession she had been given an income, accommodation and a lifetime's supply of wine. All were on a lavish scale: an annuity of £50, the keepership of The Coldharbour – formerly Lady Margaret Beaufort's London residence, where Henry and his mother had first taken refuge from the threat of the Cornish rebels in 1497 – and a tun of Gascon wine a year.

Now Henry was about to trust his first-born to her as well.

As Catherine's due date approached, Henry became all solicitude. On 28 February, shortly before she was due to begin her formal confinement by 'taking to her chamber', Henry laid on a banquet in the parliament chamber at Westminster for all the foreign ambassadors then resident in his court. He led Catherine into the chamber and placed her, to all appearances in the final stages of pregnancy, on the royal throne to preside over the proceedings. Nor did his condescension stop there, as he acted every role in the lexicon of hospitality. He served as his own master of ceremonies, directing the ambassadors and ladies to their seats in person. And he revelled in playing the good host as, refusing to sit himself, he 'walked from place to place, making cheer to the queen and the strangers'.

No one, then or subsequently, could be more charming than Henry when he felt so inclined – or felt he had to be.

Soon after the banquet the court moved to Greenwich and the queen began her formal confinement. It was now only a matter of weeks before Catherine was due to go into labour and Henry – like many expectant fathers – flung himself into a welter of preparations. First he turned his mind to the important business of the christening. The precedents of Henry's own birth and those of his siblings were pored over and. *The Ryalle Book* consulted. For *his* child was to have an entry into the world as grand as any of his or her royal predecessors. He signed the necessary warrant on 12 March. This ordered the supply of red cloth to cover the steps of the font and 'cypress' to line it, just as had been done for his own christening. The font itself was to be the great silver font of Canterbury, in which the baby Henry had been plunged by Bishop Foxe, who was now his own chief minister. Finally, and with that eye for detail which was already pronounced, he ordered another six ells (seven and a half yards) of good quality linen to make 'aprons and napkins for four gentlemen [-in-waiting] . . . according to the old use and custom in that case heretofore used'.

He or one of his assistants also noticed that an item had been forgotten for the nursery. This was the canopy 'to hang over the cradle of estate in our nursery'. Another warrant was drawn up for the delivery of the necessary materials to one of the yeomen ushers of 'our dearest wife the queen'. It was dated at Greenwich in 'the first year of our reign'. But the day – that all important day when Catherine would be delivered – was left blank.

That day never came. It was not for want of waiting. For of course calculations in these matters were never precise. Thus, probably, Henry consoled himself as Catherine remained in her courtly purdah for March. And April. And on into May.

But then he snapped. He had not had sex with Catherine since she entered her darkened, tapestry hung chamber in early March and his patience was exhausted. Moreover, inside the birthing chamber – impenetrable to men – the truth was gradually dawning on the queen's terrified entourage.

For her 'right heavy belly' began to go down of its own accord. Or, as her confessor (who *was* allowed into her chamber) put it sententiously: 'it has pleased our Lord to be her physician in such a way that the swelling decreased'. It was no thanks to her actual physician, whose false diagnosis of a continued pregnancy after her miscarriage in January had started the whole sorry business. Or to her women, who had refused to draw the obvious conclusion from her resumed periods. Or, indeed, to Catherine herself, who had let herself be persuaded, it would seem, against her own better judgment.

Wise after the event, the newly arrived Spanish ambassador, Luis Caroz, railed at the folly of supposed experts who would 'affirm that a menstruating woman was pregnant and . . . make her withdraw publicly for her delivery'.

But that did not solve the problem of how to break the news to Henry. Finally it was probably Catherine herself who plucked up the courage. Her pregnancy had been a false one. The preparations, the warrants had been in vain. The ambassadorial congratulations rang hollow.

Henry had been misled into taking part in a very public and humiliating farce.

The preparations were stood down. The great silver font was returned to its custodians at Canterbury. And Henry was left with his thoughts.

We do not know his real reactions. His councillors may have spoken for him when they made plain they were 'very vexed and angry' – though, from courtesy, they protested they blamed Catherine's women rather than the queen herself. More darkly, they also began to draw dangerous conclusions about Catherine's infertility: murmuring that 'since the queen is not pregnant, she is incapable of conceiving'.

On the other hand, her confessor blithely asserted that all was well and that 'the king my lord [Henry] adores her, and her highness [Catherine] him'.

Possibly. But there was also the problem of going public with the news and what spin to put upon it. This exercised all those in the know. Ambassador Caroz first discussed it with the council. And then, in view of the delicacy of the matter, he had an audience with Henry in person. 'I have spoken with the king', he reported home, 'as to what we are to say of the queen's confinement.' 'They find the case so difficult', he continued, 'that they do not know what to determine.'

Finally, as governments usually do in such circumstances, they decided to lie. The queen, it was blandly announced, had suffered a miscarriage. The 'news' was current in London in the first week of June and on the eighth the Venetian ambassador reported it in despatches: 'The queen', he wrote, 'has had a miscarriage, to the great sorrow of everyone.' 'They are forming fresh projects,' he added somewhat mysteriously.

But it was not only the government which lied. So did Catherine. And to her own father, to whom she repeated the official line in a letter written in her own hand. Indeed she went further. The official communiqués seem to have left the date of the miscarriage studiously vague. But Catherine, in her letter dated 27 May, informed Ferdinand that it had happened 'some days before'.

We can sympathize with Catherine's motives, since she so evidently feared her father's wrath. Do not be angry, she pleaded, 'for it has been the will of God'. Whatever its motives, however, a lie is a lie.

And one lie tends to lead to another. 'She and the king her husband are cheerful,' she protested to her father. In fact, they had just had their first serious quarrel.

This also had arisen out of her false pregnancy. Henry, as we have seen, had been excluded from his wife's bed, by both etiquette and respect for her supposed condition, for nearly three months. And the strain was beginning to tell.

Enter William Compton once more, this time in the role of Leporello to Henry's would-be Don Giovanni.

Ambassador Caroz reported the resulting imbroglio to his government in cipher and breathless haste. Edward Stafford, duke of Buckingham, he explained, had two sisters, Elizabeth and Anne. Both lived in the palace as the queen's ladies-in-waiting and both were married, Elizabeth to Robert Ratcliffe, Lord Fitzwalter, and Anne to George Hastings, Lord Hastings. Elizabeth was the elder and had long been a fixture in Henry's life. She had been his mother's principal attendant, and had kept in touch with Henry after Elizabeth of York's death, when she gave him a present of 'a pomander of gold with a red rose enamelled'. She had quickly become the favourite of Catherine of Aragon as well.

Anne was younger, fresher and – it would seem – soon caught the eye of Henry, 'who', Caroz reports knowingly, 'went after her'. Catherine's extended lying-in provided an opportunity – and Henry's resulting enforced abstinence from marital sex an incentive – for the affair to develop.

And, as usual, Henry turned to Compton to get him what he wanted.

Compton resorted to the go-between's old trick of pretending to woo Anne on his own behalf. But, bearing in mind his known place in Henry's favour, the stratagem was transparent and Elizabeth became seriously concerned at the threat to her sister's virtue. She took her brother the duke, her husband and her brother-in-law Lord Hastings, into her confidence and sought their advice. Buckingham reacted to the disparagement of his family honour with typical choleric impetuosity. He was in Anne's chamber at court when Compton entered to speak with her. The duke accosted him and 'reproached [him] in many and very hard words'.

It was now Henry's turn to lose his temper at

the insult to his confidential servant and 'he repri-manded the duke angrily'. Outraged to be upbraided by one whom he regarded as little more than a boy, Buckingham withdrew in a huff from court, while Hastings packed Anne off to a convent sixty miles away, where she was out of even the king's reach.

Once again Henry escalated the affair. The day after Anne's removal, he turned Elizabeth and Fitzwalter out of the palace. And he wanted to go further still. He believed that Elizabeth had other minions at court who went 'about the palace insidiously spying out every unwatched moment in order to tell the queen'. Henry wanted to expel all these as well until, on cooler reflection, he decided that it would cause 'too great a scandal'.

The damage was done, however, and the affair became public knowledge. As did the fact that Catherine had sided with Buckingham against her husband. 'Afterwards', Caroz reports, 'almost all the court knew that the queen had been vexed with the king, and the king with her, and thus this storm went on between them.'

Compton's position also threatened to become an issue: Catherine 'by no means conceals her ill-will towards Compton, and the king is very sorry for it'.

But then there was another twist in the extra-ordinary tale of Catherine's first pregnancy. Henry had continued to sleep with Catherine until the very eve of her confinement at the beginning of March. Clad only in his nightgown and shirt, he would have been escorted to the door of the queen's chamber by Compton. Early in the marriage William Thomas, who was almost as close to Henry as Compton, would probably have played the role of escort too. But no longer. For Thomas had quickly given up his post: he is last described as a groom of the privy chamber on 17 April 1510 and had disappeared from the privy chamber list by December. Was he tired of his existence at court? Eager for the delights of life as a prosperous Welsh country gentleman?

Or did he know too much about Catherine's first marriage with Henry's elder brother Arthur for her to feel comfortable with his presence?

After all, the Anne Stafford affair shows that Catherine was not shy of making her feelings known and that she could be a formidable and ruthless opponent.

She also – which mattered most of all – had luck. Her periods, which had resumed soon after her miscarriage in January, gave Caroz some concern. She does 'not menstruate well', he fretted, and blamed her diet. Be that as it may, and despite the infection in her uterus, she was fertile enough for Henry to impregnate her in late February or early March.

The result was bizarre: by late May, when she

finally gave up on her false pregnancy, she was *really* pregnant for the second time.

And this time all went smoothly. At the end of October the couple took up residence at Richmond. In November, the formal preparations for the lying-in and christening got under way and the prior of Canterbury was put on stand-by to send up the font. Towards the end of the month, Catherine began her confinement, which continued through the Christmas festivities. Then, on New Year's Eve she went into labour and the baby was born at half past one the following morning.

It was healthy. It was a boy. It was the best New Year's gift that Henry had ever received.

London went wild: bells were rung; bonfires lit; the streets ran with wine; thanksgiving processions of clergy wended through the City and at the Tower the gunners blasted their way through 207 pounds of gunpowder as the great cannon thundered out salute after salute.

The christening took place on the following Sunday, 5 January. A processional way, twenty-four feet wide, was made from the hall doors to the adjacent church of the Friars Observant. The way was railed, gravelled and hung with cloth of arras, as was the church itself. The ceremony was conducted 'with very great pomp and rejoicing': the king of France was godfather and the

Habsburg Archduchess Margaret godmother; the ambassadors of France, Spain, Venice and the papacy were in attendance and the boy was christened Henry.

That same day Henry, bursting with pride and love, issued a challenge to a celebratory tournament and got the preparations under way.

He then went on a pilgrimage of thanksgiving to Our Lady of Walsingham in Norfolk. He left on the eleventh and reached the shrine shortly after the twentieth. Erasmus, Henry's acquaintance and correspondent, visited Walsingham the following year and, no doubt, the king's experience was much like his.

The relic of the Virgin's milk was kept on the high altar. It was solidified, like 'powered chalk, tempered with white of egg', and protected by a crystal vial. The custodian, wearing a linen vestment with a stole round his neck, prostrated himself in adoration before proffering the sacred vial to be kissed. The pilgrim knelt on the lowest step of the altar and reverently touched the relic with his or her lips.

Then the custodian held out a board 'like those used in Germany by toll collectors on bridges'. It was for a cash offering.

Henry offered £1.13s.4d.

And, just as with the devotions in the bede-roll of his youth, his act of piety gained him remission of forty days in purgatory.

★ ★ ★

363

Henry was back at the Tower by 31 January 1511. By this time Catherine was 'churched', or ritually purified from the pollution of childbirth. She was also fully recovered from its physical after-effects and ready to preside over the joust which Henry had prepared in her honour. These took place at Westminster on 12 and 13 February and were of unparalleled magnificence. Everything was blue velvet, damask and cloth-of-gold, and the costumes and pavilions of Henry and his three fellow challengers were covered with letters of 'H' and 'K', likewise of fine gold.

Henry ran as *Coeur Loyall* ('Sir Loyal Heart'). On the first day of the tournament the prize was carried off by his principal aid, Sir Thomas Knyvet, who ran under the *nom de guerre* of *Vaillaunt Desyre*. However, Henry, as usual, stole the show by putting on an impromptu display of spectacular horsemanship, which left one observer in ecstasy:

> No man could do better, nor sit more close nor faster, nor yet keep his stirrups more surely. For notwithstanding the horse was very courageous and excellent in leaping, turning and exceeding flinging, he [Henry] moved no more upon him than he had been holding a soft and plain trot.

But this was just the overture. When Henry came in front of the queen's grandstand or tent, he performed another set of manoeuvres and 'leapt and coursed the horse up and down in wonderful manner'. Finally, he turned his horse's hooves against the massive wooden barrier or tilt which ran down the centre of the lists and 'caused him to fling and beat the boards with his feet'. The noise was ear-splitting and 'rebounded about the place as it had been shot of guns'.

Finally, Henry turned to the queen, 'made a lowly obeisance [bow] and so passed in a demure manner into Westminster Hall'.

There he quickly unarmed and returned to Catherine's grandstand, 'where shortly after . . . he was seen . . . kissing and clipping [hugging] her in most loving manner'.

It was the same at the end of the second day of the tournament, when Henry carried off the prize. This time, he was all chivalrous submission. He rode round the lists bareheaded at a slow, solemn trot, and each time he passed in front of the queen 'he forgot not his humble obeisance to the erudition and learning of all well nurtured and gentle wedded men'.

Never had Henry been so in love with Catherine as at that moment; never would he be so fully again.

That night there was a revel in the White Hall at Westminster. Henry and his fellow challengers appeared in character, with their garments covered in the gold letters 'H' and 'K' and further festooned with their *noms de guerre*, also in letters of gold: Henry as *Coeur Loyall*, Knyvet as *Vaillaunt Desyre* and so on.

But on Knyvet's codpiece appeared only the single word *Desyre*.

After the dancing was over, the king – 'in token of liberality' – called on his principal foreign guests and their servants to help themselves to the gold ornaments on his costume. He had instructed his gentlemen ushers beforehand to tell the lucky recipients that 'they should not fear to pull and tear the said garment from his body'. Nor did they. More guests soon joined in and quickly turned their attentions to the other performers. Knyvet leapt up on to a stage and made a show of resistance. But 'for all his defence, he lost all his apparel' and was stripped to his doublet and hose. So was the king and between the two of them they lost letters and other gold ornaments weighing 225 ounces.

Things now threatened to get out of hand and the guard were called in. But Henry, who had started the whole thing off, made light of it. He settled down to a great banquet with Catherine and the ladies 'and all these hurts were turned to laughing and game, [with the] thought that all that was taken away was but for honour and largess'.

'And so', the chronicler Hall concludes, 'this triumph ended with mirth and gladness.'

* * *

366

Ten days later, on 23 February, the little Prince Henry died at Richmond. Something in Henry died too.

And he never went on pilgrimage to Walsingham again.

CHAPTER 25

FRIENDS AND BROTHERS

The Westminster tournament of February 1511 was a turning point in Henry's life. He was only in his twentieth year. But it marked his coming of age.

The author of *The Great Chronicle*, an avid spectator at the event, was quite sure of this. And he puts it in straightforward terms of before and after. 'At the beginning in that field', he notes, 'was many a fearful and timorous heart for [Henry]; considering his excellency and his tenderness of age.' But his performance put all such fears to rest – for he could not only give, he could take as well:

> Anon the king called for a spear and so ran six courses or he left [off]. And broke in those six courses four spears as well and as valiantly as any man of arms might break them. And such as were broken upon him, he received them as though he had felt no dint of any stroke.

A collective sigh of relief went round the lists. The king would survive – and thrive:

> After they had seen the said courses run and his manful and deliver [agile] charging and discharging, he rejoiced so the people's hearts that a man might have seen a thousand weeping eyes for joy. And then such as were in most fear saw by his martial feats that by the aid of God he was in no danger.

It was, the chronicler concluded, a sort of revelation: for the first time, Henry had demonstrated 'the excellency of [his] person, which never before that day, as I think, was seen in proper person'.

The English is convoluted. But the meaning is clear. Henry had come out as himself – and as a man.

He had also – in the ultimate boy's dream – shown himself to be as good as, if not better than, the sporting heroes of his boyhood and youth; indeed, he now joined their ranks.

This was more than joining a club: it was initiation into a gang, a band of brothers – or rather brothers, half-brothers, brothers-in-law and blood brothers – who fought together, danced, drank and played together, did deals together and, in the end, showed themselves ready to die together.

The godfather was Sir Thomas Brandon, master of the horse. He had been the principal custodian of the chivalric tradition in the latter years of Henry VII's reign; he had helped carry it through the dark days of the Suffolk conspiracy, when jousting and Yorkist treason seemed almost synonymous; and he had been at the heart of the revival of the tournament that followed Henry's own move to court as prince of Wales.

He had even sung of the joys of jousts and jousters. The occasion was the tournament held in early March 1508 at Richmond. On the sixth, as André explains, there was a day's interruption from the sport 'while the horses were resting'. Brandon showed his versatility by stepping into the breach and entertaining the court and its guests with martial music and song: that 'night', André writes, 'a very tuneful song in praise of warriors was repeatedly sung to the lyre [?lute] in melodious fashion by [Sir Thomas] Brandon'.

Henry we know was at court; he may even have been in the audience. And now that he was king he would sing such songs himself – and write their words and music too.

> The time of youth is to be spent,
> But vice in it should be forfent.
> Pastime there be I note truly
> Which one may use and vice deny.
> And they be pleasant to God and man:

These should we covet when we can.
As feats of arms, and such other
Whereby activeness one may utter.

As Falstaff to King Henry rather than Prince Hal, Brandon seemed destined for great things in the new reign. Under a connoisseur of hunting and horseflesh like Henry, his mastership of the horse assumed an inflated importance. He joined Sir Henry Marney as one of the new king's men in the inner ring of the council, and he was given the immensely profitable office of warden and chief justice of the royal forests south of the Trent.

Henry's decision to joust publicly, if incognito, in the Richmond tournament of January 1510 was the culmination of all that Brandon stood for. The royal stables, of which he was departmental head as master of the horse, must have been in on the secret. But by then Brandon himself was probably past caring. Earlier that month, he had suddenly fallen ill. On the eleventh, the day before Henry and Compton ran in the Richmond tournament, Brandon wrote his will, and he died on the twenty-seventh.

Others would reap the harvest he had sowed. And the reapers got to work quickly. As the court regrouped at Westminster for the Shrovetide revels, Henry was lobbied to divide Brandon's offices and grants among the participants. Charles Brandon, Thomas's nephew and already one of Henry's closest cronies, succeeded his uncle as marshal of King's Bench. The office was virtually a Brandon appanage: held by the Brandon family since the middle of the fifteenth century, it controlled the Marshalsea gaol, which lay in Southwark, on the east side of Borough High Street, opposite to the Brandons' town-house on the west.

But Charles, though close to Henry, by no means monopolized his favour at this stage and more of Thomas's spoils went elsewhere. His valuable stewardship of the West Country lands of the duchies of Exeter and Somerset was given to Henry Bourchier, earl of Essex. Essex had been another mentor to the young bloods at the court of Henry VII and Henry had made this role official by appointing him captain of the greatly expanded band of spears that he had set up the previous autumn. The office of warden and chief justice of the royal forests was granted to Sir Thomas Lovell, one of the leading councillors to survive the change of reign. But the plum position – the mastership of the horse – was bagged by Sir Thomas Knyvet. Jouster, reveller, hunter and all-round hearty young man, he was probably closest of all to Henry in these earliest years of the reign.

Newly enriched, all of the grantees (apart from the superannuated Lovell) took part with Henry in the Shrovetide revel on 28 February 1510, when they were disguised variously as Russians, Prussians or Turks. But the sensation of the show, which Essex had devised and supervised, was the appearance of the leading ladies of the court, including Henry's own sister Mary, in oriental costume and 'blacked up': 'their faces, necks, arms and hands were covered with fine pleasance black, some call it Lombardeen, which is marvellous thin, so that these same ladies seemed to be negroes or blackamoors'.

Thomas Brandon had also made another, more personal, disposition in the legacies in his will. His nephew Charles naturally figures largely, getting 'all my gowns not bequeathed' and a valuable wardship. But the principal legatee was Lady Jane Guildford, the widow of another old colleague at the court of Henry VII, Sir Richard Guildford. Guildford, controller of the household and master of the ordnance and armouries, had acted as royal spy-master, naval, military and civil engineer and head of security. He had been forced to resign his offices in 1505 and had died on a face-saving pilgrimage to the Holy Land the following year, leaving Lady Jane, who was his second wife, ill-provided for. Did Brandon feel sorry for her? Was she perhaps an old flame? Either way, he left her a life interest in Brandon House in Southwark and the lands he had purchased in East Anglia.

And Lady Jane takes us (and probably Henry) back into the heart of his own youthful experience. She had been one of his mother's ladies and, as such, a familiar figure in his own childhood and that of his sister Mary. Lady Jane was possessive and fiercely loyal; she was also unusually cultured for a woman of her class, speaking French well (she had a French mother) and being able to hold her own in conversation with Erasmus 'on one or two occasions'.

All this and more she passed on to her son, Henry. Born in 1489, he was almost certainly Henry VII's godson. He was also, from his earliest youth, in household service to Henry as prince of Wales. There he attended Henry as his 'carver, cupbearer and waiter' and got to know him as few others did.

The new reign was Guildford's opportunity too. He jousted from time to time, but his real speciality was the revel – both as participant and, increasingly, as pageant-master. He first appeared in this role in 1511 in the festivities for Twelfth Night, which were held at Richmond while Catherine was still in her chamber recovering from the birth of Prince Henry. The pageant consisted of a mountain, 'glistering by night', from which issued a Lady followed by Morris dancers. 'The which mountain was with vices [screws] brought up towards the king . . . and then it was drawn back.' This was typical of Guildford, who seems to have inherited his father's engineering skills as well as his mother's literary interests.

It also provided another point of contact with Henry, who was likewise developing a strong amateur interest in mechanics and mathematics.

Alongside the Brandon circle there was another, even more powerful, grouping among Henry's sporting friends. The service rendered to Richard III by the

Howards, father and son, at Bosworth, when the former was killed and the latter captured, was regarded as exemplifying the highest contemporary ideals of chivalry and loyalty. Even Henry VII – who was not given to thinking charitably of his opponents – respected them for it. But, to judge from the surviving tournament records of Henry VII's reign, neither Surrey himself nor any of his sons had shown much interest in the mockwar of the tournament.

The only member of the clan to do so was Sir Thomas Knyvet, who had married Surrey's daughter Muriel, dowager Viscountess Lisle. The marriage took place before July 1506; the following year, Knyvet, who was in his very early twenties, was one of the four gentlemen (Charles Brandon was another) who had 'parfinished and done' the May Joust.

Henry VII's death and Henry VIII's accession brought about a striking change in the Howard attitude to jousting and the whole paraphernalia of the chivalric cult. The explanation has to be that they read the runes about Henry and *his* attitude to chivalry and – pragmatic as ever – decided that they must follow suit. Knyvet's established reputation in the tilt would have in any case acted as a passport to Henry's favour. It is also striking that Surrey's second son, Sir Edward Howard, was chosen to wear Henry VII's armour at his funeral and, as it were, impersonate his knightly valour.

But it was Henry's coronation that offered the opportunity for a grand gesture. Six knights acted as the 'enterprisers' or organizers-cum-challengers for the celebratory joust. And four of them belonged to the Howard clan: Thomas, 'heir apparent to the earl of Surrey', Edward, 'his [second] brother', Sir Edmund Howard, the third brother, and Thomas Knyvet, the brother-in-law of the other three. The other two challengers were Sir Richard Grey, younger brother of the marquess of Dorset (who was still imprisoned in Calais) and Charles Brandon. And Brandon was Edward Howard's closest friend and had chosen him to act as witness to his wedding to Anne Browne and as godfather to their two daughters.

A decade or so earlier, when Henry was still a boy, jousting had been more or less monopolized by a Yorkist family clique; now that he was king, it looked like becoming a Howard family preserve.

Or it would have done if it had not been for Henry himself. For the message was clear: it was Henry, not the Howards, who was in charge. Jousting, hunting and revelling might be what we would call pleasure and they called 'pastimes'. But Henry took his pleasures very seriously. And, like everything else he was serious about, he flung himself into them with energy, passion and commitment.

'The king of England', the Spanish ambassador Caroz reported home on 29 May 1510, 'amuses himself almost every day of the week with running

376

[at] the ring, and with jousts and tournaments on foot, in which one single person fights with an appointed adversary.' Then, as enthralled as he had been a few weeks earlier when he had seen Henry in armour for the first time, he goes into lavish detail about the foot combat:

> Two days in the week are consecrated to this kind of tournament, which is to continue to the feast of St John [24 June], and which is instituted in imitation of Amadis [of Gaul] and Lancelot, and other knights of olden times, of whom so much is written in books.
> The combatants are clad in breast plates, and wear a particular kind of helmet. They use lances of fourteen hands breadth long, with blunt iron points. They throw these lances at one another, and fight afterwards with two-handed swords, each of the combatants dealing twelve strokes. They are separated from one another by a barrier which reaches up to the girdle . . .

'There are many young men who excel in this kind of warfare,' Caroz concludes, 'but the most conspicuous among them all, the most assiduous, and the most interested in the combats is the king himself, who never omits being present at them.'

As it happens, this tournament is unusually fully documented: we have the original challenge and a list of the combatants, when they fought and who their opponents were, as well as another description in Hall's *Chronicle*. And they confirm Caroz's report at every point. Especially in terms of Henry's own assiduity: he fought more often than anybody else, and seems to have outdone even his three star aids – Knyvet, Edward Howard and Brandon – in stamina and skill.

But even Henry, it seems, got bored with devoting every Thursday and Monday for a month to the same kind of combat. Or perhaps he simply ran out of opponents. At any rate, just before the court left Greenwich for the summer progress, the king devised a new martial game: a fight with battle-axes in the presence of Catherine (newly emerged from her confinement for her false pregnancy) and her ladies. Henry kicked off, Hall notes, by taking on 'one Guyot, a gentleman of Almain [Germany], a tall man and a good man of arms'. This is Sir Guyot de Heulle, one of the king's spears: 'And then after they had done, they marched [?matched] always two and two together, and so did their feats and enterprises every man very well.'

'Albeit', Hall concludes, 'it happened the said Guyot to fight with Sir Edward Howard, which Guyot was by him striken to the ground.'

There was always a risk with this sort of violent, one-to-one combat of hard feelings as well as hard knocks. Henry had shown himself alive to this at the time of the coronation joust. He did so again on this occasion. And he (or was it perhaps the presentational genius of Guildford?) turned the peacemaking to pageantry.

The day after the fight with battle-axes, the court had moved to the Tower, en route to Richmond and the start of the summer progress. 'To the intent that there should be no displeasure nor malice', Henry gave £133.6s.8d in gold to the combatants 'to make a banquet among themselves'. The banquet took place at Fishmongers' Hall in Thames Street and – to emphasize their unity and amity – all twenty-four were dressed in 'one suit or livery' of yellow satin slashed with white. Even their shoes, hat-feathers and scabbards were of the same colour.

Then, after the banquet was over, they marched 'by torch-light' to the Tower, where they presented themselves to the king.

It is a scene that is almost filmic in conception: a band of brothers, clad in yellow from head to toe and bathed in light – now glowing now guttering – young, united, happy and saluting their chief, who was himself the youngest, happiest and boldest of them all.

Henry, we are told, 'took pleasure to behold them'. As well he might. In little more than a year he had made the world of 'Amadis [of Gaul] and Lancelot, and other knights of olden times, of whom so much is written in books', live again.

His court was Camelot and he was a new Arthur.

CHAPTER 26

WOLSEY

After the torchlit parade at the Tower, Henry moved upriver to Richmond, before leaving for Windsor and the progress. This took him in a leisurely circuit through Berkshire, Hampshire, Dorset, and Wiltshire, then looping back to Hampshire again before returning through Surrey to Richmond.

But there was nothing in the least indolent about his leisure. According to Hall, he 'exercis[ed] himself daily in shooting, singing, dancing, wrestling, casting of the bar [shot-put], playing at the recorders, flutes, virginals, and in setting of songs, making of ballets and did set two goodly Masses . . .'.

Among the 'ballets' (verses) he made may well have been this. It has a claim to be his best work of poetry; it is also the most interesting psychologically and even politically:

Though some say that youth rules me,
   I trust in age to tarry.
God and my right (*Dieu et mon droit*), and my
   duty,

From them shall I never vary,
Though some say that youth rules me.

I pray you all that aged be
How well did you your youth carry?
I think some worse of each degree.
Therein a wager lay dare I,
Though some say that youth rules me.

Pastime of youth some time among –
None can say but necessary.
I hurt no man, I do no wrong,
I love true where I did marry,
Though some say that youth rules me.

Then soon discuss that hence we must
Pray we to God and St Mary
That all amend, and here an end.
Thus says the king, the eighth Harry,
Though some say that youth rules me.

Henry, as his daughter Elizabeth was to be after him, was a master of language. Take, for instance, the first line or refrain: 'Though some say that youth rules me'. What does it mean? Is 'youth' a mere abstraction? Or is it the flesh and blood youths – Knyvet, Howard, Brandon and Guildford – with whom Henry spent so much time and shared so many passions?

Both meanings, I think, are present. And both provided Henry's councillors with headaches and opportunities. The two were unequally distributed, however. The opportunities were for those councillors with close connexions to Henry's charmed circle of youth/s. This meant, in practice, Thomas Howard, earl of Surrey, knight of the Garter, and lord treasurer.

The Howards, as we have seen, had stepped smartly into the chivalric arena by assuming a predominant part in the coronation joust. Thereafter, there was no stopping them and the rewards came thick and fast. In April 1510 Thomas Howard, Surrey's son and heir, was elected a knight of the Garter together with Henry's political favourite, Sir Henry Marney. To have one knight of the Garter in the family was a signal honour; to have father and son as members of the order at the same time was extraordinary. A few weeks later, on 1 July, Thomas Howard and his wife Anne Plantagenet (who was Henry's aunt) also received a generous land grant in settlement of Anne's claims as a co-heiress of Edward IV.

Finally, and at the same time, Henry gave Howard's father, the earl of Surrey, his heart's desire. The office of earl marshal had been hereditary in the dukedom of Norfolk. But the office, together with the dukedom itself, had been forfeit when the Howards fought on the wrong side at Bosworth. Now Henry restored the earl marshalship to Surrey. He did so on less generous terms than Surrey would ideally have wished: only granting it for life and refusing to countenance any hereditary claim.

It was enough, however. The earl marshalship carried enormous prestige as one of the three or four noble 'great offices of state'. And it was much more than merely honorific. The earl marshal was in overall charge of the college of arms, as the collegiate body of heralds was known. The heralds, collectively and individually, were responsible for the granting and policing of the coats of arms that were the badge of belonging to the rank of gentleman. They also scored and refereed tournaments and other martial contests. Finally, the earl marshal still had a residual claim to command the royal army as deputy only to the king, and bore the marshal's gold baton as testimony to the fact.

By his appointment, in short, Surrey found himself recognized as – under the king – the head and fount of English chivalry. For a king as chivalrous as Henry, it was the greatest honour he could bestow.

This headlong advance of Surrey and the Howard clan is, I think, the background to Polydore Vergil's account of the politics of the first years of Henry's reign. Vergil writes as a contemporary; he was already long resident in England, he knew all the main actors and most of the minor ones, and he was a close and shrewd observer of the political scene. He was also a bitter enemy of the man who came to dominate that scene: Thomas Wolsey. This has led some historians to discount his evidence.

But, as I have remarked before, I do not see why we should believe a man's friends rather than his enemies. The more so when Wolsey's apologist and servant, George Cavendish, writes (though long after the event) an account of his master's early years and his rise to power that is strikingly similar to Polydore's.

A complicating factor is that Polydore's evidence has rarely been used in full. This is because the standard English translation of the *Anglica Historia* is based on Polydore's autograph manuscript of about 1513, rather than the final printed Latin text of 1555. For obvious prudential reasons, the former excludes much of the sensational personal detail that appears only in the latter. After all, how to tell Henry VIII to his face – for the work was intended for dedication and presentation to him – how and why his principal minister had been manoeuvred into his favour? Four decades later, however, it was easy. Almost all the participants – including Henry himself – were safely dead, while Polydore was back in Italy and preparing for death himself.

What follows is therefore based on the 1555 text, in which Vergil – unconstrained – was at last free to speak his mind.

The key to developments, as Vergil sees it, was a power struggle between the two dominant figures on Henry's council: Thomas Howard, earl of Surrey, and Richard Foxe, bishop of Winchester and lord privy seal. 'These men', Vergil writes, 'had long nursed secret quarrels between themselves, which their rivalry made bigger and bigger every day.'

But it was more than a clash of personalities. 'Each of them', Vergil points out, 'had different interests.' Foxe was a satisfied power; Surrey, a lean and hungry one. Foxe, sitting comfortably on the vast revenues of his bishopric, was able to take a loftily disinterested view of politics, seeking only (Vergil claims) to serve the king and state. Surrey was the opposite. Since 'his patrimony . . . had been shipwrecked' in the Wars of the Roses, his aim in politics was to recover it. Which meant in turn that he put 'his own private interests' first in his dealings with the king.

The earl, 'sticking determinedly to the king's side, profitably received great kindnesses from him, which the earl might then grant, give or assign to his family or other people according to his judgment'. This is a loaded but recognizable account of the rise of the Howards as we have traced it in the first eighteen months or so of the reign. By which time it indeed seemed, as Vergil claims, that Surrey, having already 'loaded his relatives and friends with honours and riches', might 'soon entirely take over the prime positions in [Henry's] household'.

This Foxe determined to prevent. And his instrument was Wolsey.

★　★　★

385

Thomas Wolsey would eventually make an impression on contemporaries and posterity second only to Henry himself. But it would be hard to think of a more different start in life.

Wolsey, or 'Wulcy' as he usually spelled his name, was born in about 1475 in Ipswich, where his father was a butcher and grazier. He was a bright boy and was early destined for what was then the only career open to talent: the church. He went to Oxford where, as he graduated BA at the age of only fifteen, he was known as the boy bachelor. By 1497 he was a fellow of Magdalen College and was ordained a priest the following year. He was then studying for a higher degree in theology. This was an odd choice if he already harboured ambitions for the sort of administrative career that had taken his soon-to-be patron Richard Foxe to the summit of political power. At first he thrived at Magdalen, becoming in quick succession bursar, master of Magdalen College School and dean of divinity. But he resigned his fellowship in about 1502.

Had he trodden on toes, as his enemies claimed? Or was he wanting to make a name for himself in the wider world?

His first leg up came from Henry's half-blood uncle, the marquess of Dorset, whose sons Wolsey taught. This established a taste for life in a great household and he became chaplain successively to three important figures: Henry Deane, who was archbishop of Canterbury for two years before his premature death in 1503; Sir Richard Nanfan, treasurer of Calais, who died in 1507; and finally, after Nanfan's death, Henry VII.

The king sent him on two or three diplomatic missions. The outcome was not particularly successful but the whirlwind energy he showed got him his first major promotion in the church to dean of Lincoln in February 1509.

Two months later, Henry VII was dead and Wolsey was still only royal chaplain.

He did, however, already have a certain reputation at court. He was, notes Vergil, 'learned in letters . . . a wise man . . . [and] also bold and absolutely prepared to do anything'.

This, Foxe decided, was the man to take on Surrey: Wolsey was a hot iron waiting to be struck, and Foxe, with good reason, fancied himself as a human blacksmith. ('Here in England', Henry told the Spanish ambassador, 'they think [Winchester] is a fox. And such is his name.') So, 'although he did not know [Wolsey] particularly well', Foxe sang his praises to Henry. Then he primed Wolsey's ambition. That was easily done. Finally, it remained to find a suitable opening. This time death, which had so often hindered Wolsey's career by removing his patrons, struck in his favour. Thomas Hobbes, who had been appointed royal almoner at the beginning of Henry's reign, died in September 1509 and Foxe 'took care' that Wolsey should be his successor.

The almoner was in charge of the charitable doles of the royal household; his office involved personal attendance on the king and he was also a regular, if junior, member of the royal council.

It was a start.

Wolsey's first known appearance as a councillor came about 20 November 1509 when he counter-signed, as the most junior member of the board, a warrant for the issuing of a proclamation. Here, too, Foxe talked his protégé up, making sure that 'he should be received with approval and should be consulted in the council with the chief men'. He also 'made much of him publicly as well as privately by mentioning the man's discretion, vigilance and his excellent hard work'. 'Mr Wolsey *Elimosinarius* (Almoner)' duly appears at the unusually weighty meeting of the council on 21 June 1510 to consider the duke of Buckingham's claim to be hereditary constable of England.

Not for the last time, the butcher's son sat in judgment on England's premier peer.

The council was not the ultimate source of authority, however; the king was. Henry's powers might be veiled because of his age, but time would soon correct that. Wolsey grasped these truths with his usual incisiveness and it was to the king – and the king's young friends – that he bent his remarkable powers of charm and persuasion.

'Wolsey', Vergil continues, 'now began to stick

closely to the king's side, and it is wonderful to relate in how short a time he came to be accepted both by him and by his retinue of young men, which he kept as his favourites.' For Wolsey's priestly vows sat lightly upon him. He had probably begun his relationship with Mistress Lark in the last months of Henry VII's reign and she would bear him at least two children. Now, according to Vergil, 'since there was no reason for the appearance of seriousness', 'his priestly persona was discarded' almost entirely. Instead, 'together with the young men, he very often played the lute, danced, held many charming conversations, laughed, joked and generally amused himself'.

Here it is worth remembering one rather over-looked episode in Wolsey's early career. He had been a schoolmaster; if only for two terms, and tutor to the aristocratic boys of the Dorset household. And teachers, if they are any good (and Wolsey tended to be very good at anything he turned his hand to), have to understand the young. It seems clear that Wolsey did.

He applied this knowledge above all to Henry himself. And there was more to it than 'playfulness'. 'Because he could act more conveniently out of sight of witnesses', Vergil claims, 'he made a temple of all the pleasures at his house', where the king was a frequent visitor.

And there, amid sensual delights, Wolsey inculcated a series of maxims into his royal pupil. 'That the state was being badly run by many governors, each of whom was serving his own ends'. 'That the management of the kingdom's government was safer with one man rather than many'. That Henry 'would be better suited, in the flower of his youth, to turning his mind to literature and the occasional honest pleasure, rather than being weighed down with the anxieties [of business]'. 'That it was right for the government of the kingdom to be committed to someone other than Henry himself until he came to maturity'.

It was rather like the catechism of pithy sayings which Henry's old teacher Skelton had administered in his *Speculum Principis* and had probably got him to learn by rote as well. But, unlike Skelton's meandering list, Wolsey's maxims of state all pointed to a single, irresistible conclusion: 'That Henry should put Wolsey in charge of affairs'.

Perhaps. The account is of course highly coloured and we only have Polydore's word for it. But everything that can be checked – Wolsey's appointment as almoner, his admission to the council, the role of the young favourites, the Howards' dramatic accretion of power, Henry's determination to enjoy himself – is accurate. Even 'the temple of all the pleasures' sounds like one of the luxurious private closets that were to be such features of Wolsey's palaces and later of Henry's own.

Even so, something is missing. This emerges more clearly from Cavendish's parallel, if more pedestrian, narrative of Wolsey's rise. 'He was', Cavendish writes, 'most earnest and readiest among all the council to advance the king's only will and pleasure without respect to the case.'

> The king therefore, perceiv[ing] him to be a meet instrument for the accomplishment of his devised will and pleasure, called him more near unto him and esteemed him so highly that his estimation and favour put all other councillors out of their accustomed favour that they were in before.

Wolsey's role, in other words, was the same as Compton's: to get done what the king wanted to be done. But Compton dealt with the personal and the petty; Wolsey with power and politics on an increasingly grand scale.

But it started at the same point: the subversion of his council's tutelary control. Henry used Compton to end the council's ban on his participation in jousting; he used Wolsey to signal an end to its control over his free disposition of patronage. On 26 May 1511 Wolsey turned up in the chancery with a signed bill for the appointment of a certain John Whetwood to a Lincolnshire rectory. Lincolnshire was Wolsey's backyard. The signed bill, which stated that it was to be a sufficient warrant to the chancellor for the making and sealing of the patent, was the death-knell for conciliar control of patronage. Warham, conscientious and rigid, demurred. Wolsey insisted. And then he delivered the *coup de grâce*: he was giving him the letters, he informed Warham, 'by the royal command'.

That was unanswerable. Warham's only riposte was to have the incident written up with the enrolment of the grant, together with the note '*ut asseruit dictus Dominus Wul[s]ey*' – 'as the said Master Wol[s]ey claimed'.

Wolsey was teaching Henry a new lesson: to know his own power. This was the beginning. Where would it end?

And when would it extend to policy?

Over the next few years, Wolsey enabled Henry to fight and win wars and impose peace. It was, as has been well observed, a partnership that, between them, turned Henry into a northern Caesar who (as not only he thought) bestrode Europe. Wolsey also taught Henry what he could do, as opposed perhaps to what he should do. In so doing, he laid the foundations for the older, greater, badder Henry.

He also destroyed himself in the process.

INTERVIEW

From Book to TV and Back Again:
The Making of a TV Series

Historian David Starkey in conversation with director David Sington about *Henry VIII: The Mind of a Tyrant*

Sington: David, the timing of this book is interesting because you were writing it pretty much in tandem with the writing of the script for the television series, delivering your chapters to me in instalments. It was like receiving a Dickens novel in serial form! And what is remarkable is that if one reads the finished book there is hardly a comma changed. Most non-fiction books go through a process of revision and redrafting, but yours seems to have come out fully formed, which I suppose is because it is the fruit of decades and decades of study.

Starkey: It's also because it's narrative history, which of course is one of the reasons it translates relatively easily into television. I write my books as a storyteller. There is room for analysis, the inclusion of original documents and quite detailed reflections on sources, but the thing that holds the narrative together for me is the story. And what you say about the two things being written in parallel is interesting because I'm so often asked the question 'Which comes first, the book or the television series?' and the answer is that so often they come together. Virtually everything I have written, since I first really learnt how to write back with *Elizabeth* in 1999, has been conceived in parallel with a television series. For me the experience of writing for television has been completely the opposite of dumbing down because the process of scripting actually forces you to concentrate on the fundamentals: all the junk goes, the excessive detail, the unnecessary characters, the pristine little asides and academic posing – there ain't no room for none of it, it *goes*. For me it's fostered the most extraordinary discipline in writing.

I suspect that it was during my twenty-five years of academic life, after my dissertation, that my writing suffered a decline, because the whole emphasis in academia is that you *mustn't* tell a story. Academic history assumes that everything that matters is known and that all you've got to do is analyse it, and unfortunately that sort of analysis naturally exists in the realm of the complex sentence, and in the realm of the footnote. I absolutely abominate the dialogue between text and footnote. I remember how I was taught history at Cambridge: it was a world in which human beings didn't exist. I've always likened it to one of those scenes from a P. G. Wodehouse novel describing aunt calling to aunt, 'like brontosauruses across the primeval swamp'! It was abstract noun, it was class, hierarchy, bureaucracy, all of these grandiose terms with nary a human being, fact or incident – which just seems to me how *not* to write.

Sington: Having been taught a certain type of history at Cambridge, how did you find the confidence to break away from it thereafter?

Starkey: It's an interesting question. I think the answer is that I am just a rebel! My nickname in my circle at Cambridge, where I was taught by Geoffrey Elton, and was indeed for a time his favourite student, was Lucifer, who you will remember is the favourite son of God who rebels and becomes Satan in *Paradise Lost*, and I think you can say that at Cambridge I was always dissatisfied. I'm a natural non-conformist, indeed my parents were Quaker, so I was this very odd specimen, a working-class Quaker, and being working class at Cambridge was even odder. So the whole of my career has been based on being a non-conformist, on saying no. I'm a bit of an awkward squad.

Sington: I'm exactly the same.

Starkey: But you went to Harrow!

Sington: But I was a rebel at Harrow.

Starkey: A comfortable sort of rebel.

Sington: I was always a rebel at the BBC, which is why I had to leave the organisation . . .

Starkey: And why I left academic life . . .

Sington: What I've been trying to do with this series is to include more of the real David, and break away from the formal pieces to camera and so forth that have featured in your previous programmes for television.

Starkey: Yes, you've been trying to get me to be naughty on screen! In the past I've been a little *too* naughty – my personality on things like *The Moral Maze* was far too outrageous – and this period was followed by a toning down, a reduction of temperature. But that in itself can become dull, and you've been prodding me into occasional winks at the camera, which of course is something that I do very much when I am writing.

As a writer of history, you are the equivalent of an interpreter of a foreign language, because although Tudor English is very near to what we write and speak, it is at the same time radically different. The past needs the presence of a not-too-interventionist, not-too-domineering interpreter, which inevitably means that one brings one's personality into the story. But there's also the element of personal interaction with readers, to whom you are saying, 'Come on, imagine we're actually talking,' because although a book is not a dialogue, there's got to be space within the writing for the reader to pause, reflect and move on. Also what I am doing, more than anything else, is trying to get readers to have that confidence to converse with the sources and with the people that I am writing about. In the television series, I want the reader suddenly to realise that the hands that wrote these documents were actually human and they are the only reason we know anything about this period at all.

Sington: I think you've described the process of weaving a narrative that moves seamlessly from your own prose into a source and then out of it again as 'academic knitting', and it's exactly what viewers will see with the TV series, as part of the story is carried by you, then Henry in his own words, then Anne Boleyn, and so on.

Starkey: Well, if it were just me on screen it would be the equivalent of an A. J. P. Taylor lecture!

Sington: I mean that I think your programmes get more sophisticated in what they're demanding of and offering to the viewer. So this series is both the story of Henry's reign, and an analysis of his character; essentially, how does he get to be this way? I think at times, as we've joked in the past, you almost play Henry VIII. There are moments when you slip into him on camera.

Starkey: Yes, I mean, dear me, I taught for a ridiculous number of years and you need to be an actor to be a teacher, especially with a subject like history. And of course one of the things that's so striking about the Tudor period is that it is such a theatrical age; I mean the whole business of the court is pure theatre. If you go into Tudor palaces today they're on the whole rather plain and dull but that's because no room ever had permanent furniture or decorations – they were like large white-washed barns waiting for the court to turn up. And when the court did arrive it was like the night before a performance: a storm of people going into a room hanging up tapestries, installing pieces of furniture, flinging fabrics about the place, scattering hugely expensive cushions and unrolling carpets and, in the final stage before the arrival of the king, bringing out the gold and silver and treasures from the jewel house amid more posing and faffing. It's *just* like a theatre, with the audience of flunkeys standing around watching.

Sington: It's interesting that you mention your time as a lecturer because so often I was able to simply cut out a paragraph from your book and give it to you to speak on camera, which is something that can't normally be done when one is translating a work from the page on to the screen and, I suspect, goes back to your time as a teacher. Your prose is very close to speech; it's conversational.

Starkey: It's heightened conversation, not remotely naturalistic. I use words of more than three syllables! I think both in terms of writing and TV what you do is encourage people, like a good teacher, but it's got to be in an absolutely clear context. So what I like to do in writing is to use very plain English and then leaven it. There will be a moment when suddenly the whole thing starts to effervesce like a glass of champagne and the language gets more colourful. As always, Shakespeare is the model, for example that great moment in *Macbeth* when Macbeth asks: 'Will all great Neptune's ocean wash this blood / Clean from my hand?' and then answers himself: 'No; this my hand will rather / The multitudinous seas incarnadine / Making the green one red.' So you've got a line of Latinate prose referring to 'multitudinous seas incarnadine' followed by plonking Anglo-Saxon. And of course the reign of Henry VIII is the very moment at which English is shifting from a peasant dialect, a shrunken form of bastard Anglo-Saxon French, into a Latinate form in which abstract nouns are introduced. So in some ways what I'm doing when I play this game is I'm replicating my characters' experience of language.

Another of the things that is wonderful about

this period is that writing was a kind of Sunday-best activity and people had immensely good memories so that you find amazingly vivid reports of scenes which read like the very best journalism. One of the reasons I use original documentation so much in my writing is because in reading the stuff there's a sense of eavesdropping. For example, I was able to read the extraordinary handwriting of the clerk who took down the notes of the interrogation of Thomas Culpepper, who went to the scaffold for his amorous intrigue with Katherine Howard, and the notes read like the best moments in a Shakespeare comedy, where brilliant verse and prose are combined.

Sington: You've been writing around and about Henry for almost thirty years now. What sort of a relationship do you and he have?

Starkey: I feel that I increasingly know him, but then I have to remember that we don't completely know anybody. All our knowledge is solipsistic. Henry is an enormous challenge because in one sense he's been a figure of the popular imagination, he's been painted by Holbein in the greatest and most magnificently conceived royal portrait, and yet, and yet, and yet . . . we know so little of the personal trivia on which our sense of character depends. So it's always a search, it's always a leap, there's always something more to find out. For me there's a sense of perpetual fascination. I'm

402

not in love with Henry per se, as Garrett Mattingly was with Catherine of Aragon or J. E. Neal with Elizabeth I, but I am captivated by him. He really is my Cleopatra. There's something always changing, something febrile, a kind of lambent, licking, flame-like quality about him, an uncertainty that I find fascinating.

Sington: In the television series we have three actors playing him . . .

Starkey: And it's not enough! What I think is so extraordinary about Henry, and the reason I am writing his biography in two books, is that although there are qualities that run through his life – such as the quest for fame and glory, the intelligence, the musicality – it's as if a carapace develops over this once charming, sweet-tempered, understanding, loving, sympathetic man, and suddenly this horror emerges, a man of totally different qualities. And it's the horrible man that does all the memorable things. Had Henry died in 1529 he would have been completely forgotten, just another tedious late medieval king who tried to be Henry V.

But I'm fascinated too because despite the calibre of the people around him – he could pick and choose between a Cromwell, a Wolsey and a More for his ministers – he's so confident in his dealings with them. He's not a Gordon Brown, terrified of equals; *he is a big man*. And again, if you were to ask me what I felt about him I would say of course he did unspeakable things, and there is a certain pettishness about him, he does pursue vengeance in vile ways, but on the other hand *he's not small*. Everything about him is big: his horror is big, his vengeance is big and, equally, so are the positive sides of his actions. He is the person who really first envisages England as a unit, who first thinks of its coastline as a single strategic problem, and then goes about recruiting experts to advise him on fortification. And the most extraordinary thing about this amazing campaign is the language that results from it: it feeds straight into the great speeches in Shakespeare's *Richard II* about 'This other Eden, demi-paradise / This fortress built by Nature, land of England', 'this precious stone set in the silver sea', the images of the sceptred isle and of the walled garden. Shakespeare lifted it *straight* from Henry's propaganda. One of the key points I would make about Henry is that the really important period in the sixteenth century, the period when the real creativity happens, is not in Elizabeth's reign, it's in Henry's. Yes, Shakespeare and Spenser lived in Elizabeth's time but, great and glorious though they are, they were only building on the foundations that were laid under Henry; they are using the words that were coined under Henry, they're employing the linguistic forms devised under Henry. Blank verse isn't a creation of Elizabeth, it's a creation of Henry. The sonnet is a creation of Henry's reign, not

404

Elizabeth's. There is a whole work of – and I hate the word because it conjures up awful images of academic nitpicking and backscratching – but there is a world of revision to be done on Henry's reign. As you'd expect from this real revolutionary, you get a volcanic eruption of creativity in his reign which is one of the reasons why I'm perpetually interested in him. It's in art, cartography; it's in the making of armour, of music; wherever you look in this period you can see a revolution, so that for every chapel that has its intestines ripped out there is a countervailing achievement.

Sington: In fact we end the series by saying that the English national character, in so far as it still exists, is a reflection of Henry.

Starkey: Indeed. Henry is the original Eurosceptic. If you look at the language of the conflict between Henry and Thomas More in 1535 which leads directly to More's execution, what they are apparently talking about is the Roman Catholic Church but the *language* they're using is the language of modern Euroscepticism. Henry is arguing that his realm should be able to determine itself, have its own parliament, its own religion, and More is saying, 'Not a bit of it,' you're a parish, a parochial council of Europe and it's the will of Christendom, i.e. Europe, that should determine what is right and what isn't. In effect, Henry sounds rather like a magisterial version of Bill Cash!'

Sington: Henry cleverly recasts the subject of divorce from Catherine from a discussion about the validity of the marriage to a discussion about whether people in Rome should be deciding on a matter of such importance to the English succession. By putting this spin on it he allays the fears of those who would otherwise be queasy about the marriage issue. You see this echoed so much in modern politics. I hope this comes across in the series, David, that you have a very high opinion of Henry's political skills.

Starkey: Yes, he was extraordinary. What we fail to realise is that Henry is essentially a consensus politician; and in carrying through this extraordinary, extreme and dangerous manoeuvre it's as if he's walking across ice floes – and he does it successfully, he does it brilliantly! And at various stages he uses his ministers Cromwell and Wolsey to do the things he couldn't, and when they've done them all the opprobrium descends on their heads rather than Henry's. I always say that the role of a minister in the Tudor period is like that of a tissue. You're desperately important for that moment, and then you're thrown away whilst the king rides off with clear sinuses!

But what we've also been trying to do in this

series is rescue Henry. With the increased interest in historical women over the recent period, Henry's been swallowed up by his wives. That won't do – Henry is much more interesting, a much bigger character than that, so that in this series the wives are there but they are the machinery of the action rather than anything else.

Sington: We start with the enigma – how does someone charming, romantic, poetic become the monster and tyrant? There are many answers, but the one-line one is a nasty protracted divorce.

Starkey: Which is immensely modern. Like many modern divorces it sets the man against his family and friends. One of the fascinating things with Henry is that there is a kind of universal quality about him. Because he's partly mythic, as well as historical, because he's so varied, we can reflect so much off him; there is a kind of inexhaustible quality to his persona, and hard though I try, I can't quite exhaust him.